John J. Clark is a professor of finance and director of graduate studies at Drexel University in Philadelphia. Formerly a professor of economics and dean at St. John's University in Jamaica, New York, he has served as executive director of the Eastern Finance Association and as a consultant to Western Electric, Sperry Rand, and numerous other corporate and community organizations. He is a frequent contributor to professional journals on business and finance and is the author of seven other books.

A HANDBOOK FOR
ENTREPRENEURS AND MANAGERS

Business Merger and Acquisition Strategies

JOHN J. CLARK

A SPECTRUM BOOK

Prentice-Hall, Inc.,
Englewood Cliffs, New Jersey 07632

Library of Congress Cataloging in Publication Data

Clark, John J.
   Business merger and acquisition strategies.

   "A Spectrum Book."
   Includes index.
   1. Consolidation and merger of corporations—Handbooks,
manuals, etc.   I. Title.
HG4028.M4C35 1985   658.1′6   84-15963
ISBN 0–13–106345–6

10 9 8 7 6 5 4 3 2

Printed in the United States of America

Editorial/production supervision by Cyndy Rymer
and Rhonda K. Mirabella
Book design by Maria Carella
Jacket design © 1985 by Jeannette Jacobs

This book is available at a special discount when ordered
in bulk quantities. Contact Prentice-Hall, Inc., General
Publishing Division, Special Sales, Englewood Cliffs, N.J. 07632.

ISBN 0-13-106345-6

Prentice-Hall International, Inc., *London*
Prentice-Hall of Australia Pty. Limited, *Sydney*
Prentice-Hall Canada Inc., *Toronto*
Prentice-Hall of India Private Limited, *New Delhi*
Prentice-Hall of Japan, Inc., *Tokyo*
Prentice-Hall of Southeast Asia Pte. Ltd., *Singapore*
Whitehall Books Limited, *Wellington, New Zealand*
Editora Prentice-Hall do Brasil Ltda., *Rio de Janeiro*

to Margaret Theresa,
wife and first mate

Contents

Preface

This book is about business combinations—that is, the acquisition by one corporation of the control or assets of another corporation. The event is always a profound (some would say traumatic) experience for the "marrying" companies, and among the largest firms it becomes at times a public event of high drama. The latter instance often brings to the surface a public interest underscored by the media and welcomed by politicians who can make pronouncements pro or con on an issue unlikely to evoke sharp reaction from their particular constituencies.

Not all corporate marriages are made in Heaven, and not all succeed. Moreover, some are voluntary and others involuntary. In a voluntary combination, the mutual self-interest of the firms is the most enduring form of corporate love. On the other hand, shotgun weddings do take place—a quite common union in the past two decades. If one party is too myopic to appreciate the advantages of combination, the suitor may seek to force the union by an offer that "can't be refused." The ensuing contest may then enlist opposing casts of managers, stockholders, bankers, lawyers, and public officials in a donnybrook understood only by those familiar with the arcane features of corporate finance.

This book is intended as a practical guide for managers who contemplate combination as the road to corporate growth or who seek to fend off unwanted suitors. Since the success rate is no better (and may be lower) than that of conventional marriages, management is well advised to give serious consideration to the advantages and pitfalls of this type of corporate investment. Business combinations tend to come in bunches, and when managers follow the crowd, mergers are frequently undertaken on an *ad hoc* basis with too little regard for ultimate outcomes and intermediate difficulties. Short-term profit expectations govern the decision-making process, and the weaknesses of the union soon became manifest with the next downturn in business activity.

My theme, therefore, centers on the need for a well-conceived acquisition strategy. This entails more than a generalized statement of corporate objectives to identify desirable acquisitions. It will, in addition, contemplate specific decision points on the following:

1. The advantages of internal vs. external expansion
2. The most desirable type of combination
3. The legal form of the combination
4. The nature of the financial analysis required
5. The articulation of a negotiation strategy
6. The accounting options available to record the union
7. The tax options open to the parties
8. The liability of the combination to antitrust action by government or by third parties claiming personal injury
9. The technological and people problems inherent in the combination

Policies under each of these subheads need to be integrated into a comprehensive plan for intercorporate investment.

In executing the theme, emphasis centers on acquisition strategy as a component of strategic planning. Intercorporate investment is but one form of business investment that necessarily competes against alternative employments of corporate resources. Intercorporate investments should not be evaluated independently without regard to the risk–return ratios from such other projects as investment in new plant and equipment, research and development, financial structure adjustments, and so on. All proposals involving the long-term commitment of corporate resources should be evaluated as part of a comprehensive capital budgeting process. The complexities of business combinations do not exempt intercorporate investments from the criteria of capital budgeting.

Several features highlight the discussion of business combinations. These include the following:

- Brief case histories illustrating the attributes of successful and unsuccessful business combinations.
- Techniques for identifying and evaluating target companies.
- Setting up a pre-negotiation bargaining area described by maximum and minimum prices acceptable to the acquiring and acquired companies.
- Key variables in the negotiation process.
- Study of offensive and defensive tactics in a hostile takeover situation.
- At the end of each chapter, a bibliography of books and periodicals dealing with the topic discussed.

Business combinations are not phenomena of the post–World War II era. To properly understand the function and significance of business combinations, the reader has to adopt an historical perspective. The conglomerate, for example, has a longer history than one would suspect from reading the tabloids. The dimensions of the merger movement also have to be measured against the growth of the U.S. economy. In this respect, business combinations are not unique to the American enterprise system.

They are a common manifestation of private enterprise societies in the industrial age. Chapters 1 and 2 put business combinations in perspective and thereby set the stage for the discussion of acquisition strategy.

The book is not an exercise in quantitative analysis. Any reader familiar with the terminology of accounting and investments and with the concept of discounting will have no difficulty in handling illustrations of financial analysis preceding the merger event.

I wish to express appreciation to Alok K. Chakrabarti, Ph.D., for his contribution of Chapter 7, Acquisition Strategy: Behavioral Component. In the final analysis, the quality of business leadership and the skills exhibited in anticipating and mitigating people problems are crucial elements in the success or failure of any combination. I am also indebted to Thomas C. Chiang, Ph.D., for his insights on the statistical significance of merger activity *vis-à-vis* other financial and economic variables. Both researchers are associated with the Center for Research on Technology and Corporate Strategy (Drexel University).

Also, Douglas V. Austin, Ph.D. (The University of Toledo), provided valuable data on tender offers, the fruits of a long-term interest in the phenomenon of business combinations.

Classifying Business Combinations

1

Adherence to the *status quo* has never characterized industrial society. New technologies, demographic movements, availability of natural resources, socioeconomic attitudes, and other underlying factors affect the price–cost relationships of the marketplace, signaling the direction of business activity. In this environment of flux, few business firms have the good fortune to find a niche in the marketplace and enjoy unchallenged security. Most firms either adapt to the mores and trends of the market or slide into oblivion. The system breeds change and puts a premium on risk taking.

Adaptation can take the form of expansion or retrenchment. For many companies expansion is a mandatory not an optional decision in a growing economy. New product lines can secure economies-of-scale in distribution; rising costs of production can necessitate investment in new plant and equipment to remain abreast of competitors; improvements in transportation expand the market area and alter the scale of production; optimal utilization of facilities may dictate a large sales volume. The stimuli for expansion are manifold. Conversely, as business activity turns down, a different set of adjustments is required. Firms are enjoined by circumstance to cut out unprofitable product lines and divest subsidiaries with inadequate rates of return. Hard times make for lean organizations. In either case, the lesson is clear: The business firm bent on survival must assess its strengths and weaknesses and plan for expansion or retrenchment as the times demand.

This chapter deals with one kind of expansion—by combination of existing business units. Combinations are classified by type and by legal form. The potential benefits and drawbacks of each are assessed, for the choice of type and form of combination constitute important components in the formulation of an acquisition strategy. **1**

DIRECT AND INDIRECT INVESTMENT

From one point of view, business combinations are transactions in the market for corporate control [20]. However, it is not for control *per se* that executives contend. Control confers the right to manage income producing assets. Adding this element, Bradley notes:

> At least in theory, acquisitions are both capital budgeting and strategic decisions intended to maximize the value of the firm's common stock. In practice, however, other managerial objectives often come into play and in fact may be dominant [3].

From the perspective of capital budgeting, an acquisition, regardless of the supporting motivations, constitutes an investment expected to enhance the market value of the common shares. However, it may also serve the interests of the management and stockholders in ways not reflected in the market value of the common stock. Unlike personal investment, an acquisition generally has more than one sponsor and can rarely be explained by the motivation(s) of a single group or decision criterion.

Direct investment connotes the *de novo* acquisition of income producing assets. The assets represent the fruits of new production or distribution from inventory. Direct investment does not comprehend the acquisition of claims on assets (indirect ownership through corporate control) or of on-line assets from an existing producer. Direct investment relates to the creation of *new* income producing assets.

Indirect investment represents the acquisition of *existing* income producing assets by purchase or gaining control over a firm holding title to these assets. The acquiring firm purchases the assets from the selling firm or seeks control over the seller holding title to the assets. The transaction involves a change of control over existing, on-line assets.

Business combinations fall into the category of indirect investments. For this reason, they are at times criticized as detracting from the national industrial capacity. It is said that the national interest would be better served if firms invested directly in new productive capacity rather than in transactions that merely change the control of existing assets. However, the case is more complex than the criticism suggests: (1) The decision to invest in new plant and equipment will be made only if the discounted values of the projected cash flows exceed the cost of the investment, the excess termed net-present value (NPV). If this criterion is not met, companies will not invest in new plant and equipment regardless of the prevailing mood toward business combinations. Only if the NPV for indirect investment exceeds that for direct investment, would indirect investment displace direct investment.

On the other hand, NPV places greater emphasis on *short term* results; the discounting process *per se* gives greater weight to the early cash flows in the life of the project. But, in the long run, this may induce myopic decision making adverse to the interests of the company and the nation. For example, at the time of this writing, it is "cheaper" for an oil company in need of additional reserves to buy out a company with ample reserves rather than to engage in a search for new reserves. The national interest might dictate a search for new reserves. What is good for Texaco is not necessarily good for the nation. The situation exists whenever asset replacement costs exceed the market values of existing facilities.

To acknowledge that the self-interest of business firms can run contrary to the national interest simply asserts that business responds to a price system which guides the distribution of resources by risk-return criteria. The social interest remains the province of government. If government judges, for example, that new oil exploration should have a priority claim on investment funds then it must undertake the assignment itself or create a set of economic incentives for private operators to do so. Moreover, the price system itself is not always an infallible guide pointing to the survival of the firm. The NPV trap may hinder new product development and the exploitation of emerging markets that promise longer term payoffs. The travails of the U.S. auto industry may be a case in point. (2) The combination itself may create conditions (improved efficiencies, lower cost financing, larger markets, etc.) which stimulate new

---

EXHIBIT 1–1
Acquired Assets Compared With New
Investment in Manufacturing and Mining
1960–1979
(Billions of Dollars)

Year	New Investment	Acquired Assets	Acquired Assets as Percent of New Investment
1960	$16.4	$1.7	0.104
1961	15.6	2.2	0.141
1962	16.5	2.7	0.164
1963	17.5	3.2	0.183
1964	20.7	2.6	0.126
1965	24.9	3.7	0.148
1966	29.8	4.4	0.148
1967	30.2	9.0	0.298
1968	30.0	13.8	0.460
1969	33.5	12.2	0.364
1970	33.8	6.6	0.195
1971	32.2	3.1	0.096
1972	33.8	2.7	0.080
1973	40.8	3.6	0.088
1974	49.2	5.1	0.104
1975	51.7	5.5	0.106
1976	56.5	6.9	0.122
1977	64.7	10.0	0.154
1978	72.4	11.8	0.163
1979	83.8	16.0	0.191
		Average	0.172

Note: Acquisitions of mining and manufacturing firms with assets of $10 million or more.

Source: Bureau of Economics, Federal Trade Commission, *Statistical Report on Mergers and Acquisitions.* July 1981.

investment. (3) The acquiring company may have to inject new invest-ment funds in order to achieve the objectives of the combination. In his study of large conglomerates, Markham, for example, found that new capital outlays for acquired companies in a three year period following acquisition averaged 220 percent of pre-merger outlays for the same time frame[13].

From a macro-perspective, direct and indirect investment are not mutually exclusive alternatives. Salter and Weinhold report that asset acquisition by combination has had almost no effect on new invest-ment[19]. Exhibit 1–1 shows that the bulk of asset acquisition represents new investment. Over the period 1960–1979, acquired assets in manu-facturing and mining averaged 17.2 percent of new investment. Also, the two types of investment tend to covary with economic conditions. It is fair to conclude that both types of investment are essential to a healthy, dynamic economy.

Internal and External Expansion

A growing organization can achieve its goals by direct or indirect invest-ment and internal or external expansion. In the latter case, the distinction refers to the means of financing. Internal expansion implies a process of "natural" growth financed *primarily* by retained earnings. The question is one of emphasis, for internal financing would not preclude the use of debt or equity issues if appropriate to the circumstances. There are several advantages to this policy as follows:

- Opportunity to acquire assets specifically designed to the requirements of the organization.
- Opportunity to acquire low-cost resources.
- Opportunity to entrench the company as a low-cost producer in the industry.
- Absence of liability to inherited creditors or minority stockholders of an acquired firm.
- No requirement to obtain the specific consent of the stockholders.
- Avoidance of costly negotiations and the attendant problems of valuation.
- No requirement for special filings with the Securities and Exchange Commission.
- Probably, internal expansion is less apt to attract the scrutiny of the Antitrust Division of the Justice Department and/or the Federal Trade Commission.

Conversely, a policy of internal expansion suffers drawbacks:

- The pace and size of the expansion program are limited by the amount of funds which the firm can generate through retained earnings and securities issues.
- The expansion program may strain the liquidity position of the firm.

It is probably correct to generalize that most larger firms followed a policy of internal expansion when relatively small and closely held. After they achieved substantial size, internal growth was supplemented or replaced by a policy of external expansion.

External expansion refers to expansion through business combinations. This can be financed by cash and/or an exchange of securities. External expansion has the following advantages:

- The pace and size of the expansion program are not circumscribed by the limitations of internal resources.
- It need not constitute a drain on working capital. External expansion can be accomplished by an exchange of securities.
- It is faster; existing assets are immediately acquired.
- It may be cheaper if reproduction costs exceed book value.
- It may not increase the productive capacity of the industry and may reduce the number of competitors.
- As an added benefit, the expanding firm may inherit the managerial skills, customers, goodwill, patents, and other intangible assets of the acquired firm.
- Tax elements and accounting options may further enhance the attractiveness of external expansion.

There is always another side of the coin, however. The disadvantages of external expansion merit careful examination. These are:

- Consent of the stockholders of one or both parties to the transaction may be required.
- Costly and perhaps lengthy negotiations may precede any agreement. Lawyers, accountants, investment bankers, and others have a role in the drama and demand a fee for their act.
- Dissident stockholders may have to be bought off.
- The acquiring firm may have to assume some or all of the liabilities of the selling company.
- Funds may have to be invested to adapt the acquired assets to the needs of the purchasing company.
- After the combination, the acquiring firm may face challenging personnel problems in integrating two managerial teams married to familiar traditions and loyalties.
- Expansion by combination will, given the nature of the beast, most likely attract the attention of the Justice Department and/or the Federal Trade Commission. In addition, there may be special filing requirements with the Securities and Exchange Commission and other Federal agencies.
- Whether initiated by government or parties of interest, the path of external expansion is marred by potential legal actions that impede the process.

TYPES OF COMBINATIONS

Business combinations are classified according to the similarity or relationship of the products marketed by the participating companies. The FTC utilizes the following classification scheme for collating data on combinations:

FTC Code 1 = Horizontal Mergers
FTC Code 2 = Vertical Mergers

FTC Code 3 = Product Extension Mergers
FTC Code 4 = Market Extension Mergers
FTC Code 5 = Pure Conglomerate Mergers[18].

However, not all combinations fall neatly into one slot or the other. The FTC, for example, regards three, four, and five as subsets of conglomerate combinations. Market extension combinations, at times, more nearly approximate horizontal mergers than conglomerates. Similarly, product extension combinations may closely parallel vertical combinations. Accordingly, in order to best illustrate the notion underlying each type of combination, we shall attempt to cite cases that fall clearly into one classification or another rather than concentrate on those that make up the gray areas between the classes.

1. Horizontal Combinations: According to the FTC, "a merger is horizontal when the companies involved produce one or more of the *same*, or closely related, products in the *same* geographic market" [*italics added*] [18]. The problem with this definition is that the relevant geographic market changes with the modes of transportation and communication. An alternative definition to the FTC rule simply states that the horizontal combination is the joining of two or more companies at the same stage of production.

During the period 1948–60, Foremost Dairy Products acquired fifty-nine local companies; Borden acquired thirty-five; and National Diary Products acquired fifteen [9]. The merger of the Chase National Bank with the Bank of the Manhattan Company and the Manufacturer's Trust Company with the Hanover Bank, all operating in the New York City market area, constitute two further illustrations of the horizontal class combination. The FTC also classified the following as horizontal combinations: Coca Cola Bottling (NY) and Franzia Bros. Winery (1973); Sun Oil Company and Calvert Exploration (1974); Phillips Petroleum and Cardinal Petroleum (1974); Buttes Gas & Oil and Chapman Drilling (1974); St. Regis Paper and Michigan Carton Co. (1974).

The horizontal combination offers management several inducements:

- The number of competing units is reduced. (On the other side of the coin, it may make the combination vulnerable to antitrust prosecution.)
- The combination may capture a larger proportion of the total market and at the same time reduce distribution costs relative to competitors.
- The combination may economize on working capital—bring about a decline in the ratio of working capital to sales.
- Added economies may result from the elimination of duplication in facilities, management personnel, purchasing practices, and improved utilization of fixed assets.

In sum, the economic rationale of horizontal combinations rests upon the creation of economies-of-scale in production and distribution of the product.

*2. **Vertical Integration:*** According to the FTC, "a merger is vertical when the two companies involved had a potential buyer-seller relationship prior to the merger"[18]. Under a single management, this form of combination brings together firms which produce supplementary products— products at different stages of the production process.

The initiating firm may seek to extend its operations backward in the direction of suppliers or forward toward the consumer or in both directions. Many of the nation's industrial giants achieved their status through vertical integration. At the peak of its development, the United States Steel Corporation had extensive holdings in iron ore reserves, coal and coke properties, railroad and water transportation companies, natural gas facilities—all integrated to produce a variety of steel products (pig iron, steel ingots, wire, tubes, pipe, structural steel and specialty steel). General Motors and Ford Motor integrated parts and accessory suppliers and moved forward into sales and service[9].

The benefits of vertical integration include:

- Reduction in buying and selling costs incurred when separate companies own two stages of production.
- Reduction in materials handling costs.
- Assures, in some cases, access to critical materials in potentially short supply or to key raw materials used in the production process.
- Given an assured supply of materials, vertical integration allows improved coordination of production and inventory scheduling from one stage of production to another.
- Control of distribution outlets contributes to improved production planning.
- Integration economizes working capital especially in reducing the need for "safety-stock" inventories.
- Coordination of marketing and technological capability may encourage successful innovation.
- Vertically integrated industries generally have high entry barriers which may discourage new competition.

Vertical integration is not only a series of pluses. The minuses include:

- Vertical integration can result in a capital intensive industry. Recent studies show that capital intensification correlates with low profitability unless operating cost savings are very substantial[4].
- The minimum efficient scale of operation for each stage may differ from the volume needed for the production of the end product. One or more of the stages may accordingly operate at a less than optimal level. The evidence suggests that successful vertical integration presupposes a higher share of the market relative to competitor shares. General Motors, for example, with the largest share of the American car market buys 10 to 15 percent of its standard components from outsiders; Ford with a smaller market share buys from 40 to 50 percent.
- If technological change makes one or more stages of production obsolete, the integrated system will have difficulty in quickly adapting and may face the prospect of heavy fixed asset write-offs. Vertical integration reduces flexibility.
- Different industries (stages of production) generally have distinctive forms

of organization, control systems, and management styles. The "manufacturing mentality" may not easily appreciate retail attitudes. The problems of mixing different stages of production are illustrated by the shift of U.S. oil companies from emphasizing station ownership to franchise control and the troubles of clothing manufacturers in managing retail outlets[4].

• Like the horizontal combination, vertical integration runs a serious probability of an antitrust challenge. Chapter 10 discusses this problem.

Recent vertical combinations include DuPont's acquisition of Conoco; Texas Instruments' forward movement into calculators, watches and related products; Pillsbury's acquisition of Burger King; Standard Oil of Indiana's acquisition of Pasco Oil and Gas's Wyoming properties.

Buzzell surveyed 1,649 manufacturing-processing businesses over four-year periods in the 1970s to measure the profitability of vertical integration. Using the Profit Impact of Marketing Strategies (PIMS) data base the study concluded:

> A. Vertical integration can lead to higher profits if not accompanied by increased capital intensity.
>
> B. For industrial product manufacturers, backward integration slightly increases return on investment (ROI); for consumer manufacturers, forward integration increases ROI.
>
> C. Vertical integration worked best for firms with relative market shares of 60 percent or more.
>
> D. The data did not support the hypothesis that integration provides insurance against the effects of inflation.
>
> E. In both mature and growing markets, high levels of integration correspond to high rates of new product introduction[4].

*3. **Product Extension:*** By FTC criteria, "a merger is considered to be product extension in type when the acquiring and acquired companies are functionally related in production and/or distribution but sell products that do not compete directly with one another. An example of a product extension merger would be a soap manufacturer acquiring a bleach manufacturer"[18].

The merger of two local breweries represents a pure horizontal combination. The product extension combination, by contrast, adds to an existing product line complementary products which utilize similar distribution channels or which have a technological link to the acquiring firm's product line. Combinations that appear to fall into this category include: Sperry-Rand's acquisition of Univac (RCA); American Motors Corporation's acquisition of Kaiser Jeep; Honeywell's acquisition of Computer Control; Emerson's Electric's acquisition of Fisher Radio; and more recently the Prudential Insurance Co. of America's acquisition of the Bache Group, and American Express Co.'s acquisition of Shearson Loeb Rhoades (both in 1981). Another illustration of this kind:

> On January 31, 1983, Allied Corp. announced plans for a friendly takeover of Instrumentation Laboratory (IL), a maker of biomedical and analytical instruments. Allied indicated the acquisition would expand its health and

scientific products business begun with the acquisition of Fischer Scientific Co. in 1981. Instrumentation fits well with Fischer's world wide sales and service organization which will now accommodate IL's customer base; in turn, IL gives Allied high technology products to expand its position in the fast growing diagnostic portion of the clinical laboratory market[21].

4. Market Extension: The FTC definition states "a merger is considered to be market extension in type when the acquiring and acquired companies manufacture the same products, but sell them in different geographic markets. An example of a market extension merger would be a fluid milk processor in Washington acquiring a fluid milk processor in Chicago"[18].

Mergers in this category add to the product market served by the acquiring firm. The acquisitions capitalize on existing channels of distribution, on the advantages of national-media advertising, and on the stability of a mass consumer market[3]. Dairy, beer, cement, and oil producers have been good candidates for this type of acquisition with motivations similar to those in horizontal combinations. The beer industry presents an interesting study of the transition from pure horizontal combinations to the market extension type. The thrust of combination moved from local breweries serving a single state or metropolitan area to regional combinations serving several states to national brewers selling in almost all states. For example,

> . . . the Stroh Brewing Company, prior to its 1980 acquisition of the F.M. Schaefer Brewing Company, operated out of one plant in Detroit, Michigan. In 1957, it sold beer in seven states; by 1980, it shipped into eighteen states from Detroit and considered it possible to market to most states east of the Mississippi on a profit[1].

For the industry as a whole, the number of brewing plants declined from 750 in 1935 to eighty-two in 1980; the number of independent companies declined from 404 in 1947 to forty-one in 1980; in 1947, the five largest brewers accounted for 19.0 percent of sales and the ten largest accounted for 28.2 percent, but the respective figures for 1980 were 75 and 93.8 percent of sales. Mergers among brewers, although much publicized in the press, accounted for only an insignificant amount of the increased concentration. Successful Justice Department prosecutions of brewery combinations simply encouraged brewers to expand by internally financed direct investment. The economies-of-scale and distribution over a widening market area provided the return to stimulate new investment[1]. Antitrust policy influenced the mode of expansion, but industry size and structure adapted ultimately to the requirements of the marketplace.

The FTC introduced its classification scheme in 1948. At that time, market and production extension mergers were often referred to as circular combinations; that is, a merging of firms with distinct product lines that shared a step in the production chain, namely, common distribution channels, similar research and development facilities or compatible technologies. General Mills, General Foods, DuPont, and many of the combinations under three and four would meet this criterion today. But the reader will

EXHIBIT 1–2

Acquisitions of Large Mining and Manufacturing Firms,
by Type of Acquisition 1966–1979
(in Millions of Dollars)

Type of Acquisition	1966 No.	(%)	$	1967 No.	(%)	$	1968 No.	(%)	S
Horizontal (1)	8	(.105)	263.0	7	(.051)	1021.0	9	(.052)	373.0
Vertical (2)	8	(.105)	216.6	13	(.094)	409.9	13	(.075)	725.7
Conglomerate:									
Market Extension (4)	1	(.013)	499.6	1	(.007)	435.3	1	(.006)	749.0
Product Extension (3)	41	(.539)	1725.7	84	(.609)	4133.2	102	(.586)	4736.3
Pure (5)	18	(.237)	624.7	33	(.239)	2258.9	49	(.282)	5996.0
Total	76			138			174		
Average Value Per Acquisition			$ 43.8			$ 59.8			$ 72.3

Type of Acquisition	1969 No.	(%)	$	1970 No.	(%)	$	1971 No.	(%)	$
Horizontal (1)	12	(.087)	2114.4	9	(.099)	930.0	7	(.119)	567.1
Vertical (2)	12	(.087)	800.9	3	(.033)	244.3	1	(.017)	10.6
Conglomerate:									
Market Extension (4)	6	(.043)	342.5	7	(.077)	855.4	3	(.051)	52.8
Product Extension (3)	63	(.457)	3609.7	36	(.396)	1994.6	25	(.424)	769.0
Pure (5)	45	(.326)	4175.7	36	(.396)	1880.0	23	(.390)	1060.14
Total	138			91			59		
Average Value Per Acquisition			$ 80.0			$ 64.9			$ 41.7

Type of Acquisition	1972 No.	(%)	$	1973 No.	(%)	$	1974 No.	(%)	$
Horizontal (1)	14	(.233)	538.7	18	(.281)	593.5	21	(.339)	1374.8
Vertical (2)	10	(.167)	234.6	7	(.109)	499.6	3	(.048)	47.6
Conglomerate:									
Market Extension (4)	0	(.000)	0	6	(.094)	480.2	3	(.048)	337.8
Product Extension (3)	22	(.367)	799.2	12	(.188)	420.3	15	(.242)	1010.1
Pure (5)	14	(.233)	313.0	21	(.328)	1155.2	20	(.322)	1701.0
Total	60			64			62		
Average Value Per Acquisition			$ 31.4			$ 49.2			$ 72.1

EXHIBIT 1–2

Continued

Type of Acquisition	1975			1976			1977		
	No.	(%)	$	No.	(%)	$	No.	(%)	$
Horizontal (1)	4	(.068)	167.0	14	(.171)	825.5	26	(.257)	1183.9
Vertical (2)	3	(.051)	100.3	4	(.049)	205.6	4	(.040)	752.8
Conglomerate:									
Market Extension (4)	1	(.017)	35.9	8	(.096)	700.6	0	(.000)	0
Product Extension (3)	25	(.424)	1265.4	27	(.329)	1131.4	38	(.376)	2863.1
Pure (5)	26	(.441)	3383.9	29	(.357)	3438.7	33	(.327)	4204.4
Total	59			82			101		
Average Value Per Acquisition			$ 83.9			$ 76.8			$ 89.2

Type of Acquisition	1978			1979		
	No.	(%)	$	No.	(%)	$
Horizontal (1)	22	(.198)	3055.4	5	(.052)	295.8
Vertical (2)	13	(.117)	1619.3	5	(.052)	934.7
Conglomerate:						
Market Extension (4)	0	(.000)	0	2	(.021)	43.5
Product Extension (3)	37	(.333)	2999.9	41	(.423)	4615.7
Pure (5)	39	(.351)	3050.6	44	(.454)	6977.4
Total	111			97		
Average Value Per Acquisition			$ 96.6			$132.6

Summary

Year	Number of Acquisitions	Average Value Per Acquisition
1966	76	$43.8
1967	138	59.8
1968	174	72.3
1969	138	80.0
1970	91	64.9
1971	59	41.7
1972	60	31.4
1973	64	49.2
1974	62	72.1
1975	59	83.9
1976	82	76.8
1977	101	89.2
1978	111	96.6
1979	97	132.6

Source: Federal Trade Commission, *Statistical Report on Mergers and Acquisitions.*
July 1981.

observe from Exhibit 1–2 that FTC inserts market and product extension combinations as subsets of the conglomerate type. The FTC format recognizes that the five classes denote movement over a spectrum from specialization to diversification. In essence, the advantages of the pure horizontal and vertical combinations are the benefits of specialization. Product and market extension combinations also manifest in some degree the economic virtues of specialization but exhibit qualities attributable to diversification. At the opposite end of the spectrum, the pure conglomerate stands or falls on the advantages of diversification.

5. *Pure Conglomerate:* The FTC states "this category involves the consolidation of two essentially unrelated firms. An example would be a shipbuilding company buying an ice cream manufacturer"[18]. A prominent feature in the merger wave of the 1960s—the pure conglomerate joined under one management, companies with different product lines "having little or no common elements as they relate to raw materials, production technology, or marketing demands"[9]. The primary objective appeared to be a high level of diversification.

Steiner's definition of a conglomerate has a somewhat legalistic hue but does not basically contradict the preceding descriptions. He regards "conglomerate mergers as being ones that do not have a primary direct impact on competition within an economic market." His definition combines product extension and pure conglomerates but excludes market extension types[20]. Steiner's conglomerate participates in several economic markets but does not adversely affect the degree of competition in any single market.

Salter and Weinhold define the pure conglomerate as an "unrelated diversifier . . . pursuing growth in product markets where the key success factors are unrelated to each other. Such a company, whether an actively managed conglomerate or a more passively managed holding company, expects little or no transfer of functional skills between its various businesses (divisions)." By contrast, the product extension and market extension conglomerates are related diversifiers that use their skills "in a specific functional activity or product market as a basis for diversification"[19].

Mueller cites ITT as a prime example of the multi-faceted nature of the pure conglomerate:

> In 1960, International Telephone and Telegraph Corporation (ITT) ranked fifty-first among the nation's largest industrial companies manufacturing telecommunications equipment and operating telephone communication systems. Under Harold S. Geneen, ITT adopted an aggressive diversification policy to move away from a single product orientation. Between 1961 and 1968, ITT acquired fifty-two domestic and fifty-five foreign corporations operating in eighty countries. The more prominent acquisitions included: Hartford Fire Insurance Company, Grinnell Corporation, Canteen Corporation, Rayonier Corporation, Continental Baking Company, Avis Inc., Sheraton Corporation, Levitt & Sons, Inc., Bobbs-Merrill Publishing, and Marquis *Who's Who*. ITT also acts as an operator for a significant number of NASA and Defense Department installations. The conglomerate controls approximately one-third of Europe's telecommunications business[16].

To cite another example, Textron markets a product line comprising polyurethane foam, engine blocks, camshafts, fiberglass boats, outboard motors, lawn mowers, golf carts, bathroom fixtures, cooking ware, work shoes, rocket engines, helicopters, nuclear research, machine tools, rolling mills, textiles, and watch bands. Naturally, in such diverse product lines as ITT and Textron, one can see some residuals of the product and market extension types but the emphasis clearly comes down on diversification.

THE CONGLOMERATE CONTROVERSY

Conglomerates have replaced the nineteenth century trust as an object of public fear and suspicion. In the media, conglomerates are always "giants" or "international" or members of the "military-industrial complex." Yet none of these adjectives describe a conglomerate or address the issues. How do we justify the imposition of a common system of control over diverse enterprises? What, in particular, can the pure conglomerate do to improve productive efficiency and to stimulate technological advancement? The advantages of specialization are manifest and popularly accepted. This is not so for diversification. Review of the literature since the 1960s yields different explanations of the conglomerate's role.

Before looking at the literature, however, we should dispense with a conventional hang-up regarding the nature of corporate enterprise. Traditional economic theory views the corporation as a single product firm functioning in a market which may be highly competitive, monopolistically competitive, oligopolistic, or monopolistic. This outlook associates the firm with a particular industrial process. Consequently, it cannot *adequately* model the price behavior of multiproduct integrated firms (General Motors) and certainly not the decision making criteria of the pure conglomerate enterprise[2]. Rather than locate each firm in a given industry (for example, U.S. Steel as a producer of steel products), it appears more realistic to view the corporation as a pool of capital—liquid and fixed assets—which, *over time*, moves into projects promising a return in proportion to a defined level of risk. The projects may lie outside the scope of the firm's present operations. The period of transition in moving from product line to product line depends, in some part, on the time required to recapture the investment in fixed assets.

The objective is corporate survival. The alternative is a lower rate of return on investment and eventual demise of the firm. Which course holds the greater benefit for society may be arguable. However, at the level of personal interest, the former alternative will likely be preferred by the management, stockholders, and creditors. Thus, at this writing (1982), only 11 percent of U.S. Steel's operating income flows from steel products. Allied Supermarkets, Inc., which operates food processing plants and supermarket outlets, grew out of the A.C.F. Brill Motors Company, a manufacturer of busses[9]. The pool of capital concept tells us something about the cycle of acquisitions and dismantlings marking the corporate life of certain conglomerates (United Technologies for one). In this respect, the pure conglomerate parallels the investment company.

An early justification for the conglomerate held that modern management techniques—systems analysis—could be applied across-the-board to diverse enterprises. Good management rested less upon accumulated experience than upon an ultra-rationalization of the production/distribution process. Sophisticated, quantitatively oriented management, emanating from the top, generated the *apparent* synergy reflected in conglomerate earnings and higher market values of the common shares. Litton Industries, under the leadership of Tex Thorton, operated ninety-seven diverse enterprises and typified the *avant-garde* management style of the sixties.

> Earnings per share of Litton common stock doubled from 1960 to 1962, more than doubled again from 1962 to 1965, and very nearly doubled again from 1965 to 1967. This profit performance became reflected in the astronomical rise in the value of its common stock which rose from $6 per share in 1960 to $104¾ in early 1968[16].

However, in their enthusiasm to apply systems analysis and cost-benefit criteria, experienced managers were ofttimes displaced and production disrupted. The Litton ship building operation suffered the twin pangs of new technology and inexperienced management. Executives of other conglomerates also found it difficult to manage the assets of unrelated businesses. Litton's common stock fell to $68 in 1968 and to $2½ in 1974. By 1982, Litton stock traded in the range $36 to $59½.

Other analysts explained the emergence of conglomerates in the 1960s in financial terms. Curley observed when the P/E ratio of the acquiring firm exceeded the P/E ratio of the acquired firm, market price per share increased when in fact no growth in real earnings occurred. Exhibit 1–3 is a modified version of his illustration. The exhibit assumes the

---

EXHIBIT 1–3
Financial Synergism

	Acquiring Firm A	Acquired Firm B	Combined Firm
Constant Annual Earnings	$4 M	$2 M	$6 M
Shares Outstanding (S)	3 M	3 M	
Conversion Ratio: 1A = 4B			3,750,000 shares
EPS	$1.33	$.67	$1.60
P/E	40	20	40
Market Price Per Share (MV)	$53.20	$13.40	$64

Synergism

Pre-Combination Value of Firms (MV × S):		
$159,600,000 A + $40,200,000 B	=	$199,800,000
Post Combination Value of Firm ($64 × 3,750,000)	=	240,000,000
Transitory Synergism		$ 40,200,000
Share to Acquired Company		
($48,000,000 − 40,200,000)	=	7,800,000
Share to Acquiring Company		
[($64 − 53.20) × 3,000,000)]		$ 32,400,000

Source: Modified version of Table (p. 10) in Anthony J. Curley, "Conglomerate Earnings Per Share: Real and Transitory Growth," *The Accounting Review* (July 1971).

following: no real growth in earnings as an immediate consequence of the combination, no change in the P/E ratio of the acquiring company which is now applied to the combined earnings, and the transaction is recorded as a pooling[8].

The transitory growth accruing from the combination must be confirmed by subsequent performance or it will evaporate; the combination needs at a minimum to maintain current growth rates and risk posture. Per Curley, transitory synergism can occur only when the ratio of aggregate earnings ($^{B}/_{A}$) exceeds the ratio of stock prices ($^{B}/_{A}$); in this case, $.50 > .125$. But some warnings are in order. If the acquiring and acquired firms are proximate in size, the risk posture of the combination will likely change and with it the P/E ratio. Apart from the size factor, if the covariance of the cash flows is higher after the combination, the combination has intensified risk and requires a higher ROI to sustain the market values of the common shares.

An alternative financial approach to the conglomerate looks at changes in debt capacity. The essence of the debt capacity argument for conglomerate mergers is that the combination of two cash flow streams, which are imperfectly correlated, reduces the probability of bankruptcy and thus lowers the marginal cost of debt. This enables the merged firm to exceed the total premerger debt capacity of the combining firms since debt service costs are reduced and the risk of default lessened. In effect, the combination provides a type of coinsurance—the equity of one party serves as a buffer against the potential bankruptcy of the other party to the merger. Importantly, this effect could *not* be achieved by investor's manipulating their own portfolios. As put by Lewellen:

> When a lender diversifies, he 'spreads the risk' by lending small fractions of his total portfolio to each of a number of different enterprises . . . but he cannot thereby affect the probability that any given borrower will be forced to default . . . (On the other hand,) mergers transform all the original loans into something akin to *reverse* income bonds; the crucial payments of interest are made when charges are not earned[10].

A survey by Weston and Monsinghka showed that conglomerates utilized leveraging to raise returns on net worth, although their returns on total assets were not significantly different from those of non-conglomerates [17,23].

The thrust of the Weston-Monsinghka survey, however, purported to show that conglomerates tended to acquire firms with less than average rates of return for their industry but having good prospects for revival. The combination's synergism, accordingly, came from bringing the substandard returns of acquired firms up to their industry average by redeployment of asset and managerial resources. Thus, W & M contended, conglomerates preserved the values of ongoing organizations and avoided the costs of bankruptcy. This function made the conglomerate in effect a new industry[23].

Conn took issue with the W & M explanation of the conglomerate mode of operation. His survey of 159 mergers in the period 1954–1969 revealed no significant difference in the rates of return for acquiring and acquired firms *vis-à-vis* industry averages[7]. Nor was there evidence of defensive diversification by conglomerates; that is, a firm with a sound financial position doing business in a mature industry with a low growth rate acquiring a firm in an industry paying higher returns on investment plus brighter growth prospects.

In respect to the W & M hypothesis and the Conn dissent, one could reason *a priori* that if conventional capital budgeting criteria were applied by the conglomerate management, funds would flow toward the more profitable lines and away from projects with lower rates of return. In the Penn-Central debacle, the more profitable investments in subsidiary projects siphoned funds from the railroad and hastened the bankruptcy of the latter.

It was mentioned above that the pure conglomerate in acquiring and divesting subsidiary companies paralleled the operations of an investment company. From this perspective, the benefits of unrelated diversification by the pure conglomerate stem from the application of modern portfolio management theory to the business firm. This theory views the business firm as a portfolio of investments or projects subject to systematic and unsystematic risks. Systematic or *nondiversifiable* risk refers to the variability of a portfolio's return compared to the return on all securities in the market—the market portfolio. The systematic risk depends upon the inherent characteristics of the firm's underlying assets and financial structure. Systematic risk is measured by the Beta statistic.

Unsystematic risk or *diversifiable* risk arises from factors not captured by the correlation of the firm portfolio and the market portfolio. In a properly structured portfolio the unsystematic risk, which is specific to each investment in the firm portfolio, can be diversified away. Therefore, the pure conglomerate could *in theory* relieve its shareholders of unsystematic risks. Thus it performs an investment company function.

But can the pure conglomerate perform an investment company function more efficiently than the shareholder acting independently on his own behalf? Mason and Gondzwaard researched the issue. They found in the period 1962–1967 that investors could have earned higher returns from randomly selected portfolios of securities in industries with conglomerate representation than by purchasing conglomerate shares directly[14]. In other words, an investor seeking diversification can accomplish the objective himself more efficiently by adjusting his personal portfolio instead of direct investment in conglomerate stocks. The independent shareholder would have achieved superior results despite transaction costs and the conglomerate's use of financial leveraging.

What can be collected from the available evidence to compose an economic/financial rationale for the pure conglomerate? The following arguments were cited to support the case for the pure conglomerate:

1. The nature of corporate enterprise—the urge to survive.
2. Synergism resulting from the application of modern management techniques—systems analysis and cost benefit analysis.

3. Synergism resulting from the transferability of the acquiring company's P/E ratio to the acquired company's earnings.
4. Synergism resulting from the effects of enhanced debt capacity.
5. Synergism resulting from improving substandard earnings of acquired firms.
6. Synergism resulting from diversification—the application of portfolio theory to the business firm.

The evidence in each case was mixed and in some instances the particular feature was not *sui generis* to the conglomerate form. What functions can the pure conglomerate perform better than other types of business organizations? Salter and Weinhold synthesized the potential benefits from conglomerate diversification[19]. The following are included:

1. Centralization of Cash Balances: The conglomerate can act as banker for its operating subsidiaries. The working capital's needs of subsidiaries vary with their seasonal peaks and lows. Central management can route cash from one unit to another and reduce the total organization's reliance on outside sources of funds.

Also, the increased stability of the conglomerate's total operating income enables it to borrow funds at lower interest rates than its individual companies. Further, with increased stability of cash flows, the combination can afford to carry a larger burden of debt. The blending of these elements raises the leverage factor and reduces the weighted average cost of capital. Bear in mind, since interest payments are tax deductible, that shareholders shift some part of the financial risk to government.

On the other hand, realization of these financial economies depends on the conglomerate's portfolio mix of low and high risk units and a high Debt/Equity (D/E) ratio.

2. Better Facilitates Long-Run Profit Maximization: Long-run profit maximization is facilitated when the conglomerate manages a large number of unrelated firms as a single enterprise. Each unit operates in a different product market and on a different cash flow cycle. Central management can recycle the net cash inflows of some units to support the cash flow needs of other units with good long-term prospects. Positive economic benefits accrue from the reinvestment of cash flows at optimal rates of return on projects chosen from a greater variety of options. The larger number of available projects from which to choose enables conglomerate management to better apply capital budgeting techniques than single product firms. Under the risk–return decision criteria of capital budgeting, funds flow to projects with higher rates of return relative to risk and away from projects with less favorable long-term prospects.

Another way of stating this concept of a conglomerate portfolio is to view it as making up some business units with a low future growth potential but a strong current position. These "cash cows" or bonds create a cash flow to feed other elements in the portfolio—units with high growth potential but in need of investible funds. The latter must be managed for long-term results, becoming "savings accounts" of the former.

3. Improved Access to Information: Since the conglomerate operates in a diverse group of industries, it may well become a center for information not generally available to investors; that is, data on the competitive position and potential of companies in different industries. Supported by these data, the conglomerate management is in a superior position to evaluate specific projects and long-term trends[19].

For the product related and market extension conglomerates, we can add the potential benefits of transferable skills and resources between the acquiring and the acquired companies—the residual advantages of specialization. Synergism is created when the combination leads to a greater income stream than could be realized by the companies operating independently and/or a reduction in the variability of the income stream compared to that experienced by companies operating independently.

These are *potential* benefits of conglomeration. Realization, as in any type of business combination, depends upon the quality of management at the core. That these potentials of conglomerate organizations are not always realized in practice is underscored by the conclusion of Dennis C. Mueller. Mueller found that conglomerate mergers generally do not improve the market value of the acquiring firm's common stock. His view is that corporate expansion frequently pursues other objectives than stockholder welfare and economic efficiency. Size brings with it political power and influence[15].

MODELING MERGERS

The conflicting evidence on the operations of conglomerates cited above arises from the deficiencies of the research undertaken. The assumptions made by the researcher affect his conclusions. We have already noted the conflict between traditional microeconomic theory that stresses the advantages of specialization and modern portfolio theory that seeks strength in diversification. A researcher conceptually inclined to one theory will base his research on a particular set of assumptions. These assumptions determine the type of model used to evaluate the data.

The selection and availability of the data also color results. Data is not always available in a form best suited to the research design. Less precise surrogate data may have to be inserted. The size of the sample differs from one research report to another so that the body of evidence becomes highly variable. Firms included in one survey may be excluded from another. Results, therefore, are not comparable. Moreover, the time frame spanned tends to vary with each research project. Even if the number and selection of firms were identical in each survey, results would differ with the time frame of the study. The firm lives in a dynamic economy and its performance reflects macroeconomic movements from period to period.

The statistical methodology used to manipulate the data itself rests upon certain assumptions. Applying different methodologies to the same data base can lead to contrary interpretations. As chapter 10 shows, the same data base can be used to demonstrate that the U.S. economy is becoming more or less competitive and more or less concentrated in fewer business units.

Finally, modeling focuses on the effects of business combinations in the form of statistical generalizations. Motivation is reduced to a unidimensional assumption. Financial analysis, for example, generally assumes the objective of the firm is to maximize the market value of the common shares and that management acts on behalf of the stockholders. However, others contend the large corporation with scattered stock ownership is run for and in behalf of the management group. Whatever the case, motivations are rarely so simplistic. The business firm is both an economic and political organization. As a political organization, the decisions reflect the attitudes of groups with diverse interests—shareholders, managers, employees, public pressure groups, and government agencies. The modeling process does not allow for the interplay of mixed motives and, while it provides some insight to business decisions, it can never fully explain a firm's behavior. Samuel Richardson Reid makes the point:

> The emerging body of literature devoted to developing a behavioral theory of the firm has contributed much to our understanding of the corporate entity. Even allowing for the extension of classical profit maximization models to take risks and costs of analysis explicitly into account, it has become evident that such models do not adequately reflect the objective functions used by managers in making decisions[22].

This is especially true in relation to the complexities of merger analysis.

METHODS OF COMBINATION

Business combinations may also be classified by the method or legal form of the combination. Methods of combination, in turn, can divide into formal arrangements—purchase of assets, merger or consolidation, holding company, leases, and trusts—and informal arrangements—gentlemen's agreement, pools, community of interest, and interlocking directorates. The method of combination is an important component of the acquiring firm's acquisition strategy for it can affect the success of the combination and the future options open to management. The factors for consideration in choosing a method of combination include:

- *Degree of management control:* Some methods of combination are best suited to the application of a decentralized management philosophy (the holding company, for example), others to centralization of management authority—the merger.
- *Flexibility:* Must the acquiring firm assume all the assets and liabilities of the acquired firm, including the less desirable ones—the merger—or only those assets in which it has direct interest—purchase of assets?
- *Permanence:* If the acquisition does not justify expectations, is it difficult to divest the acquired firm?
- *Financing:* What type and size of capital outlay is required to effect the combination? Leasing, for example, allows the firm to acquire assets without expenditure of capital funds.

• *Taxation:* Does the transaction give rise to taxable income or will it qualify as a tax-free exchange? What is the tax status of the enterprise post-combination? Tax considerations may favor the merger or consolidation over the holding company form.

• *Accounting:* The method of combination interlocks with the accounting decision on recording the combination as a purchase or a pooling.

• *Ease in setting up the combination:* This depends upon state law. In some states, a majority of the outstanding shares are required to approve a combination; while in other states, two-thirds of the shares are required.

Formal Combinations

1. Purchase of Assets: The managements of the acquiring and acquired firms execute a sales contract under which the acquiring firm purchases all or some of the seller's assets, and assumes all, some, or none of the seller's liabilities. The sale of the RCA computer division to Sperry-Univac falls into this category. Similarly, after deregulation of the airlines, US Air and Piedmont purchased DC 9s and 727s from the trunk airlines to open up new routes.

The advantages to the purchase of assets include:

• The sale may not require the approval of the selling corporation's stockholders. Unless the sale changes the character of seller's business—the sale of goodwill or property forming an integral part of the business—the transaction might not require the consent of the stockholders.

• In contrast to the merger approach, purchase of assets has an inherent flexibility. The acquiring corporation may purchase only those facilities pertinent to its operations and may or may not assume any liabilities. Consideration may take the form of cash, securities, or some combination thereof.

• It may create tax shields if the sale results in a tax loss.

• The acquiring corporation does not inherit the personnel or management problems of the selling firm.

• Where state law prohibits the merging or consolidation of domestic and foreign corporations, purchase of assets may be the only practical method to affect the combination.

On the other hand:

• If the sale requires the consent of the shareholders, the usual problems of minority rights arise. Creditors, however, cannot object in the absence of fraud, and their liens follow the property subject to the attachment.

• Unless the transaction can qualify as a tax-free exchange, it may result in substantial tax liabilities to the selling company if a gain is realized.

• Whether the transaction involves all or some of the selling firm's assets, the negotiators must tackle the problem of valuation.

2. *Consolidation and Mergers:* Under *consolidation*, a new corporation is organized to assume all the assets and liabilities of the combining corporations. The latter are then dissolved. A *merger* involves the absorption by an existing corporation of the assets and liabilities of another corporate entity. The latter is then dissolved.

In 1967, a new company, McDonnell Douglas Corporation, was formed to consolidate the McDonnell and Douglas corporations. Douglas shareholders received 1.75 shares of the new firm's common stock for each Douglas share. McDonnell shares were swapped on a one-to-one ratio. In 1937, Nash Motors absorbed the Kelvinator Corp. and changed its name to Nash-Kelvinator Corp. Then, in 1954, the Nash-Kelvinator Corp. changed its name to American Motors Corporation, and merged with the Hudson Motor Car Company.

The advantages of the merger/consolidation route include:

- The transaction can generally qualify as some form of tax-free exchange.
- The transformation is permanent and gives the management of the surviving corporation full and complete control.
- The method favors the exercise of centralized authority.

The offsetting factors are:

- The arrangement is inflexible. The acquiring corporation must assume all the assets and liabilities of the seller, including those of incidental importance.
- Stockholders of both corporations must consent to the combination. Dissenting stockholders may demand an appraisal of their holdings and payment in cash. Dissenters may also sue to test compliance with the legal formalities stipulated by state law.
- Negotiators must wrestle with the question of valuation, choice of accounting method, and the tax status of the selling firm's shareholders.
- The perennial managerial problem of blending two previously distinct managerial teams remains.
- The permanent nature of the arrangement makes dismantling difficult if the acquisition should subsequently prove to be a poor choice.

3. *Holding Company:* A holding company is a corporation which holds stock in other companies for purposes of exercising control. It is the actual or intentional exercise of control that distinguishes the holding company from the investment company or mutual fund. Both the holding company and the investment company seek a return on their investment, but the holding company also asserts control to effect a self-defined objective.

A pure holding company's assets consist solely of the securities issued by subsidiary corporations and its chief sources of income are the dividends, interest, and fees received from the subsidiary units. The United States Steel Corporation and American Home Products were formed *initially* for the purpose of acquiring stocks in operating companies. In many instances, the holding company is also an operating company. General

Motors, for example, has operating divisions for the production of cars and other manufactured products but it is also a holding company for General Motors Acceptance Corporation and other foreign and domestic subsidiaries. In 1981, the agreement to combine Standard Brands Incorporated and Nabisco provided for the establishment of a new corporation, Nabisco Brands, to set up two wholly owned subsidiaries to absorb Standard Brands and Nabisco respectively. This is an interesting example of combination simultaneously using the holding company and merger methods.

The flexibility of the holding company format has proved adaptable to the varied needs of industrial, banking, and public utility enterprises. In the latter case, not without scandal.

The following factors recommend the holding company form of effecting expansion:

- It is not necessary to secure the consent of stockbrokers of the subsidiary corporations, and the need to pay off dissenters does not arise.
- The parent acquires a going concern intact without loss of goodwill.
- If cash is paid to purchase subsidiary stock, a sum far less than the net value of the subsidiary's assets need be invested to acquire control. The parent has only to gain sufficient outstanding shares to ensure control, and where the subsidiaries have large blocks of long-term debt outstanding, this can represent a small portion of the total assets brought under control.
- The pyramiding of debt leverages the parent's investment; the parent need not assume the liabilities of the subsidiary corporations.
- It may make possible a combination of enterprises which legislation would not permit under a single corporate roof. By the late 1960s, virtually all the nation's larger commercial banks converted their corporate structures to holding company form to enable them to enter lines of business—data processing, insurance, mutual fund sales, investment advisory services, and leasing—in which as banks they could not directly participate.
- The form facilitates decentralized operations over state and national boundaries.

The following factors detract from the holding company format:

- The structure may prove unstable. If the subsidiary fails to pay dividends on its preferred stock or misses an interest payment, the parent's investment may prove forfeit, or its control jeopardized.
- The income tax works to the disadvantage of the holding company in at least two ways. If the holding company owns less than 80 percent of the subsidiary's stock, it must pay a tax on 15 percent of the dividends received from the subsidiary. This 15 percent is subject to tax at 46 percent or whatever rate applies to the parent's tax bracket. Also, the holding company device creates three levels of taxation on the same income: the operating companies on the original income earned, the parent holding company in receipt of dividends from the operating company, and the holding company's stockholders on the dividends they receive from the parent.

• Maintaining separate corporate entities duplicates expenses: franchise taxes, annual meetings, officers' salaries, etc.

• Minority interests of the subsidiary corporations can prove troublesome. The minority is there to challenge intercorporate transfers, accounting methods, and inventory control or practices that appear to "exploit" the subsidiary corporations.

• Because of historical abuses, the holding company device is regulated by the SEC under the Public Utility Holding Company Act of 1937 and the ICC under the Interstate Commerce Act.

• The parent company must own 80 percent or more of the subsidiaries' voting stock and 80 percent of all other shares in order to file a consolidated return. This tends to negate the advantage of acquiring control by a majority or less of the voting shares.

Figure 1–1 illustrates the structures of an industrial holding company.

4. Leasing: Some economists have predicted that before the close of the century over 80 percent of the nation's capital formation will be subject to lease agreements—everything from land, factories, and equipment to aircraft, railroad cars, ships, delivery vehicles, and motor cars, as well as a variety of information processing and retrieval system.

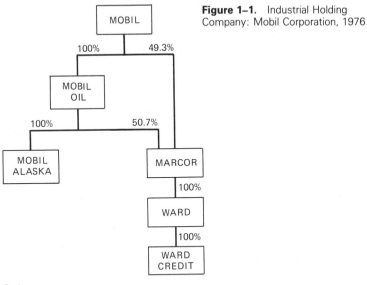

Figure 1–1. Industrial Holding Company: Mobil Corporation, 1976

Code:
    Mobil Corporation ("Mobil")
    Mobil Oil Corporation ("Mobil Oil")
    Mobil Alaska Pipeline Company ("Mobil Alaska")
    Marcor Inc. ("Marcor")
    Montgomery Ward & Co., Incorporated ("Ward")
    Montgomery Ward Credit Corporation ("Ward Credit")
Source: 10K Report to Securities and Exchange Commission, 1976.

The leasing industry grew very slowly at the start of the twentieth century but has grown almost explosively since World War II. Leatham estimates the growth rate to have been 30 percent yearly during the 1950s, 15 percent to 30 percent during the 1960s, and 15 percent during the 1970s. According to Rochwarger, the value of the equipment owned by the leasing industry by the end of 1975 was expected to be $100 billion, compared to $75 billion at the end of 1973. Further, he estimated that total revenues received by lessors, including manufacturers, captive leasing companies, independent leasing companies, banks, and bank holding companies, increased by 20 percent a year from 1964 to 1974. The American Association of Equipment Lessors currently estimates the value of equipment under lease (1981) in the U.S. at $100 billion, an increase of 150 percent from 1974 estimates of $40 billion[5,6].

A lease is defined as an agreement whereby the owner of a particular asset (lessor) enters into an agreement (lease) with the user (lessee) for the latter to use the asset for a specified period of time. Leases can be classified by type and analyzed from the position of the lessor and the lessee. This, however, requires lengthy discussions outside the scope of the present volume. Suffice to say, the general advantages of leasing include:

1. Leases provide an alternative source of obtaining facilities and equipment for firms that have limited capital budgets. In fact, capital projects can be analyzed on the basis of ownership or leasing and the respective NPV or IRR calculated for each alternative.

This budgeting procedure provides wide visibility with respect to alternative capital acquisition plans: some may be purchased and others leased, with the goal of selecting the most profitable combination.

2. Frequently, equipment may be leased over a longer period than would be available through conventional financing. Usually, equipment loans run for a period that is substantially shorter than the economic life of the asset, whereas leases can be obtained for nearly the total length of the asset's life. This results in spreading the cost over a longer time period.

3. Leases are normally quoted at fixed rates or may be tailored to meet the cash budgets of the lessee. This avoids the risks associated with short- or intermediate-term financing and refinancing. Recall that many intermediate-term loans have balloon repayment features whereby the bulk of the principal is due at the end of the loan and, if the firm maintains its credit rating, forms the basis for a new loan. Such refinancing exposes the firm to added risk, as interest rates may change.

4. Leasing may conserve existing sources of credit for other uses and usually does not restrict a firm's borrowing capacity. Many loan indentures do restrict additional borrowing. Further, some firms which cannot raise the needed capital to purchase an asset due to marginal credit standings may be able to lease. Moreover, under the terms of the Economic Recovery Act of 1981, the sale and leaseback provisions permit the sale of tax credits for cash thereby adding to working capital.

5. Leasing generally provides 100 percent financing, since a down payment is not required.

6. Leasing is quick and flexible as opposed to raising funds and making capital expenditures. The restrictive covenants usually found in loan indenture agreements are generally not included in lease agreements. Further, lease terms and options can be tailored to the specific need of the lessee. For example, lease payment schedules may be arranged to meet the seasonal cash flows of the lessee.

7. The total acquisition cost, including sales taxes, delivery and installation charges, and so on, may all be included in the lease payment. These front-end costs may be substantial and thereby result in heavy initial cash outflows, if assets are purchased. This can be avoided through leasing.

8. Leasing can assist the process of cash budgeting by permitting accurate prediction of cash needs. This would be a desirable feature over short-term loans but less so over long-term financing.

9. The entire lease payment is tax-deductible to the lessee. When land is involved in the lease this is especially important, since land otherwise may not be depreciated.

10. Leasing avoids the costs of underwriting and floating new issues of stocks and bonds. Also, the public disclosure surrounding such offerings is avoided when a firm does not have to go to the capital markets to secure funds.

11. Leasing may avoid the risk of obsolescence. In fields which are changing rapidly such as computer technology, ownership may be a distinct disadvantage when new products are introduced. But risk avoidance has a price that will be factored into the cost of the lease by the lessor[6].

De facto, the lease represents a form of indebtedness. Under FAS #13 (Financial Accounting Standards Board), the financial leases must be capitalized and shown as an asset and liability on the firm's balance sheet.

5. *Trust:* Until their successful prosecutions under the Sherman Anti-trust Act of 1890, the trust device was used to organize some of the nation's largest business combinations. Under the trust technique, the stockholders of competing companies tendered their shares to a trust and received, in exchange, trust certificates—receipts for their shares. Trust certificates could be purchased or sold on the market in the same manner as common stock. The trustees, on the other hand, exercised the rights of the stockholders and imposed a common control over the competing companies.

The trust technique may not be entirely dead. Recently (*The Wall Street Journal*, October 22, 1982), it was announced that Forstmann-Leff Associates and the Ryder System (a leasing company) are planning a joint venture to channel funds from private pension funds into the direct purchase of securities. The joint venture will take the form of a holding company (Forstmann, Leff, Kimberly) capitalizing at $85 million (80 percent Ryder and 20 percent Forstmann-Leff) to sponsor a California trust to solicit funds from pension managers for the purchase of existing companies. The trust will manage the acquired companies and collect fees from the pension funds for managing their investments. The earnings of the trust will be passed back to Forstmann, Leff, Kimberly and ultimately as dividends to the partners in the joint venture. The advantages to the participants in the structure are said to include:

- For Ryder, the opportunity to diversify from its truck-leasing base into less capital intensive service business.
- For the pension funds, in return for the loss of liquidity from holding widely traded securities, control over financial management and dividends of the acquired companies.
- The acquisitions represent a purchase of assets recorded at cost that typically will be less than the book values carried by the selling firm. The trust thus gets the benefit of higher depreciation tax shields.
- All of the capital put into each transaction will be equity funds.

It was estimated that if pension fund managers put 5 percent of their assets into the trust the funds would finance $50 billion dollars in takeovers.

Informal Methods of Combination

These involve gentlemen's agreements, pools—a simple written agreement among competitors to co-operate in some form of market control, community of interest—co-ordination of policies by a small group who control separate corporations; such as, members of a family or acquaintances, and interlocking directorates—two or more corporations which have some part of their board membership in common. Existing law makes each of these forms subject to prosecution in addition to endemic weaknesses of the informal method of combination.

Voluntary chains, on the other hand, provide some of the benefits of formal combination for small business concerns. The members of each chain retain their individual identities but contract with a central organization for certain management functions—purchasing, advertising, credits and collections, marketing, and so on. At one time or another the following were voluntary chains: Independent Grocers Alliance, United Rexall Drug Co., and Howard Johnson.

SUMMARY   The classification of business combinations represents more than a statistical compilation by the Federal Trade Commission. The different types and methods of combination stand as decision points in the implementation of an acquisition strategy. Each type and method of combination brings with it advantages and disadvantages that have to be blended with other considerations (accounting, tax, managerial, legal, etc.) to formulate terms of acquisition consistent with the strategic objectives of the combination.

NOTES   1. Adams, Walter. *The Structure of American Industry.* New York: Macmillan Publishing Co., 1982. pp. 224, 218–248, 432–434.

2. Bailey, Elizabeth, and Ann F. Friedlaender. "Market Structure and Multi-

product Industries." *Journal of Economic Literature*. September 1982. pp. 1024–1048.

3. Bradley, James W., and Donald H. Korn. *Acquisition and Corporate Development*. Massachusetts: Lexington Books, 1981. p. 64.

4. Buzzell, Robert D. "Is Vertical Integration Profitable?" *Harvard Business Review*. January–February 1983.

5. Clark, John J., and Pieter Elgers. *The Lease/Buy Decision*. New York: The Free Press, 1980. pp. 1–10.

6. Clark, John J., Thomas J. Hindelang, and Robert E. Pritchard. *Capital Budgeting*. Englewood Cliffs, New Jersey: Prentice-Hall, 1984, pp. 384–385. Reprinted by permission.

7. Conn, Robert L. "Performance of Conglomerate Firms: Comments." *The Journal of Finance*. June 1973. pp. 754–758.

8. Curley, Anthony J. "Conglomerate Earnings Per Share: Real and Transitory Growth." *The Accounting Review*. July 1971. pp. 519–528.

9. Husband, William H., and James C. Dockeray. *Modern Corporation Finance*. Homewood, Illinois: Richard D. Irwin, 1966. pp. 598–599, 600, 600–602.

10. Lewellen, Wilbur G. "A Pure Financial Rationale for the Conglomerate Merger." *The Journal of Finance*. May 1971. pp. 532–533.

11. Lynch, Harry H. *Financial Performance of Conglomerates*. Boston: Harvard University Press, Division of Research, 1971. pp. 66–102.

12. Mace, Myles L., and George C. Montgomery. *Management Problems of Corporate Acquisitions*. Massachusetts: Division of Research, 1971.

13. Markam, J. W. *Conglomerate Enterprise and Public Policy*. Boston: Harvard University, Graduate School of Business Administration, 1973. pp. 88–89.

14. Mason, R. Hal, and Maurice B. Gondzwaard. "Performance of Conglomerate Firms: A Portfolio Approach." *The Journal of Finance*. March 1976. pp. 39–48.

15. Mueller, Dennis C. "The Effects of Conglomerate Mergers: A Survey of Empirical Evidence." *Journal of Banking and Finance*. Vol. 1. p. 339 1977.

16. Mueller, Willard F. "Conglomerates: A Nonindustry." in Walter Adams' *The Structure of American Industry*. New York: Macmillan Publishing Co. 1982. pp. 432–434, 435.

17. Renshaw, Edward F. "The Theory of Financial Leverage and Conglomerate Mergers." *California Management Review*. Fall 1968.

18. *Report of the Federal Trade Commission on the Merger Movement*. 1968. pp. 108–109.

19. Salter, Malcolm S., and Wolf A. Weinhold. *Diversification Through Acquisition*. New York: The Free Press, 1979. pp. 7, 15, 130–156.

20. Steiner, Peter O. *Mergers*. Ann Arbor: University of Michigan Press, 1977. pp. 2, 21.

21. *The Wall Street Journal*. January 31, 1983.

22. U.S. Senate Hearings, Part 5. *Economic Concentration*. 1966. p. 1915.

23. Weston, J. Fred, and S. K. Monsinghka. "Tests of the Efficiency Performance of Conglomerate Firms." *The Journal of Finance*. September 1971. pp. 919–936.

Historical Perspective

2

Chapter 1 classified business combinations by type and method of combination. The chapter sorted out the *potential* advantages and possible pitfalls of each type and method. As might be suspected, success or failure depended more often than not upon the quality of leadership. This chapter examines the phenomena of merger waves—those spurts in merger activity—that have marked the evolution of post–Civil War industrial society. The study looks to identify the underlying factors which create the incentives for entrepreneurs to invest in business combinations.

MERGER STATISTICS   Chapter 1 referred to the deficiencies of the data on the types of business combinations. Unhappily, the quality of the data is even less reliable for the historian tracing the course of business combinations from the late nineteenth century.

Data on merger activity, covering the longest span of time, *by number of acquired firms* in manufacturing and mining from 1895 to the present depends upon two series:

1. Ralph L. Nelson's *Merger Movements in American Industry, 1895–1956.* New Jersey: Princeton University Press 1959. Nelson used the *Commercial and Financial Chronicle* as his prime source of data.

2. Willard L. Thorp's "The Merger Movement." in TNEC Monograph No. 27, 1941, and "The Persistence of the Merger Movement." *American Economic Review, Supplement* (March 1941). Thorp took his data primarily from the *Standard Daily Trade Service* beginning in 1914. Thorp's survey covered the period 1919–1939 and was continued by the Federal Trade Commission after 1939 to the present.

Figure 2–1. Business Consolidations: Manufacturing and Mining 1895–1979

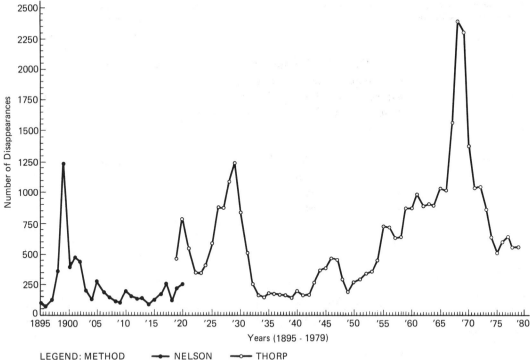

LEGEND: METHOD —•— NELSON —○— THORP

Figure 2–1 charts the Nelson- and Thorp-FTC data recording mergers in manufacturing and mining from 1895 to the present. The data must be considered an approximation of overall merger activity for:

• Some types of combinations were/are not included—gentlemen's agreements, cartels, leases, interlocking directorates, and companies for which data were not publicly available. As government regulation of business activity became more pervasive reporting requirements changed. In 1903, the predecessor of the Federal Trade Commission—the Bureau of Corporations—was formed. The Securities Acts of 1933 and 1934 created and defined the authority of the Securities and Exchange Commission. Thus, the quality of the data is uneven, although tending to improve over time.

The criteria established by the FTC for inclusion in the series are governed by the characteristics of the acquired firm. These are:

1. the acquired company must be in an industry in which the Commission has jurisdiction; 2. the acquisition must represent the purchase of 50.1 percent or more of the stock or assets of the company acquired; 3. an independent company, subsidiary or division of another company must be acquired; 4. *the acquired assets should be $1.0 million or more.* For example, acquisitions of banks, railroads, and airlines are not included in the series. However, acquisitions by banks, railroads, airlines, etc. of companies meeting the above mentioned criteria are included. Similarly, acquisitions that **29**

involve the purchase of a plant or land which does not constitute an independent company, subsidiary, or division are not included. No count is made of partial acquisitions (where less than 50.1 percent interest is acquired), and such acquisitions do not appear in any tables or lists . . . [italics added][8].

The FTC also publishes data on acquisitions defined as large mergers—acquisitions of manufacturing and mining companies *with at least $10 million in assets*. (See Exhibit 2–1). These data are included in the previous series on manufacturing and mining covering acquired assets of $1.0 million or more.

- Over the life of the series, combinations among smaller business units are understated. This is unfortunate as the potential benefits of economies-of-scale are greater for smaller business units than for medium and large business organizations.
- Exclusions from the series also tend to understate the rising importance of the service industries, especially after World War II.
- Frequently, parts of an acquisition are divested by the acquiring firm. Since the acquisition of a divested firm is incorporated into the total count of acquired assets, this results in double counting[3].
- An acquisition by one firm is sometimes part of a later acquisition by another firm. For example, U.S. Steel was a consolidation of ten previous consolidations. The assets of the previous consolidations were again counted in the U.S. Steel merger—another instance of double counting[3].
- The assets of acquired companies are recorded at book values in Exhibit 2–1. Book values (or accounting numbers) are historically oriented and reflect generally accepted accounting customs and conventions. Accounting standards which are reflected in the pronouncements of the American Institute of Certified Public Accountants and the Financial Accounting Standards Board, have changed significantly since the beginning of the aggregate merger series. This makes book values suspect as a basis of valuation except for relatively short time frames. Moreover, if the acquired assets are listed at book values in the series, the values of the acquired companies will be understated in periods of rising prices and overstated in periods of falling prices. Either way, the magnitude of merger activity will either be overstated or understated. In 1972, for example, $2,052.5 million was paid for assets with a book value of $1,860.3. By contrast, in 1968 (a peak year in merger activity), $11,930.7 million was paid for assets with a nominal value of $12,554.2 million. Book values based upon original cost always lag current price movements.
- Over the life of the series, the declining value of the dollar and the growth in the size of the economy tend to magnify the relative size of merger activity in more recent years. For example, from 1968 to 1977, the number of large mergers in manufacturing and mining increased 35 percent but the average size per merger increased 69.55 percent.

The FTC also publishes data on the number of completed mergers broken down by manufacturing, mining, trade (wholesale and retail), and

EXHIBIT 2–1

Large Acquisitions in Manufacturing and
Mining by Year, 1948–1979(1)

	Year	Number of acquisitions	Assets[1] ($ millions)
	1948	4	63.2
	1949	6	89.0
Third Merger Wave	1950	5	186.3
	1951	9	201.5
	1952	16	373.8
	1953	23	779.1
	1954	37	1,444.5
	1955	67	2,165.7
	1956	53	1,882.0
	1957	47	1,202.3
	1958	42	1,070.6
	1959	49	1,431.1
	1960	51	1,535.1
	1961	46	2,003.0
	1962	65	2,251.9
	1963	54	2,535.8
	1964	73	2,302.9
	1965	64	3,253.7
	1966	76	3,329.1
	1967	138	8,258.5
	1968	174	12,580.0
	1969	138	11,043.2
	1970	91	5,904.3
	1971	59	2,459.9
	1972	60	1,885.5
	1973	64	3,148.8
	1974	62	4,466.4
	1975	59	4,950.5
Fourth Merger Wave(?)	1976	82	6,301.8
	1977	101	9,166.6
	1978	111	10,724.3
	1979	97	12,867.1
	Total	2023	$121,857.5

[1]Acquired firms with assets of $10 million or more.

Note: Not included in above tabulation are companies for which data were not
publicly available. There were 346 such companies with assets of $8,161.2
million for period 1948–1974.

Source: Bureau of Economics, Federal Trade Commission.

EXHIBIT 2–2
Number of Mergers

Year	FTC: Number of Completed Mergers and Acquisitions	W. T. Grimm Number of Mergers	Mergers and Acquisitions (Journal): Number of Mergers
1960	1,345	—	—
1961	1,724	—	—
1962	1,667	—	—
1963	1,479	—	—
1964	1,797	1,450	—
1965	1,893	2,125	—
1966	1,746	2,377	—
1967	2,384	2,975	1,354
1968	3,932	4,462	1,829
1969	4,542	6,107	1,712
1970	3,089	5,152	1,318
1971	2,633	4,608	1,237
1972	2,839	4,801	1,263
1973	2,359	4,040	1,064
1974	1,474	2,861	825
1975	1,047	2,297	859
1976	1,171	2,276	1,058
1977	1,183	2,244	1,139
1978	1,245	2,106	1,346
1979	—	—	1,420

Sources: FTC, *Statistical Report on Mergers and Acquisitions*, various years; *Mergers and Acquisitions Journal*, various years; W. T. Grimm, various years.

services. This series is compared with the W.T. Grimm and *Mergers and Acquisitions Journal* data in Exhibit 2–2.

The analyst of merger activity must exercise care in the selection of an appropriate statistical base.[1] Selection of the overall manufacturing and mining series or the large manufacturing and mining series or the series on total completed mergers may provide differing answers to such questions as: Is the American economy becoming more or less competitive? Does merger activity exhibit a secular trend? Can merger activity be significantly explained by movements in other economic variables? Is merger activity importantly affected by institutional changes in antitrust judgements, legislation, tax codes, technological innovation, and so forth? Are there comparable spurts in merger activity in other industrialized states?

---

[1]The last report of the FTC's, *Statistical Report on Mergers and Acquisitions 1979*, was issued in 1981. The FTC has indicated it will no longer publish annual reports on merger activity, although it will continue to monitor business combinations.

In his analysis of merger movements and business cycles (1895–1956), Nelson tested the following explanatory variables in relation to merger activity: stock prices, the volume of trading in the stock market, the index of industrial production, new incorporations, and the reference cycle[24].

Stock prices were subsequently chosen as a preferred indicator over the volume of stock trading. Rising stock prices, for example, provide a more meaningful interpretation of investor attitudes in a period of constant trading activity than a rising volume of trading activity in a period of stable stock prices do.

Nelson's study reached the following conclusions:

1. Merger data showed no clear secular trends. This was held to reflect the absence of underlying forces upon which the trend concept is based. Nelson's analysis centered on large mergers. However, he acknowledged that mergers among smaller firms were unlikely to follow the same pattern.

2. Merger activity exhibited the closest average lead or lag with stock prices at the business reference-cycle peaks and with business incorporations at reference-cycle lows.

3. In prosperity, merger activity related most closely to stock prices. In contraction, merger activity related most closely to the Index of Industrial Production and business conditions.

4. Merger activity tended to correlate with economic growth in the general economy but particularly with the growth rate in industries susceptible to the lure of merger.

5. Not all business-cycle upturns or downturns were accompanied by corresponding changes in merger activity. In the expansions of 1911–12 and 1921–23, the number of mergers actually declined. In these cases, however, the rise in industrial production was not accompanied by a similar rise in the stock prices. Similarly, the 1953–54 business downturn did not witness a similar downturn in merger activity. The modest rebound from the depression low which took place between 1933 and 1937 did not generate a marked change in the number of mergers. The evidence suggests that a cyclical expansion has to be substantial before it affects the level of merger activity.

6. Nelson reviewed H. W. Macrosty's *The Trust Movement in British Industry*. Macrosty's work covered the period 1887–1904. The points of interest were as follows:

   a. In both the U.S. and Britain, there was no evidence of major merger movements prior to the last fifteen years of the nineteenth century.

   b. British merger activity also tended to respond to conditions in the financial markets. Exhibit 2–3 compares merger activity in the U.S. and Britain to stock prices and industrial production.

Nelson's study ended in 1956 prior to the merger wave of the 1960s and well before the end of the long post–War prosperity. Do Nelson's **33** variables continue to relate significantly to merger activity? Do other variables provide insight into periodic spurts in merger activity?

Chiang and Clark using annual data on merger activity in manufacturing and mining for firms with assets of $1 million or more, regressed the number of mergers to the S & P Index of Common Stock Prices and the Index of Industrial Production for the period 1919 to 1979[6]. For the explained variable and the combined explanatory variables, the estimated coefficient of correlation (r) was 0.758 and the more stringent coefficient of determination (R^2), 0.575. Disaggregating the results by variable yielded:

	r	R^2
Number of Mergers and S & P Index	0.641	0.411
Number of Mergers and Index of Industrial Production	0.475	0.226

The financial variable—S & P Index—was the dominant variable both in periods of expanding and contracting merger activity.

In his seminal work, Nelson stated:

> . . . changes in the capital market permitted developments in merger activity which in turn *caused* further changes in the capital market. [italics added].

and later

> The findings concerning the role of the capital market in merger movement lent considerable support to the thesis that the development of the capital market was a major *cause* [italics added][26].

Chiang and Clark tested further for the presence of a *causal* relationship between merger movements and stock prices in the U.S. economy. They found:

1. There was no causal relationship running from a change in stock prices to merger movements.

2. There was no reverse causation from changes in merger activity to stock prices.

3. But the evidence strongly supports the conclusion that merger movements are highly correlated contemporaneously to changes in stock prices.

The relationship between the Index of Industrial Production and merger movements did not at first glance square with the conventional wisdom. The authors found:

1. A unidirectional causality running from merger activity to industrial production.

2. The relationship between the number of mergers and the Index of Industrial Production was shown to be negative. This would apparently suggest that an increase in merger activity leads to a decline in the Index of Industrial Production. However, other explanations are possible and the hypothesis requires much additional investigation.

3. There was no indication that changes in the Index of Industrial Production caused changes in the merger movement.

The importance of financial variables in merger activity has the following explanations:

1. The financial markets reflect the attitudes of the business community regarding future performance of key economic variables which affect merger activity.

2. The financial markets mirror, although imperfectly, the present and anticipated state of the economy.

3. Valuation discrepancies between potential acquirers and sellers come to focus on the securities markets. Gort notes:

> . . . when security prices are low relative to their mean value over a period of years, managers and long-term investors will tend to consider the shares of their firm undervalued. The stockholders of firms that are potential acquirers, on the other hand, can be expected to resist acquisition prices that are far above those at which the individual investor can purchase securities in the open market on his personal account. Consequently, valuation discrepancies of the type needed for acquisitions to occur will be far more frequent in periods of high than in periods of low security prices[12].

Trends in Merger Activity

Nelson observed:

> The merger series exhibited no clear trend. . . . the discontinuous pattern on merger activity suggests that the concept of a secular trend, may be inapplicable to mergers[26].

However, Nelson's statement applies to the deterministic analysis of calculating a trend line. The simplest form of the latter technique is the linear trend model which states that the dependent variable [the number of mergers] correlates with time units [annual data]. The relationship assumes a *constant amount of change* in the dependent variable per unit of time. Another version of the linear trend allows for a *constant rate of change* per unit of time.

Chiang and Chakrabarti applied both versions to the period 1919 to 1979 using the data from Figure 2–1[5]. They found that merger activity is positively correlated with time. In the particular case, the number of mergers increased by an average of 11 per time unit and had a 20 percent growth rate. Although the empirical evidence supported the hypothesis that merger activity is positively correlated to time trend, and the estimated coefficients are statistically significant at the 99 percent confidence level, the R^2 values were low (0.172 for the arithmetic trend and 0.187 for the rate of change model). This lends at least partial support to Nelson's findings.

But there are other approaches to time series analysis. Chiang and Chakrabarti also used an autoregressive trend model on the same data for the same time period. The autoregressive model describes the effect of a unit change in the preceding period on the following period data. Applied to mergers, the question asked is whether a change in the number of mergers in one period affects the number of mergers in the next period. Or, to what extent is current merger activity explained by the numbers of the previous period? The authors conclude that merger activity is highly correlated to that of the previous year. The R^2 values are 0.762 and 0.847 respectively for the *absolute* amount of change and the *rate* of change. A 10 percent change in the *number* of mergers for period one would generate a 9.2 percent change in period two.

The authors devised a general model by superimposing the autoregressive technique on the linear trend model. For the general model, the R^2 values were further improved to 0.817 and 0.884 respectively for the absolute amount of change and the *rate* of change. A 10 percent variation in the *rate* of change in period one would cause an 8.5 percent change in the *rate* of merger activity in period two.

Finally, in order to investigate possible changes in the series pattern, the authors divided the sample data into two sub-periods: 1919–1948 and 1949–1979. The first period covers the later part of Nelson's study, while the second period covers, for the most part, post-Nelson years. The results show a downward trend in the number of mergers for the period 1919–1948 and an upward trend for the period 1949–1979.

However, the existence of a trend in the annual number of business combinations is only significant in relation to the growth in the size of the economy and the population of business firms. A simple upward trend in the number of combinations does not tell us whether the economy is becoming more or less competitive or more or less concentrated in fewer firms. The evidence on these points is a very mixed bag indeed. Chapter 10 takes up this discussion.

Business combinations in the United States are not a phenomenon unique to the post–Civil War period. Railroad combinations predated the late nineteenth century combinations in manufacturing. The New York Central, for example, was formed in 1853 to consolidate ten small railroads running between Albany and Buffalo. In 1867, Vanderbilt acquired control of the New York Central. He had previously acquired control of the New York and Hudson River Railroad and the New York and Harlem Railroad[25]. However, discernible waves in merger activity emerged in the post–Civil War era and may have been spurred by the economic effects of the War. Depending upon the historian, the period from 1879 to the present incorporates four or five merger waves.

1879–1890: The Trust Era: The Trust Era is generally acknowledged to have begun with the organization of the Standard Oil Trust by Rockefeller in 1879. The Standard Oil Trust controlled 90 percent of U.S. oil refining capacity and pipelines. Impressed by the Standard Oil model, other trust combinations followed, namely, Sugar Trust (Havemeyer), National Lead Trust, Cottonseed Oil Trust, Linseed Oil Trust, and Distillers and Cattlefeeders Trust[20]. The Sugar Trust, at one point, attained a 95 percent market share.

The trusts began a generation of horizontal combinations. But the potential efficiencies of horizontal combination were not the sole or even the primary motivation underlying the trust movement. The promoters of the trusts sought security from the rigors of competition and protection from the fluctuations of the business-cycle. As Dewing put it:

> The trust form of organization was admirably adapted to the purposes of industrial consolidation. There was unity of management; yet the individual corporations, *hitherto competing*, retained a separate corporate individuality and each maintained a measure of independence. Nor was it necessary for the promoters of the consolidation to secure all the stock of the smaller corporations. A bare majority would give the necessary control over the board of directors, and, through the board of directors, control over the policy and the administration of the subsidiary corporation. In a real sense, the trust was too efficient [italics added][9].

By 1890, the peak of trust activity had passed. As a result of popular agitation, Congress passed the Sherman Anti-Monopoly Act of 1890. In the same year, a New York court declared the Sugar Trust illegal under the common law principle that no corporation, through its stockholders or otherwise, had power to give over its rights, powers, and duties to a board of trustees.[32]. The business recession of 1893 also dampened merger activity.

Other forms of business combinations, primarily mergers and holding companies, were utilized during the Trust Era. American Tobacco was organized in 1890, Diamond Match Company in 1889, United States Rubber Company in 1892, and General Electric Company in 1892[20].

These represented a transition from the Trust Era to the First Merger Wave.

1895–1905: The First Merger Wave: Institutional changes and improved business set the stage for a surge in business combinations. Assisted by lawyers from New York, New Jersey, in 1893, broadened its incorporation law to permit one corporation to hold stock in another. The specific intent was to attract large industrial combinations and increase state tax revenues. New Jersey's action set off competition among the states to ease restrictive provisions on corporate combinations[9]. Between 1895 and 1920, New Jersey accounted for 54 percent of all merger capitalizations and 47 percent of all firm disappearances through merger[20]. The change in the form of combination from trust to holding company was not one of substance. Both forms accomplished the same purpose in approximately the same manner. Yet, in the change of form, legality was substituted for illegality.

The emergence of an organized large scale capital market was prerequisite to the financing of a large volume of business combinations. A mature financial market could marshal the capital funds of domestic and foreign investors and channel them to business entrepreneurs and promoters. Between 1875 and 1900, issues listed on the New York Stock Exchange increased from 150 to 400. The number of shares traded annually jumped from fifty million in 1895 to 250 million in 1901[20,26,31].

The wave of mergers between 1895 and 1905 involved an estimated 15 percent of all manufacturing assets and employees[28]. Over 3,012 firms disappeared through merger and total authorized capitalizations approximated $6.91 billion. Through horizontal combinations, the following firms achieved dominant market positions: U.S. Steel (1901) with 65 percent market share, American Can (1901) with 90 percent market share, American Tobacco (1890) with 93 percent market share, International Paper (1898) with 66 percent market share, American Tin Plate (1899) with 95 percent market share, American Smelting and Refining (1902) with 90 percent market share, International Harvester (1902) with 85 percent market share, and National Starch Manufacturing (1890) with 70 percent market share[3]. E. I. DuPont de Nemours absorbed sixty-five firms resulting in an 85 percent market share. It was in Stigler's words "merging for monopoly"[30].

Apart from the institutional environment, researchers have adduced several motivational and technological factors to explain the 1895–1905 merger wave. These included:

1. The Expectation of Monopoly Benefits Through Market Control: As the nineteenth century progressed, larger amounts of capital were required to finance new technologies of mass production. Mass production, although holding out the promise of lower unit costs, also increased fixed costs relative to total costs. Individual business units became more vulnerable to the rigors of competitive price cutting as well as cyclical variations in economic activity. A high degree of market control would decrease the menace of price cutting and together create the strength to ride out down-turns in business activity. This was at least the expectation; ultimate realization was another matter. But business decisions are based upon expectations conditioned by a finite knowledge of the extant situation.

In ninety-two industries marked by significant merger activity, seventy-eight combinations controlled over 50 percent of the market, fifty-seven controlled over 60 percent, and twenty-six controlled over 80 percent. Eighty-six parent corporations accounted for 1,465 of the 3,012 firms that "disappeared" between 1895 and 1904[21,24].

2. Economies-of-scale: Economists tended to view the 1895–1905 merger wave as a phase in a general movement toward large scale production resulting in lower unit costs, declining prices, and larger total profits from volume output. It is doubtful, given the managerial problems accompanying business combinations, if the economies-of-scale could have provided an immediate motive to combination; however, taking a longer view they might have constituted a substantial incentive.

Lynch, in particular, casts a skeptical eye on the economies-of-scale rationale. He noted that the economies-of-scale are most manifest in medium or small business units rather than larger companies. However, merger activity tended to concentrate in the large firm category. Second, the combinations taking place resulted in multiplant operations. Manufacturing economies-of-scale would appear after production was integrated by investment in larger replacement facilities. In this connection, Sherer stressed the relationship between the economies-of-scale and monopoly power:

> But if new plant and equipment must be built, why should the acquiring firm waste its resources buying out a plant of suboptimal scale instead of proceeding forthwith to the construction of the efficient plant? . . . the answer turns on the monopoly elements. The firm may perceive that adding the output associated with a plant of minimum optimal scale to existing industry output would unduly depress prices . . . there simply does not appear to be much opportunity to realize plant scale economies through merger, unless an interaction effect with monopoly elements exists[29].

On the other hand, horizontal combinations can yield shorter term savings in administrative and marketing costs. Third, observed merger activity appeared in a wide spectrum of industries—ninety-two in the surveys cited above. Technological developments generating savings in manufacturing costs would not likely surface uniformly in such a wide variety of industries within the span of one decade. Lynch concluded that "while scale economies probably provide one important source of motivation, it was not a dominant motivation"[20].

3. Rewards of Promotion: Promoters and underwriters undoubtedly added to the magnitude of the merger wave. These agents of combination sought out merger situations, brought together former competitors, organized new corporations, arranged the exchange of stock, and marketed new securities to finance the combination. The House of Morgan, already experienced in railroad combinations, helped to organize General Electric, International Harvester, and the United States Steel Corporation. In the latter case, $150 million in stock (one-seventh of the total issued) was credited for promotion and underwriting services[17]. Promoters did not create the basic conditions favorable to combination but in their enthusiasm may have pushed the movement to an unwarranted extreme:

> Because investors were captivated by the prospects of pursuing this road to fortune, and because there were no effective controls on the quality of information disseminated in connection with new capital stock flotations, unscrupulous promoters arranged mergers with little chance of achieving real monopoly powers simultaneously issuing misleading prospectuses, planting rumors, and priming the market to convince investors otherwise[29].

4. Psychological Factors: Business decision-making is the human response to a conceived set of economic conditions. Business decisions, therefore, always reflect a variety of psychological needs. In reference to the motivations for business expansion, Dewing notes:

> On the whole they are not economic, but rather psychological; they are motives incident to the struggle for conquest and achievement. . . . All motives for expansion . . . arise out of the perception that there is increased strength, excellence, or value in increased size . . . the world . . . measures the success of a corporation by increased size, and secondarily by increased profits[9].

Some managers satisfy a creative impulse in fashioning combinations, some have a tendency to take speculative chances, and others search for security. Whatever the particular psychological content, managers play the game of mergers while stockholders put up the stakes. The distinctiveness of personality *vis-à-vis* economic imperatives on the course of the 1895–1905 merger wave, however, is not measurable. It will remain an intangible factor in subsequent merger cycles.

The downturn in merger activity began in 1901 as some combinations failed to realize their expectations and stock prices softened. Panic hit the stock market in 1903–1904 when the economy went into recession. In 1904, the decision of the Supreme Court in the Northern Securities case contributed to the general business pessimism. The Court held the unification of Great Northern and Northern Pacific Railroads in a single corporation, violated Section One of the Sherman Act which prohibited "*every* combination in the form of trust or otherwise" in restraint of trade. By inference, the principle could apply to mergers in manufacturing and mining[31]. The first merger wave had ended. The contours of the first wave are depicted in Figure 2–1.

How successful and by what criteria did these mergers succeed or fail? Shaw Livermore surveyed 328 industrial combinations formed in the period 1888–1905 and followed their performance through 1932. Success was defined in terms of average earnings on capitalization in four time frames: 1901–08, 1909–16, 1917–24, and 1925–32. The 328 combinations were divided into a Primary Group—combinations with power to influence conditions in their industry—and a Secondary Group—combinations which did not possess this market power at the time of formation. Livermore set up five categories of success-failure:

- *Success:* Firms that survived without change and that maintained profitability.
- *Limping Successes:* Firms that survived but sustained significant losses during the period of observation.
- *Rejuvenations:* Firms that underwent reorganizations involving management and stockholders but not creditors.
- *Early Failures:* Combinations that were liquidated or reorganized with losses to stockholders and creditors within the first decade after formation.
- *Later Failures:* Combinations that survived for a decade before experiencing failure as defined above.

Exhibit 2–4 presents the results of Livermore's study. Adding rejuvenations (which involved losses to stockholders), 43 percent of the 328 combinations failed. Of the remaining combinations, 44.5 percent were unqualified successes and 8.5 percent were limping successes[18].

EXHIBIT 2–4
Success/Failure of Industrial Mergers
Formed During Period 1888–1905

	Primary Group No. (%)	Totals	Secondary Group No. (%)	Summary No. (%)
Early Failures	53 (32.6)			
Later Failures	10 (6.1)			
Total		63 (40.4)	78 (45.3)	141 (43.0)
Limping Success		17 (10.9)	11 (6.4)	28 (8.5)
Successes	56 (35.9)		80 (46.5)	136 (41.5)
Rejuvenations	10 (6.4)		3 (1.8)	13 (4.0)
Outstanding Successes	10 (6.4)[A]			10 (3.0)
		76 (48.7)		
Total		156(100.0)	172(100.0)	328(100.0)

Source: Shaw Livermore, "The Success of Industrial Mergers." *Quarterly Journal of Economics.* November 1955. pp. 68–96.

A = Subdivision of success comprising companies which enjoyed continuously high earning power and were leaders in U.S. industrial and technological progress. The group included:

	1901–08	1909–16	1917–24	1925–32
American Can	2.88	5.10	7.50	10.90
American Tobacco	14.17	13.75	11.26	14.41
Corn Products Refining	3.15	3.03	10.01	11.11
DuPont	7.86	29.75	11.31	12.42
Eastman Kodak	16.36	31.15	22.65	15.49
General Electric	11.30	11.08	12.44	12.87
National Biscuit	6.27	6.79	10.58	16.62
Otis Elevator	4.23	5.17	11.04	13.73
Quaker Oats	7.91	11.31	8.46	14.73
United Fruit	13.89	11.96	16.48	8.52

In another study, Dewing surveyed thirty-five combinations mostly executed between 1890 and 1892 and 1897 and 1900. Dewing obtained the audited earnings of each component unit prior to the combination. These were compared against the actual earnings of the first year after the combination and the anticipated earnings published by bankers and promoters. Only thirteen of the thirty-five had first-year earnings equal to the earnings of the component units prior to the combination, and only four had earnings comparable to promoters' forecasts. The average earnings for ten years were, in twenty-two cases, less than the earnings of the independent plants, and in thirty cases, less than the anticipated earnings[9].

Livermore attributed successful combinations to "astute business leadership." Dewing, by contrast, cited the causes for failure. These included:

- Inadequate supply of talent to manage a large group of plants.
- The need to purchase large quantities of raw materials which, instead of reducing costs, actually increased purchasing costs. Competitors buying in smaller lots were better able to play the market.
- The increase in overhead costs actually made the combination less flexible in responding to the challenges of the business-cycle. Big business was as much vulnerable to the cycle as small business.
- The combinations moved slowly in modernizing their inherited plant and equipment thus foregoing the economies-of-scale[9].

1922–1929: The Second Merger Wave: As in the First Merger Wave, changes in the institutional structure opened new avenues for merger activity. In Standard Oil Co. v. United States, 221 U.S. 1 (1911), the Supreme Court held that only unreasonable restraints of trade were illegal under the Sherman Act. In U.S. v. United Shoe Machinery Co., 247 U.S. 32 (1918) and U.S. v. United States Steel Corporation, 215 U.S. 417 (1920), the Court went further in asserting that a dominant market position did not *per se* violate the Sherman Act. The firms in question did not drive all competitors from the field. Moreover, while both companies controlled more than 80 percent of the output in their respective industries, the Court noted they had not abused their positions and were efficient producers.

Congress responded to the Rule of Reason with the Clayton Act (1914). The Act prohibited one corporation from acquiring the *stock* of another corporation if the effect were to substantially lessen competition. However, the Act referred only to *stock* acquisitions, not *asset* acquisitions, and appeared at first glance limited to horizontal combinations. Moreover, in Thatcher Manufacturing Co. v. FTC, 272 U.S. 554 (1926), the Court held that if a corporation used a stock purchase as a step toward acquiring the assets of another corporation and completed the transaction before the FTC acted, the transaction could not be undone under the Clayton Act. Thus, while the books showed there was more restrictive legislation aimed at business combinations in the 1920s compared to 1895–1905, court decisions still left ample room for maneuver.

The merger wave that began with the upturn in business activity in 1922 contained a greater diversity of combinations than found in the 1895–1905 period. The characteristics of the Second Merger Wave included:

- The formation of numerous electric, gas, and water utility holding companies[28].
- The firms involved tended to hold smaller market shares—they were second line companies. Some of the better known combinations included: Bethlehem Steel, Allied Chemical, Republic Steel, Kraft, and Continental Can. Stigler described the process as "merging for oligopoly"[30].
- The combinations showed greater geographic diversification by bringing together firms doing the same thing in different communities; for example, food retailing and department store and motion picture theater chains[11]. National Dairy and Allied Stores were also formed in this period. Here, we see the seeds of the market extension conglomerate described in the previous chapter.
- Many combinations represented a joining of firms producing different products but utilized similar channels of distribution. Motivation lay in the economies-of-merchandising as opposed to the manufacturing economies-of-scale in the 1895–1905 wave[9]. IBM, General Foods, and Allied Chemical were products of the era. The reader will note the similarity with the product extension conglomerate of the next merger wave.
- Vertical integration played an important role especially in the metals industries[22].

Accordingly, Lynch depicts the 1920 wave as one of transition:

> While horizontal combinations leading to oligopolistic market conditions apparently remained an important feature, it appears that a significant, but undetermined, proportion of the mergers during this period would today be classified as conglomerate of the geographic market extension or product extension variety . . . the achievement of market power and economies of large-scale production must be considered motivations of reduced importance in comparison with the turn-of-the-century period[20].

Along with the renewal of merger activity, "big business" moved to improve its capacity to manage large amounts of capital. Sparked by new organizational forms at General Motors, Sears Roebuck, Standard Oil of New Jersey, and DuPont, business began to move from the centralized, functionally specialized type of organization to a decentralized, divisional system. Top management monitored divisional performance by return on invested capital while leaving more of the "how" to the discretionary authority of divisional managers[4,13]. Academia moved to fill the expanding demand for business leaders. In 1912, the Wharton School of the University of Pennsylvania gained college status. The University of California, University of Chicago, New York University, Dartmouth College, and Harvard followed suit after the turn of the century. In the early twenties, the Harvard Business School adopted the case method of study. Clearly, the concept of a managerial class was emerging. The activities of The Taylor Society, which had been founded to preserve and extend the ideas of Frederick W. Taylor and his associates, contributed to the concept of scientific management[16].

The Second Merger Wave played second fiddle to the financial speculations of the "flapper" era. The stock market crash of 1929 and the following worldwide depression led to a steep drop in the number of mergers. During the 1930s, many of the utility empires collapsed into bankruptcy and many major companies underwent reorganization.

Looking back on the 1920s and 1930s, Dewing identified three types of industrial consolidations which seemed to achieve "a modicum of success"[7]. These were found in three groups:

• *The Automatic Industry:* The production process allowed the substitution of automatic tools for hand labor bringing about declines in unit production costs. The economies-of-scale were sufficient to offset the "wastes and limitations that accumulate as size grows." Dewing cited the aluminum and metal industries as pertinent illustrations.

• *The Integrated Industry:* Subject to the essential principle that output of the acquired company be less than the amount which synchronizes with the parent's scale of production, Dewing noted two conditions justifying vertical integration: First, the producer of a raw material can reach the ultimate consumer only through an additional and unique fabricating process; by acquiring the fabricating firm, the parent gains access to two different markets—the semifabricated and fabricated markets. The second condition being where the acquiring firm needs some raw material not easily obtainable. Successful vertical combinations included Anaconda's acquisition of the American Brass Company, GM's acquisition of plate glass manufacturing subsidiaries, and the Great Atlantic and Pacific Tea Company acquisitions of production subsidiaries. Dewing stressed, unless undertaken with care, vertical-integration could lead to ruin.

• *The Retail Distribution Chain:* The retail chain took the distributor to the door of the customer. The economic characteristics for successful operation made up the following: a primary distribution business, a product sold in small quantities to a great number of people, profit per small individual sale necessitating uninterrupted large volume, the market area for any small distribution unit, and a permanent group of buyers for each distribution unit. The formula met with conspicuous success in different fields, namely, dairy products such as the National Dairy Products Company (1923) and the Borden Company (1876), small retail stores such as The Great Atlantic and Pacific Tea Company (1858), Woolworth's (1879), J.C. Penney (1902), the mail order business (Montgomery Ward and Sears Roebuck), and public utilities.

1950–1969: The Third Merger Wave:

The Third Merger Wave was preceded by an increase in the number of mergers in 1946 followed by a decline in 1948 and 1949. After 1950, however, the intensity of merger activity increased to a peak in the late 1960s.

Following the pattern of the previous waves, institutional changes had laid down a new set of ground rules. In general, the law on mergers was more restrictive. The Cellar-Kefauver Act of 1950 amended Section Seven of the Clayton Act to include asset acquisitions as well as stock acquisitions; in addition, adverse effects on competition between the acquiring and acquired companies *or elsewhere* were brought within the scope of the Act[30]. A series of court decisions tended to foreclose horizontal and vertical combinations even when loosely defined as product extension or market extension. These were as follows:

• U.S. v. E.I. DuPont de Nemours & Co., 353 U.S. 586 (1975): The Court held that DuPont's acquisition of 23 percent of General Motors' stock foreclosed one-third of the total market for automotive finishes and one-fourth of the total market for automotive fabrics.
• Brown Shoe Co. v. U.S., 370 U.S. 294 (1962): The Court rejected the acquisition of Kinney by Brown Shoe which would have given Brown control over 7.2 percent of the nation's total retail shoe outlets.
• U.S. v. The Philadelphia National Bank, 374 U.S. 312 (1963): The Court blocked the merger of Philadelphia National Bank and the Girard Bank on the grounds that the combination would secure control of 30 percent of the commercial banking business in the Philadelphia metropolitan area.
• FTC v. Proctor & Gamble Co., 386 U.S. 568 (1967): The Court ordered the divestiture of the Clorox Company by P & G since liquid bleach was a feasible avenue of diversification for P & G. Proctor & Gamble had previously considered entering the market *de novo* but acquired Clorox when the opportunity promised a better market share[31].

Previously, in U.S. v. Aluminum Company of America, 148 F2d 416 (1945), the Court ruled that ALCOA had violated the Sherman Act by controlling 90 percent of the manufacture of newly refined aluminum. Thus the "rule of reason" no longer applied.

Consequently, by the middle of the 1960s, vertical and horizontal combinations even in the form of market or product extension conglomerates were vulnerable to antitrust prosecution. However, the peril diminished as the degree of market or product affiliation declined and the share of the market diminished. For the time being, the courts left the pure conglomerate relatively untouchable.

Between 1948 and 1968, horizontal mergers among large manufacturing and mining firms declined from 31.0 percent to 6.8 percent, vertical mergers increased slightly from 10.3 percent to 11.4 percent, market extension conglomerates declined from 6.9 percent to .005 percent, product extension conglomerates increased from 46.6 percent to 59.2 percent, and pure conglomerates increased from 5.2 percent to 24.3 percent. The number of mergers in the latter category rose from four in 1948 to 173 in 1968. The FTC recorded 3,932 combinations of all types in 1968 compared to 1,345 in 1960[10].

In some respects, the Third Merger Wave represented a break with past experience and, in other respects, a maturation of trends developed in the Second Wave. The prominent features of the Third Wave were as follows:

- Most acquirers were small or medium-sized companies combining with companies of comparable size in other industries (narrowly defined).
- Increase in the pure and product related conglomerates.
- Increased importance of diversification as a motive behind business combinations and a decrease in the monopoly power motivation.
- Since the conglomerate allowed for corporate growth without an apparent concentration of market power, the period has been described as "merging for growth"[28].
- Sharp decline in horizontal mergers.
- Most mergers were inspired and negotiated by management. The role of the investment banker shifted from promoter to consultant.

Exhibit 2–5 lists the more acquisitive conglomerates active in the Third Merger Wave.

The Third Wave receded after 1969 with the decline in stock market values and the advent of the 1973 recession.

1976–19 ?: The Fourth Merger Wave: Salter and Weinhold postulate a Fourth Merger Wave beginning in 1975. Although the Supreme Court used the doctrines of potential competition (the P & G case cited above) and reciprocity (discussed in Chapter 10) to chip away at the position of the pure conglomerate, by 1979, 45.4 percent of the acquisitions of large mining and manufacturing firms were classified as pure conglomerates. Product extension and pure conglomerates together totaled 87.7 percent of large merger activity. Horizontal and vertical combinations fell to 10.4 percent of the total.

A number of other features appear to distinguish this latest merger

---

EXHIBIT 2–5
The Population of Acquisitive
Conglomerates

Automatic Sprinkler	MSL Industries
Automation Industries	Nytronics
Bangor Punta	Occidental
Condec	Ogden
FMC	Royal Industries
W. R. Grace	The Signal Companies
Gulf & Western Industries	Teledyne
Hydrometals	Textron
ITT	TRW
Walter Kidde & Company	Tyco Laboratories
Litton Industries	U.S. Industries
Ling-Temco-Vought	Vernitron
Mid-Continent Manufacturing	White Consolidated Industries
Mongram Industries	Whittaker

Source: Harry H. Lynch, *Financial Performance of Conglomerates;* Boston: Division of Research, Harvard University, Graduate School of Business Administration, 1971, p. 73. Used with permission.

wave. The combinations of the 1960s were mostly financed by the exchange of common stock and the issuance of convertible securities. After 1975, the payment of cash or cash equivalents became the principle form of consideration. This form of consideration tied in with a growing number of hostile tender offers which doubled after 1975. In a great many cases, one firm's acquisition was another's divestiture. In 1976, divestitures involved over half of all acquisitions compared to an average 10 percent in the 1960s. (The number of divestitures may contain a message concerning the quality of corporate decision-making related to the original acquisition.) Finally, the new wave witnessed the re-entry of established corporate giants to the acquisitions arena: DuPont, Mobil, General Electric, United Technologies, Philip Morris, R. J. Reynolds, Pepsico, and others.

Research on Merger Waves: More time and effort has been expended (largely by academics) on evaluating the outcomes of the Third and Fourth Wave mergers rather than Second Wave combinations. These studies, while suggestive, do suffer the deficiencies of merger research discussed in Chapter 2. Summaries of the more important research follow.

Reid and others surveyed 478 of the 500 largest firms and classified them according to their level of merger activity for the period 1951–61; forty-eight did not engage in mergers, 214 had one to five mergers, 142 had six to ten mergers, and seventy-four had eleven or more mergers. He found that the intensity of merger activity was related to two sets of variables: growth variables (changes in sales, assets, and number of employees) and profits-to-stockholders variables (changes in market prices and capital gains). The study concluded that firms that merged tended to be more amenable to managerial interests than to stockholder interests. The higher the level of merger activity, the better the performance of growth variables and the worse the performance of profit variables[27].

Hogarty studied forty-three firms with a high level of merger activity in the period 1953–64. The performance of the merging firms was compared against the average performance in the acquiring firm's industry. Included in the comparison were stock prices and dividend policies. Hogarty defined an aggressively merging firm as one acquiring aggregate assets of 20 percent or more of its preacquisition level. He found such firms did not have a better stock market performance than the average firm in their industry. In fact, many performed worse. A small number exceeded average performance. In another article, Hogarty pessimistically concluded: "A host of researchers working at different points of time and utilizing different analytical techniques and data, have but one major difference: whether mergers have a neutral or negative impact on profitability"[15].

Weston and Mansinghka concentrated on sixty-three conglomerate companies compared to two control groups randomly selected from *Fortune*'s 500 industrials and 250 nonindustrials. The survey data spanned two periods: 1958–68 and 1960–68. Acquiring firms had greater than average growth rates compared to the control groups. This included stock prices and was attributed to merger activity, and not to internal growth.

The improved return on net worth of conglomerates was explained by leveraging effects. At the start of the periods, the earnings of conglomerates were lower than the control groups' but by 1968 the conglomerates had closed the gap. The latter phenomenon suggested to Weston and Mansinghka that the economic rationale of the conglomerate lay in elevating the profitability of substandard performers to their industry average—the defensive diversification of overspecialized companies referred to in Chapter 2[33].

In a second article, Chung and Weston developed a pure financial synergy model which hypothesized that the cost of capital for acquiring firms would be equal to or less than their industry average and for acquired firms it would be greater than their industry average. As a corollary, the financial leverage of acquiring firms will be greater than for acquired firms. Acquired firms were hypothesized as relatively risky but having superior investment opportunities.

Chung and Weston sampled eighty-three acquired firms in pure conglomerate mergers for the period 1948–1977. Industry indexes were constructed on the basis of five firms per industry. From these comparisons before and after the merger event, they concluded the following:

1. Acquiring firms could not avail themselves of the investment opportunities in their own industries.
2. Acquiring firms functioned in mature industries with lower growth rates.
3. Acquiring firms, therefore, looked to growth industries to maximize the value of investment opportunities.
4. For the two years prior to the merger event, acquired firms performed below average for their industry. At the same time, acquiring firms tended to perform slightly above their industry average.
5. Since the acquired firm, for other reasons, could not internalize the investment opportunities of its industry, merger might benefit the acquired firm in addition to serving the objectives of the acquirer[7].

Haugen and Langetieg examined fifty-nine industrial mergers of firms listed on the New York Stock Exchange. Each merger was carried through by a stock swap and the acquiring company had no other mergers in a seventy-two month period surrounding the combination. In each case, the two combining firms were matched against two other independent firms from the same industry—the control group. Thus, two groups of paired firms were constructed; the two groups paralleled each other except that the merged firms united at the midpoint of the seventy-two month study period. The paired firms in both groups were *de facto* analogous to two stock portfolios. Haugen and Langetieg concluded that mergers did not produce effects different from those obtainable by the informal purchase of both company shares by an investor. The investor could equal or better the benefits of combination by adjustments to his personal portfolio[14].

Mandelker studied 241 firms from the FTC merger listings from 1948 to 1967 and used the Capital Asset Pricing Model to test for merger induced synergism. He offers the following conclusions:

1. Mergers are a mechanism in which the market displaces incompetent management. Replacement of incompetent management may create gains for the acquirer. The incumbent management of the acquired company stands at risk.

2. Stockholders of the acquired firm tend to benefit the most. Mandelker estimates abnormal returns of approximately 14 percent, on average, in the seven months preceding the merger.

3. Acquiring firms tend to earn a return appropriate to their risk posture. There is no evidence of abnormal returns or losses from merger for acquiring firms.

4. The market discounts merger effects about seven months prior to announcement[21].

Louis examined the ten largest conglomerate acquisitions made during 1971 from the 500 largest industrial corporations. A conglomerate acquisition was defined as any combination which gave the acquiring company a significant stake in the new line of business. The 1981 earnings per share of the acquiring firms were calculated on the basis of what they might have been if the mergers had not taken place. These adjusted data were then compared to the actual 1981 earnings per share. The comparisons are not flattering:

Acquiring Company (A) Acquired Company (B)	Hypothetical 1981 EPS	Actual 1981 EPS
Schering (A); Plough (B)	$4.08	$ 3.31
Heublein (A); Kentucky Fried Chicken (B)	4.11	4.09
Squibb (A); Lanvin-Charles of the Ritz (B)	2.01	2.10
RCA (A); Coronet Industries (B)	(0.28)	(0.19)
Northwest Industries (A); Buckingham (B)	N.A.	14.20
ITT (A); O. M. Scott & Sons (B)	4.54	4.58
American Cyanamid (A); Shulton (B)	4.08	4.11
General Host (A); Cudahy (B)	N.A.	2.95
Nabisco (A); J. B. Williams (B)	4.36	4.21
Johns-Manville (A); Holophane (B)	1.27	1.53

In four cases, the hypothetical earnings per share exceeded the actual EPS, and in four other cases the reverse was true. The analysis is flawed, however, by the realization that factors other than the combination could have influenced the actual and hypothetical earnings[19].

Clark and Elgers studied 246 combinations taken from the FTC major merger series for the period 1957–1975. The merger must have been an isolated event neither preceded nor followed by another merger by the same firm over a twenty-four-month interval. The research methodology employed the Sharpe-Lintner Capital Asset Pricing model. The researchers found that, contrary to popular belief, the success of corporate mergers is unrelated to the behavior of the securities markets. Conglomeration as a merger motive caused significantly better returns to equity than vertical and horizontal combinations. Moreover, a larger proportion of the merger gains to conglomerates persisted after the merger event. Also, the notion that conglomerate mergers are more likely to confuse investors was not substantiated[8].

On the other hand, Mueller, after an extensive survey of the empirical literature, concluded that conglomerates as a rule do not enhance the profitability or stock value of acquiring firms. The managements of acquiring firms apparently pursue goals not related to stockholder welfare and economic efficiency. Mueller states:

> ... the empirical literature draws a surprisingly consistent picture. Whatever the stated or unstated goals of managers are, the mergers they have consummated have, on the average, not generated extra profits for the acquiring firms, and have not resulted in increased efficiency[24].

In assessing the beneficial effects of business combinations, it is possible to find published research to support almost any hypothesis. We might assert with equal certainty that business combinations have, on balance, yielded neutral or negative returns to stockholders of the acquiring firms; that half or more of the combinations fail to meet expectations or result in financial loss to the shareholders of the acquiring firm; and that one of six mergers fails outright. Whatever the truth, the weight of evidence warrants a skeptical posture regarding the process of business combinations and the quality of decision making in top management.

The decision to merge is a capital budgeting decision. The firm's capital budget also evaluates projects involving internal expansion, research and development, refunding, divestitures, and other long term commitments, which also compete for investible funds. How does the success/ failure rate on these projects compare to that on mergers and acquisitions? We simply do not know. Mergers are spotlight events and attract follow-up studies. The consequences of less spectacular strategic decisions, good or bad, are not tabulated for public consumption. We might surmise, however, that if the same quality of managerial talent and effort is applied to all capital projects—external as well as internal expansion—then the corporate batting average on strategic decisions may not be very impressive.

There is also the question of to whom the benefits or losses of combination accrue. A combination that fails to satisfy the ambitions of stockholders may prove quite satisfactory to the management and promoters concerned. The converse is also possible. On the community level, if a less-than-optimally efficient combination limps along on the momentum of sheer size, does this constitute failure by the standards of the work force or by the creditors?

Time is a factor. When is a combination deemed to have failed—one, two, ten, or twenty years after the effective date of organization? Losses to the initial stockholders may be more than offset by subsequent gains to those investors buying in at a later date. Lever Brothers, for example, apparently used up two decades before achieving the administrative and marketing economies-of-scale projected by Lord Leverhulme in 1906[93].

A merger is a business deal with elements of drama beyond the experience of normal business activity. What does our survey tell us about the motivations of the parties? For one thing, they are complex and interrelated. The fact that business combinations are initiated by managers and promoters does not prevent tangible benefits from reaching the stockholders. For example, management may initiate a combination motivated by desire for prestige and power, yet that same combination may generate economies-of-scale which add to the market value of the common shares. The growth variables important to managerial pomp and circumstance are not mutually exclusive from the profits-to-stockholder variables, although Reid reports an inverse relation between the two. Undoubtedly, one can cite many cases where management profits at the expense of stockholders—a condition not limited to merger deals—and cases where promoters feed off both parties. Yet management cannot preside indefinitely over an empire with declining stock values. Market forces are not that impotent.

Our survey indicates a potpourri of motives—financial, operational, and psychological—underlying corporate acquisitions. To identify and assess the relative importance of these motives is not an easy assignment. Frequently, researchers will attempt to probe motivations by questionnaires or personal interviews. But businessmen are not always candid about their objectives when going public or may actually not appreciate the complexity of interrelated motives and personality factors at work. Another approach deduces motivation by examining the effects of the combination. The method assumes that a rational entrepreneur intends what he brings about. However, the history of mergers is well-filled with unintended effects. A firm may acquire a dominant market position via a series of mergers undertaken for quite different reasons. The following list represents the results of both approaches.

Acquiring Firms: Steiner has an extended list of motives taken from a survey of the literature[31]. The bulk of these apply primarily to acquiring companies:

1. A desire to limit competition or achieve monopoly profits.
2. A desire to apply unutilized market power.
3. A response to shrinking opportunities for growth and/or profit in one's own industry due to shrinking demand or excessive competition.
4. A desire to diversify to reduce the risks of business.
5. A desire to achieve a large enough size to realize an economical scale of production and/or distribution.
6. A desire to overcome critical shortcomings in one's own company by acquiring the necessary complementary resources, patents, or factors of production.
7. A desire to achieve sufficient size to have efficient access to capital markets of inexpensive advertising.
8. A desire to fully utilize particular resources or personnel controlled by the firm, with particular focus on managerial skills.
9. A desire to displace an existing management.

10. A desire to utilize tax loopholes not available without merging.

11. A desire of managers to create an aggressive image alert to new opportunities.

12. The desire of management to build an empire.

Baker and others investigated the relative importance of merger motives between firms engaging in different types of mergers. His questionnaire sample covered the chief financial officers of 175 firms headquartered in the U.S. with at least one acquisition of $5 million or more between January 1, 1978 and January 1, 1979. The merger types and related responses to the survey were as follows:

Merger Type	*Responses*
• *Horizontal:* One in which two companies in the same line of business are combined.	66
• *Congeneric:* One involving related enterprises but not producing the same product or providing the same service.	54
• *Conglomerate:* One in which two companies in unrelated lines of business are combined.	29
• *Vertical:* One in which a company either expands forward toward the ultimate customer or backward toward the source of supply.	4
• *Other Combinations:* Where a company engaged in more than one merger during the period and represented more than one type of merger.	22
Total	175

Exhibit 2–6 ranks the average responses by type of merger and motivation. Baker and others acknowledge that this type of research runs the risk of disingenuous responses and the presence of unconscious deep-seated drives[2].

However, listing merger motives *ex post* hardly fills the need to identify "which motives are decisive in accounting for levels of merger activity, and for changes therein"[28]. At present, the research does not have a framework of analysis and methodology of research to penetrate this screen.

Acquired Firms: Many combinations are initiated by the selling firm. Sherer cites several motivations typical of selling firms[29].

1. The seller may be experiencing financial difficulties and looks to new ideas, management, and financial resources to salvage the operation. At the time Heublein acquired Kentucky Fried Chicken, the latter had fallen on hard times[19].

2. Owner-managers may lack the heirs or qualified successors to carry on the enterprise. Merger may be the route to perpetuating the work of a lifetime. Raytheon's acquisition of Beech Aircraft Corporation resulted from an active search by the latter to find a worthy buyer to carry on the business.

3. The firm may have grown to a size where new managerial techniques, which cannot be supplied by the present ownership, are required.

4. Income and estate tax problems often induce the sale of owner-managed firms.

EXHIBIT 2–6
Average Response for Merger Motives

Number	Motive	Average† Horizontal (N = 66)	Congeneric (N = 54)	Conglomerate (N = 29)
1	To effect more rapid growth	3.74 (1)	3.89 (1)	3.86 (1)
*2	To gain economies-of-scale	2.96 (2)	2.33 (9)	2.14 (7)
**3	To increase market share	2.94 (3)	2.61 (7)	1.79 (12)
**4	To expand geographically	2.91 (4)	2.02 (12)	2.10 (8)
5	To increase the market value of the stock	2.82 (5)	3.15 (3)	2.66 (3)
**6	To expand or improve the product mix	2.70 (6)	2.67 (6)	2.52 (4)
**7	To spread risk through diversification	2.49 (7)	3.61 (2)	3.31 (2)
8	To enhance the power and prestige of the firm	2.38 (8)	2.30 (10)	2.24 (6)
9	To invest the firm's idle capital	2.30 (9)	2.19 (11)	1.93 (11)
**10	To acquire technical knowledge and expertise	2.03 (10.5)	3.02 (4)	2.03 (9)
**11	To counter cyclical or seasonal sales	2.03 (10.5)	2.70 (5)	2.14 (5)
*12	To obtain managerial talent	1.80 (12)	2.41 (8)	1.74 (13)
13	To obtain tax advantages	1.61 (13)	1.67 (13)	2.00 (10)
14	To gain better control over supply sources and/or retail outlets	1.59 (14)	1.56 (15)	1.45 (14)
15	To defend against a possible takeover	1.49 (15)	1.59 (14)	1.35 (15)

*Chi-square significant at the .05 level
**Chi-square significant at the .01 level
†The scale used was no opinion (0), not important (1), slight importance (2), moderate importance (3), great importance (4), and maximum importance (5). Numbers in parentheses ( ) indicate relative ranking of motive.

Source: H. Kent Baker, Thomas O. Miller, and Brian J. Ramsperger. "A Typology of Merger Motives," *Akron Business and Review* (Winter 1981), p. 26.

5. Owner-managed firms may seek the benefits of diversification by selling out to more diversified corporations.
6. Sale may result from an offer that cannot be refused.

Promoters: The objectives of promoters inspiring business combinations are more translucent:

1. Attractive consulting and underwriting fees.
2. A desire to reap promotional or speculative gains accompanying new security issues or changed price/earnings ratios.

The reader will observe that the objectives cited by Steiner, Baker, and Sherer are more easily accomplished in a rising stock market and **53** economic expansion. The transitional problems generally accompanying business combinations are ameliorated by a high level of business activity. Moreover, optimists promote combinations and the vigor of a bullish stock market does much to bolster a rosy view of future prospects. We should not be surprised, therefore, by the association of merger waves with industrial activity and a rising stock market, discussed earlier. Conversely, one might hypothesize that combinations effected in periods of recession would, in greater degree, manifest defensive motivations—risk avoidance, cost reduction, diversification, and so on.

If as Dewing stresses, psychological factors mostly account for the "urge to merge," then we might anticipate an undercurrent of imitation running through periods of heightened merger activity. Some "in thing" (whether that be diversification, horizontal combination, economies-of-scale, etc.) appears to characterize each merger wave. The influence of the imitative factor in any series of merger decisions is, of course, impossible to measure. But if merger waves do indeed contain an imitative element, then it might serve to push the wave beyond the limits of prudence and undermine the quality of decision making. This, too, we can only hypothesize, lacking reference to specific research.

SUMMARY

This chapter has examined the statistics of merger activity in post–Civil War United States. Although the data clearly depicts periods of rising and falling merger activity, it would be premature to speak of merger cycles as a phenomenon similar to the business cycle. More likely merger waves are subsets of a rhythmic expansion and contraction in fundamental socio-economic variables. However, associating the rhythm of merger activity with other economic indicators casts some light on the conditions precedent to the rise and fall of the number of business combinations.

In this respect, there appear to be at least two conditions essential to the completion of a merger deal. First, the owners of the acquired firm (seller) must, for some reason, be willing to sell at a price lower than the full value of their facilities to the acquiring firm (buyer). Second, market imperfections prevent the acquisition price from being bid up to the cost of acquiring comparable assets through new construction. Market imperfections may be the consequence of restrictive practices in financial or industrial markets; institutional factors (tax laws, antitrust legislation, or other business regulations which impede price adjustments); the distortions introduced by inflationary or deflationary movements, and so forth[26].

Last, the quality of the evidence suggests due caution in generalizing about the characteristics and social effects of merger activity. Chapter 10 continues this theme in discussing the issue of public policy and business combinations.

NOTES

1. Ansoff, Brandenburg, Portner, and Radosevich. *Acquisition Behavior of U.S. Manufacturing Firms 1946–1965*. Nashville, Tennessee: 1971, reported in Peter O. Steiner's *Mergers*. Ann Arbor: University of Michigan Press, 1977. pp. 30–31.

2. Baker, H. Kent, Thomas O. Miller, and Brian J. Ramsperger. "A New Look at Merger Motives." Paper presented at the Eastern Finance Association Annual Meeting. April 22–25, 1981.

3. Brozen, Yale. *Mergers in Perspective*. Washington, D.C.: American Enterprise for Public Policy Research, 1982.

4. Chandler, Alfred D. *Strategy and Structure*, New York: Anchor Books, 1966. p 489.

5. Chiang, Thomas C. and Chakrobanti, Alok K. *Trend and Stochastic Movements in Merger Series*, Center for Research on Technology and Corporate Strategy, Drexel University, 1984.

6. Chiang, Thomas C. and Clark, John J. *Merger Movements and Stock Market Prices*, Center for Research on Technology and Corporate Strategy, Drexel University, 1984.

7. Chung, Kwang S. and J. Fred Weston. "Diversification in a Strategic Long-Range-Planning Framework." In Michael Keenan and Lawrence J. White's *Mergers and Acquisitions*. Massachusetts: Lexington Books, 1982. pp. 315–347.

8. Clark, John J. and Pieter Elgers. "Merger Types and Shareholder Returns: Additional Evidence." *Financial Management*. Summer 1980.

9. Dewing, Arthur Stone. *The Financial Policy of Corporations*. Vol. 2. New York: The Ronald Press Company, 1953. pp. 859–862, 812, 878–879, 883–889, 877, 898.

10. Federal Trade Commission. *Statistical Report on Mergers and Acquisitions*. Bureau of Economics, 1975.

11. Galbraith, John Kenneth. *The Great Crash*. New York: Houghton Mifflin, 1955.

12. Gort, Michael. "An Economic Disturbance Theory of Mergers." *Quarterly Journal of Economics*. November 1969. pp. 624–42.

13. Gray, E. *The Chrome Collossars (GM and Its Times)*. New York: McGraw-Hill Book Company, 1980.

14. Haugen, Robert A. and Terrence C. Langetieg. "An Empirical Test for Synergism in Mergers." *The Journal of Finance*. September 1975. pp. 1003–1014.

15. Hogarty, Thomas F. "The Profitability of Corporate Mergers." *Journal of Business*. July 1970. pp. 317–327.
———. "Profits from Mergers: The Evidence of 50 Years." *St. John's Law Review*. special ed. Vol. 44: p. 389. Spring 1970.

16. Kiernan, Charles J. "The Rise of the Collegiate School of Business." In John J. Clark and Blaise Opulente's *Business Education*. New York: St. John's University Press, 1960. pp. 1–26.

17. Kptoss, Herman E. *American Economic Development*. Englewood Cliffs: Prentice-Hall, 1955. pp. 276–281.

18. Livermore, Shaw. "The Success of Industrial Mergers." *Quarterly Journal of Economics*. November 1955. pp. 68–96.

19. Louis, Arthur M. "The Bottom Line on Ten Big Mergers." *Fortune*. May 3, 1982. pp. 84–89.

20. Lynch, Harry H. *Financial Performance of Conglomerates*. Boston: Division of Research, Graduate School of Business Administration, Harvard University, 1971, p. 21, 22, 27–28, 33–34.

21. Mandelker, Gerson. "Risk and Return: The Case of Mergin Firms." *Journal of Financial Economics*. December 1974. pp. 303–335.

22. Markham, Jesse W. "Survey of Evidence and Findings on Mergers." *Business Concentration and Price Policy*. Princeton, New Jersey: Princeton University Press, 1955. p. 157.

23. Moody, John. *The Truth About the Trusts*. New York: Moody Publishing Company, 1904. p. 487.

24. Mueller, Dennis C. "The Effects of Conglomerate Mergers: A Survey of the Empirical Evidence." *Journal of Banking and Finance.* Vol. 1. 1977. p. 339.

25. Myers, Gustavus. *History of the Great American Fortunes.* New York: The Modern Library, Random House, 1936. Part III.

26. Nelson, Ralph L. *Merger Movements in American Industry 1895–1956.* Princeton, New Jersey: Princeton University Press, 1959. pp. 90–91, 102.

27. Reid, Samuel R., John Bossons, and Kalman H. Cohen. "Mergers for Whom— Managers or Stockholders?" Working Paper No. 14. Workshop of Capital Market Equilibrating Process, Carnegie Institute of Technology, 1966.

28. Salter, Malcolm S. and Wolf A. Weinhold. *Diversification Through Acquisition.* New York: The Free Press, 1979. pp. 10, 11.

29. Sherer, F. M. *Industrial Market Structure and Economic Performance.* Chicago: Rand McNally & Company, 1971. pp. 113, 117–119.

30. Stigler, George J. "Monopoly and Oligopoly by Merger." *American Economic Review.* May 1950, pp. 68–96.

31. Steiner, Peter O. *Mergers.* Ann Arbor: University of Michigan Press, 1977. pp. 152, 154, 269, 30–31.

32. The People of the State of New York v. The North River Sugar Refining Company, 121 N.Y. 582.

33. Weston, J. Fred and Surenda K. Mansinghka. "Test of Efficiency Performance of Conglomerate Firms." *Journal of Finance.* September 1971. pp. 919–936.

ACQUISITION STRATEGY
Scope and Content

3

Acquisition of one firm by another should spring neither from the whim of corporate impulse buying nor from mere conformity with the temper of the times. The roots of decision run deeper. Proposals to acquire ongoing business units, we have stressed, constitute capital budgeting decisions since they relate to the allocation of investible funds. A proposed acquisition stands as one project in a set from which the company's capital budget is constructed. Capital budgets are normally evaluated against criteria established by the strategic objectives of the firm. These same criteria, therefore, apply to the evaluation of potential acquisitions.

The development of an acquisition strategy begins with the company's strategic planning:

> Buying a company on its balance sheet and profit-and-loss statement performance, without delving into the component factors of its operation and potentials, without knowing your company, and without comparing these two groups of knowledge to determine the integration benefits and savings possible, can lead to frustration and disillusionment [10].

The first step in articulating an acquisition strategy consistent with long-range company objectives is to know your own company. For example, what operational areas hold promise of future growth? What rate of growth can the company sustain without having to change its financial structure? What are the internal political and financial implications of changing the financial structure? How is growth defined and how is it expected to pay off? A multitude of similar basic questions arise in a properly outlined analysis prior to effecting a business combination.

The components of an acquisition strategy make up the subject matter of this chapter. However, there are some prerequisites to review preliminary to the discussion. **57**

Assumptions

Textbooks in financial management, if they look at the topic of business combinations, generally assume that the rationale of the enterprise is to increase the wealth position of the common stockholders. This may be stated as maximizing the market value of the common shares or maximizing the present worth of the common shares over their preacquisition values. The assumption undoubtedly holds a measure of truth, but the study of business combinations, we have seen, does not lend itself to easy generalization.

The problem with assuming that business combinations seek to maximize the market value of the common shares is that it hides another assumption; namely, that the corporation is managed primarily for the benefit of the stockholders who are *in law* the owners of the company and *in theory* the group to which management bears ultimate responsibility. The latter assumption does not always work out in practice. Concern for the common stockholders, to cite one instance, did not appear to motivate the response of McGraw-Hill management to the takeover attempt by American Express. In January 1979, American Express offered to buy McGraw-Hill shares for $34 paying a premium of 36 percent over the current market price. When this was rejected, a second offer of $40 per share was tendered paying a premium of 60 percent. McGraw-Hill also rejected the second offer. Although corporate management is not legally required to sell the firm when presented with an apparently attractive offer, the McGraw board resisted all attempts to put its judgment to the test of stockholder approval[4,10].

Earlier writers viewed major corporations as fundamentally under the thumb of the managers. Adolph A. Berle and Gardner Means in *The Modern Corporation and Private Property*, 1932, demonstrated that, although owned by the stockholders, actual control of many enterprises rested with the management, which pursued its own interests to the detriment of the shareholders. Personal management advantage in these cases substitutes for maximization of stockholder wealth. The Berleites of today might declare that the levels of executive compensation in Exhibit 3–1 do not indicate an overwhelming concern to maximize stockholder returns. The average compensation in Exhibit 3–1 for 1974 was $647,533 and in 1983, $4,911,467, an 868 percent increase in the 9-year period. *Business Week* (May 4, 1974) reported that:

> . . . executive pay scales are being examined today by the institutional investors whose buying decisions can have a dramatic effect on the performance of the company's stock. One large institution has already asked a compensation consultant to analyze the effect of executive salaries on the earnings per share and return on investment of all companies in its portfolio.

The debate continues. For our purpose the point is made. The business community still comprises many companies managed with the shareholder foremost in mind. Other companies may look upon the shareholders as a group to be placated by sophisticated public relations while man-

EXHIBIT 3–1
Fifteen Highest Paid U.S. Executives

1974

	Executive	Title	Company	Total Individual Compensation*
1.	Michael C. Bergerac	pres.	Revlon	$1,595,000
2.	Harold S. Geneen	chmn.	ITT	789,000
3.	J. Kenneth Jamieson	chmn.	Exxon	677,000
4.	William F. Laporte	chmn.	American Home Products	600,000
5.	Rawleigh Warner, Jr.	chmn.	Mobil Oil	596,000
6.	William S. Paley	chmn.	CBS	588,000
7.	Leonard H. Goldenson	chmn.	ABC	582,000
8.	Maurice F. Granville	chmn.	Texaco	579,000
9.	Charles J. Pilliod, Jr.	chmn.	Goodyear	564,000
10.	Meshulam Riklis	chmn.	Rapid-American	545,000
11.	Bob R. Dorsey	chmn.	Gulf Oil	544,000
12.	Elton H. Rule	pres.	ABC	525,000
13.	John D. Harper	chmn.	Alcoa	516,000
14.	Frank T. Cary	chmn.	IBM	511,000
15.	Williard F. Rockwell, Jr.	chmn.	Rockwell International	502,000

1983

	Executive	Title	Company	Total Individual Compensation*
1.	William S. Anderson	chmn.	NCR	$13,229,000
2.	Philip Caldwell	chmn.	Ford Motor	7,292,000
3.	David Tendler	co-chmn.	Phibro-Salomon	6,921,000
4.	Thomas S. Murphy	chmn.	Capital Cities	6,083,000
5.	Daniel B. Burke	pres.	Capital Cities	4,349,000
6.	William S. Cook	pres.	Union Pacific	4,301,000
7.	Edward R. Telling	chmn.	Sears Roebuck	4,221,000
8.	Gerard A. Fulham	chmn.	Pneumo	3,915,000
9.	Donald E. Petersen	pres.	Ford Motor	3,783,000
10.	George Weissman	chmn.	Philip Morris	3,718,000
11.	James F. Bere	chmn.	Borg-Warner	3,705,000
12.	Andrew S. Grove	pres.	Intel	3,395,000
13.	Richard R. Rogers	pres.	Mary Kay Cosmetics	3,106,000
14.	John F. Welch, Jr.	chmn.	General Electric	2,831,000
15.	James A. Wood	pres.	Pneumo	2,823,000

*Includes Annual Compensation and Long-Term Compensation
1. Total compensation includes salary, bonus, and long-term income.
2. The top fifteen are not a stable group. They reflect the shifting fortunes of particular companies and industry groups.
Source: Reprinted from the May 12, 1975 and May 7, 1984 issues of *Business Week* by special permission, © 1975 and © 1984 by McGraw-Hill, Inc.

agement takes care of itself. A growing number of companies have fallen under the spell of corporate bureaucrats and travel the comfortable road of "satisfaction," not maximization. Apropos of the latter group, Galbraith observes:

> In general, the technostructure will increase its investment as its retained earnings increase. Having taken care of its stockholders and creditors, and therewith assured its own security, it then devotes funds to the next highest priority among its goals, which is growth. And if the funds so available are

59

inadequate, the technostructure will increase its earnings or withhold more from the stockholders[5].

However we view the issue of corporate control, acquisition strategy has to acknowledge the presence of *at least* four interested parties—the management and stockholders of the combining firms. Each party has a self-interest to protect that may conflict with the concerns of the others. Moreover, the parties are not homogeneous classes but may comprise satellite groups with conflicting objectives. In the American Express/ McGraw-Hill encounter, the result was undoubtedly influenced by a rather discordant family ownership which controlled 20 percent of the common stock and an additional 29 percent stock holding by financial institutions[4,10]. We can rarely attribute a business combination to a single motivation, although the 10K report to the Securities and Exchange Commission invariably states the combination reflects the best interests of the stockholders. The astute analyst will look for a variety of motives that shape the terms of combination.

Financial analysis preceding a business combination focuses on the benefits and costs of the union. The relevant benefits and costs are the *incremental cash inflows and outflows of the combination over the total cash flows of the independent companies.* The incremental cash flows measure the total cash impact of the combination—all cash flows directly or indirectly stemming from the venture and that would disappear if the combination were cut short. Cost reductions and revenue increases are of equal significance in measuring the cash flows of the proposed combination, since each conveys an incremental cash effect. Also, the tax effect of the combination requires estimation, for the effects on tax liabilities of the combination are frequently indirect and often substantial.

Cash Flow Analysis

Cash inflows typically include the after-tax effects of additional operating revenues—less incremental operating expenses such as selling, administrative, and manufacturing outlays—and/or reductions in present operating expense levels. Indeed, for many combinations, reductions in expense items may be the only identifiable benefits. A major selling point of the Penn-Central merger, for example, was anticipated annual savings of $80 million in operating expenses, an amount sufficient to restore the profitability of the system[2]. Cash outflows, on the other hand, include anticipated expenditures for later renovation, expansion, overhaul, and so on.

Financial analysis alone does not allow a definitive conclusion regarding the desirability of the combination. The incremental cash inflows and outflows represent *forecasted* performance over some time frame. The one certainty about a forecast is that it will in some degree miss the mark. Results may be better or worse than forecasted. In the Penn-Central case cited above, the projected savings never materialized and indeed subsequent investigation showed that there were no grounds for such a projection in the first instance. Pan American's acquisition of National Airlines predicted incremental revenues from the integration of national and international air routes plus operational savings accruing from the merger of maintenance facilities. Neither set of aspirations has been attained to date, although the general industry downturn undoubtedly influenced the unhappy outcome. Needless to add, in forecasting incremental cash flows, the methodology of forecasting should be clearly outlined.

Qualitative Factors

Incremental cash inflows and outflows are forecasts of money incomes and money costs. Unfortunately, the money denominator does not reflect qualitative factors which may influence the destiny of the combination. A major challenge in any combination lies in organizing, for two independent organizations, a single management team working toward a set of common goals. However, experience proves that individual corporate loyalties die hard. A major contributing factor to the "wreck" of the Penn-Central was the persistent rivalry between Pennsylvania Railroad and New York Central executive personnel[2]. The painful evolution of General Motors from a decentralized collection of independent firms to a centralized managerial structure is well-filled with inherited animosities[6]. Other qualitative factors which may not enter the cash flow estimates include new technologies, changes in the institutional structure (tax laws, regulatory strictures, antitrust policies), international crises, and so forth.

Valuation

Finally, the marshalling of quantitative and qualitative data culminates in the process of valuation. The value of the acquired company depends on its potential contribution to the fulfillment of the acquiring firm's long-range objectives. The acquired firm is valued in terms of its potential contribution to the acquirer. As might be expected, the literature reveals a variety of valuation techniques ranging from short-term earnings per share projections to sophisticated discounted cash flow approaches and computer models. Each methodology rests upon certain assumptions and, given the same data, may yield quite different assessments. The appropriate technique is the one in which the assumptions most closely match the circumstances of the proposed combination.

Synergy

Chapter 5 tackles the problem of measuring synergism. At this point, we may simply state that the social justification and ultimate success of a business combination is determined by the presence of synergism. Synergism occurs when the market value of the combined enterprises exceeds the sum of their separate market values prior to the time when the securities markets discount their intention to "marry." Investors will place a higher value on the combined enterprise if they anticipate larger earnings for a given level of risk, a reduction in risk posture at the same level of earnings, or some otherwise favorable trade-off between risk and return. Specific sources of synergism might include replacement of incompetent management, economies-of-scale, extension of the product line, improved market control, reduction of business risk by restructuring operations, reduction in financial risk by revamping the capital structure, and so on.

Although the notion of synergism is easily understood, the identification and measurement of the synergism attributable to a particular combination gets rather involved. The following factors corrupt the calculation in practice:

1. If synergism appears, is it simply the consequence of riding an upward movement in the economy? Typically in capital budgeting, projects look better in the expansion phase of the business cycle than in recession. Thus, it occasions no surprise that merger activity tends to peak in periods of economic expansion and fall off when the economy turns down.

2. If synergism be measured by the increment in equity values, has the combination "beat the market" by earning a return above that warranted by the risk inherent in the combination? Or is synergism the product of security market imperfections—incorrect valuation of the merging firms?

3. Time is also a factor. Many mergers depend upon the reconstitution of the management team and the resolution of human relations problems. New control is always an upsetting event. Hence, it may be months or years down the line before the expectations of the promoters are realized. Over the same period, the economy or industry may have moved to higher levels of activity carrying the combination along and blurring attempts to measure the specific benefits of a single merger.

4. In framing the combination, the choice of accounting method (purchase or pooling) can favorably influence earnings per share without any basic change in the risk–return trade-off due to the merger. Does the market respond to the accounting numbers or to cash flow? Research is divided on the question.

5. Where a firm pursues an aggressive acquisitions policy, the overlapping results of successive combinations make it difficult to trace the synergistic effects of any single acquisition. Similarly, in the case of multiple product lines, the increased market value of the enterprise postcombination may derive from the enhanced market acceptance of an existing product line independent of the combination. An almost insoluble problem of disaggregation develops under these circumstances.

If the market is efficient, the enjoyment of synergism is restricted to the stockholders at the time the market discounts the merger. The new market price reflects the combination's anticipated earnings in relation to its adjusted risk posture. Only the present stockholders reap the capital gains. Subsequent holders buy in at the adjusted price which allows a return in proportion to the risk posture of the merged units.

In all events, the dynamics of the economy generally compel management to assess the wisdom of the combination. What is the contribution of the acquired firm to the market value of the enterprise? Would the market value of the combination be enhanced by divestiture of the acquired firm? The answer to the latter question was affirmative in the case of The International Nickel Company of Canada, Limited (INCO) and ESB Incorporated:

> International Nickel Company of Canada, Limited (INCO) mines, refines, and markets nickel in a variety of forms from Canadian ores. The Company also produces and markets from these same ores substantial amounts of copper and platinum-group metals, as well as iron ore, and limited quantities of cobalt, gold, silver, sulphur, selenium, and tellurium. In addition, INCO produces and markets foundry additives and a wide range of nickel and high-nickel alloy rolling mill products. The Company is also actively engaged in increasing production from present sources and in the exploration for and development of new sources of nickel and other metals as well as other resources.
>
> ESB Incorporated is primarily engaged in the manufacture and sale of electric batteries and related items. The Company also manufactures and sells several other product lines, no one of which accounted for 10 percent of net sales or income before income taxes. The more important products in each of the principal lines of business are as follows:
>
> - Dry cell batteries for use in flashlights, lanterns, and so on.
> - Batteries for automobiles, trucks, and transportation vehicles.
> - Industrial batteries for use in forklift trucks, voltage regulation, and similar industrial uses.
> - Specialty batteries for a variety of military and space applications.
>
> The INCO-ESB merger was exceptionally interesting for several reasons:
>
> 1. It represented a widely publicized takeover of an American firm by a Canadian suitor.
> 2. After the ESB merger, no significant acquisitions by INCO occurred. Accordingly, the analysis is simplified in estimating any synergistic effects identifiable with the INCO-ESB merger.
> 3. To enter the battery business, INCO had to outlast United Technologies Corporation—an aerospace giant—in a spirited 1974 bidding contest for ESB. The management of ESB sided with United Technologies Corporation.
>
> The INCO-ESB merger took place in 1974 and the consensus of financial opinion leaned to the belief that the move would benefit INCO. Expectations were not realized. A history of earnings before taxes for the ESB batteries and related products of INCO follows:

	(millions)	*Return on original investment*
1974 (yr. of acquisition—August 1974)	$7	.00003
1975	17	.00007
1976	16	.00007
1977	15	.00007
1978	33	.00014
1979	36	.00015
1980	(24)	(.00010)

Effective December 1981, the INCO's Board of Directors approved a program of withdrawal from the battery and related products business.

INCO recorded a provision for the loss on disposition of its battery and related products businesses of $245 million after tax relief of $46.9 million. The provision included net losses expected to be incurred by the various businesses after November 1981, until the estimated dates of disposition, as well as anticipated losses on disposition.

As a consequence of the ESB experience, INCO decided to rethink its acquisition strategy. INCO concluded divestiture would enable it to concentrate the company's financial strength and management resources on primary metals and other natural resources and alloy products in accordance with a long-term objective of achieving profitable, sustainable growth in those businesses involving technology broadly compatible with the company's skills[9].

ACQUISITION STRATEGY

Acquisition strategy is a major element in the firm's strategic plan. However, it constitutes more than a broad statement of intent. The articulation of an acquisition strategy may begin with a preamble but involves statements of policy on particular decision points. These components, of course, vary with the type of business and the objectives of the firm. Nevertheless, a degree of generalization is possible. At a minimum, an acquisition strategy should spell out the firm's position on the following questions:

1. *Direct or Indirect Investment:* Does the firm plan to expand *internally* using funds generated by retained earnings or by the issuance of new securities or *externally* by combination with an ongoing business? Or will the firm resort to a prudent combination of both approaches? There are advantages and disadvantages associated with internal and external modes of expansion.

2. *Type of Expansion:* Does the firm seek to expand by vertical or horizontal integration; by product extension, market extension, or pure conglomerate form? The issues involved here include: working capital requirements, fixed asset investments, effectiveness of operations control, market control and penetrations, diversification of product lines, potential for antitrust actions, managerial efficiency, risk posture, and so forth.

3. *Legal Form of Combination:* Whether expansion is arranged by purchase of assets, merger, consolidation, holding company, or leasing, the implications go beyond the legal niceties. The specific legal form of the combination can affect the style of management (centralized or decentralized), tax liabilities, accounting considerations, method of financing, and ease of divestiture.

4. *Compatible Technologies:* Will expansion relate to product lines which bear an affinity to the product line of the acquiring company? Or does the acquisition represent a departure from the familiar operations of the firm? At issue here is the transferability of management skills and organizational integration.

5. *Accounting Options:* Conventional accounting practice offers the option of recording a combination as a purchase or as pooling. Other options relate to asset cost recovery, the valuation of inventories, the structure of leasing arrangements, asset write-offs, and so on. The choice of accounting options affects the bottom line of the income statement and may "instantly" improve earnings per share. If we assume that accounting numbers influence the market value of the common shares (and management people tend to accept the gospel), then the choice of accounting options is a significant component in an acquisition strategy.

6. *Tax Options:* Tax considerations surface in every business transaction and more so in business combinations. Whether the transaction will qualify as a taxable or tax-free exchange interacts with the choice of accounting options and the legal form of the combination. The pervasiveness of the tax issues compel their inclusion in the formulation of an acquisition strategy.

7. *Antitrust Action:* An acquisition strategy must assess the probability of antitrust action by the Justice Department or state authorities. Some forms of combination are more likely to attract prosecution than others. Suffice to say, if the acquisition is substantial in its impact on the degree of competition, management should seek an informal review by the Justice Department. This may protect the parties against the criminal provisions of the antitrust laws if not the civil penalties.

8. *Behavioral Problems:* Corporate loyalties can be retained and used to advantage in a decentralized organizational structure or a conscious effort can be made to build new allegiances. What cannot be done without risk of managerial chaos is to distribute corporate offices in the combined enterprise on some favor basis without regard to the management styles of the incumbents. Chapter 7 deals with the human resource component in business combinations.

9. *Defense Against Takeover:* Acquisition strategy is not the sole function of acquisitive firms. The prevalence of unfriendly tender offers suggest that corporate management consider the vulnerability of the company to a takeover and devise defensive tactics *before the event*.

For example, Beech Aircraft Corporation, knowing it was ripe for acquisition because of the age of the founding family and because of its place as one of the country's largest makers of general aviation aircraft, set forth its criteria for an acceptable merger partner and actively sought out a firm that would maintain the Beech identity and management. After discussions with General Dynamics and Grumman, Beech selected the Raytheon Company as its preferred partner[10]. Contrast the behavior of Beech with that of McGraw-Hill. When presented with the possibility of a takeover by American Express, McGraw-Hill, caught without a defensive strategy, had to hastily employ Morgan-Stanley to outgeneral the attacker[4,10].

10. *Nature of Consideration:* Whether the decision be for direct or indirect investment, the question of how to finance the acquired assets takes high priority. Consideration may be cash, long-term debt, preferred stock, common stock, or some combination thereof. The choice depends upon the liquidity and financial structure of the acquiring firm as well as the preferences of the seller. For example, SOHIO used the excess liquidity derived from its Alaskan pipeline venture to acquire Kennecott. By contrast, Humana, with a D/E ratio of three to one, resorted to a combination of cash and preferred stock with a contingent dividend of $2.50 to acquire American Medicorp[3]. The consideration package also interacts with the accounting treatment of the combination. If the assets are acquired for cash, debt, or preferred stock, the transaction constitutes a purchase and the potential benefits of pooling are forfeited.

11. *Divestiture:* The firm's present worth represents a trade-off between risk and return. That trade-off can be improved by an appropriate acquisition or by a judicious divestiture. When Heublein disposed of Hamm's Brewery, it absorbed a $26.5 million dollar write-off but return on equity increased to 20 percent, well above the minimum established by corporate policy[7].

12. *Financial Objectives:* What is the minimum return on assets (ROA) desired by the acquiring firm? Will the acquiring firm be required to invest new funds in the acquired firm to achieve the ROA goal? Does the acquired firm have an earnings growth rate sufficient to offset any temporary dilution in earnings per share?

The preceding list of decision points in the development of acquisition strategy is by no means exhaustive. It follows, therefore, that the decision to expand by combination merits more attention than the temporary deliberations of an *ad hoc* committee appointed when the occasion arises. A firm seriously contemplating indirect investment does well to establish a staff of key personnel meeting periodically to monitor likely candidates for acquisition and to survey operating units for possible disposal. Such a standing committee would also draft a detailed acquisition policy for submission to top management and update that policy to keep abreast of changing circumstances. This would coordinate acquisition strategy with the strategic objectives of the firm and place proposals to acquire or divest business units in the context of the firm's capital budgeting criteria.

Given the confidential nature of the subject matter, the standing committee (few in number but high in rank) should have direct access to the chief executive officer and chairman of the board. Other parties, internal and external, can be drafted into the discussion process on a need-to-know basis when the time arrives to fashion concrete proposals.

Careful planning will increase the probability of a successful acquisition, but no amount of planning can guarantee success in an arena fraught with so many hazards. Louis listed the following second thoughts of management on some prominent acquisitions ten years after the event[8]. (See table opposite.)

In "A Tale of Two Acquisitions," Hall traces out the application of two relatively similar acquisition strategies[7]:

Case 1: In 1966, Heublein, the fifth largest liquor company in the U.S., acquired Hamm's Brewing. Heublein had three strategic objectives: to make Smirnoff vodka the number one liquor brand in the world, to continue a

Acquiring Company (A) Acquired Company (B)	What the Acquirer Said About the Acquisition	
	Then	Recently
Schering (A) Plough (B)	The two companies complement each other well. Schering's research and international operations will benefit Plough.	Schering's international people didn't adapt well to consumer products. That synergism took longer than we thought.
Heublein (A) Kentucky Fried Chicken (B)	Gives us a strong position in fast foods; provides immediate new dimensions and promising prospects.	We learned the hard way; we made our share of mistakes; we took too long to move down the learning curve.
Squibb (A) Lanvin-Charles of the Ritz (B)	The proxy statement can't spell out the growth opportunities that we believe lie ahead of Lanvin-Charles of the Ritz	We made some mistakes because we didn't understand the business. But our direction was correct.
RCA (A) Coronet Industries (B)	Should provide valuable diversification in an important consumer growth area.	We will consider the sale of Coronet when market conditions warrant.
Northwest Industries (A) Buckingham (B)	Buckingham is a fine company with a strong earnings record.	Of importance in 1981 was the unsolicited cash sale of our beverages segment; sale was a proper strategic move.
American Cyanamid (A) Shulton (B)	Brought us a fine name with an excellent product line.	We'd be a much more cyclical company if we didn't have Shulton. Synergy in research took too long to come.
General Host (A) Cudahy (B)	Represents a significant step toward our goal of acquiring businesses with proven earnings.	The divestiture of Cudahy's meat business will minimize our vulnerability to this cyclical, commodity-driven business.
Johns-Manville (A) Holophane (B)	Establishes Johns-Manville as a prominent entity of lighting fixtures and components.	During much of the past decade, Holophane has distinguished itself as a contributor to our sales and earnings.

10 percent annual sales growth, and to maintain a return on the common equity above 15 percent. Based upon these strategic objectives, Heublein established acquisition criteria: that the acquired product line or company have a growth potential at least equal to Heublein's existing product line, that the new product line or company utilize the same distribution channels and marketing techniques as Heublein, and that the acquired products have a gross profit margin to support the Heublein distribution, advertising, and merchandising programs. In a purchase transaction, Heublein acquired Hamm's common stock in exchange for a 5 percent convertible preferred stock.

Hamm Brewing Company was a family-owned, regional brewer located in St. Paul, Minnesota. Hamm, ranked as the ninth largest brewer in the U.S., saw its share of the market decline during the 1960s from 4.5 percent to 3.7 percent. The company's sales organization spanned thirty-one midwestern, western, and southwestern states through exclusive franchise to 480 independent wholesalers.

Heublein moved promptly to revamp Hamm's product line, distribution, and advertising:

67

1966: Introduced a tapper keg and Hamm's "Real Draft Beer" in aluminum cans.

1967: Expanded the Los Angeles brewery and phased out the Houston brewery; entered the Detroit market; sales rose 8 percent to set a record high in Hamm's history.

1968: Introduced Velvet Glove Malt Liquor and new packaging for all Hamm products.

1969: Heublein reorganized its subsidiaries and divisions into profit centers; Hamm sales failed to meet expectations; appointed a new president for Hamm to develop an aggressive marketing strategy; entered new markets in Louisiana and Indiana; set up a new advertising campaign.

1970: Hamm met tough competition in expanding sales.

1971: Heublein acquired Kentucky Fried Chicken and set up a group structure of organization; Hamm put in a group with Smirnoff and the import divisions; Hamm had a profitable year and penetrated the Nashville, Toledo, and Dayton markets.

1972: Hamm again hit heavy competition in its western and midwestern markets; sales declined and Hamm did not contribute to corporate profits; to fight the competition, Hamm acquired a new product (Burgermeister), a new president, new advertising, and new packaging.

1973: More losses and Heublein announced decision to divest Hamm.

On the surface, the error in Heublein's strategy lay in the belief that promotion and distribution policies were the critical variables in making Hamm a winner. But Hamm's production facilities were undersized, old, inefficient, and poorly integrated. Too late did Heublein face up to the technological and manufacturing problems of Hamm. (Heublein repeated the error in the Kentucky Fried Chicken acquisition.) On the other hand, Heublein's problems with Hamm sprang fundamentally from an acquisition strategy that neglected to emphasize that an acquired firm has to be managed as a total business entity, not simply as a marketing problem. A synoptic appraisal of Hamm would have impelled Heublein to assess all facets of the Hamm operation and define its objectives in relation to the assets and limitations of Hamm. Heublein's lack of foresight triggered an inconsistent set of marketing strategies which papered over the real issues until time ran out.

Case 2: In 1969 Philip Morris (PM) acquired Miller's Brewing. PM, by 1969, serviced 16 percent of the U.S. cigarette market and 6 percent of the international market. Common shareholders earned 16.2 percent on their investment. However, looking down the road, PM anticipated a lower growth rate in sales as domestic consumption of cigarettes leveled off. On the plus side, given PM's market position, cash flow would increase substantially. PM needed a growth business in which to invest this cash flow. Like Heublein, PM sought an investment where the marketing skills of the organization could be best applied. The brewing industry seemed to promise a good match of management skills and investment opportunity for PM.

PM purchased 53 percent of Miller's stock from W. R. Grace Company and the remaining 47 percent from the De Rance Foundation. The total purchase price was $227 million. Miller produced one product—Miller High Life Beer—one of three nationally distributed premium priced beers in the

U.S. market. By 1969, Miller was the eighth largest domestic brewer with
a 4.4 percent market share. Miller owned modern production facilities in the midwest, west, and southwest and distributed its product through a network of 705 independent beer wholesalers in fifty states. PM's stated long-term objective for Miller was to increase its share of the premium beer market rather than seek short-term profit advantages.

1970:   The capacity of the Fort Worth brewery was enlarged and a site purchased for a new eastern brewery; Miller sales organization was overhauled; sales increased but operating income continued to decline.

1971:   PM puts in a new management team of personnel from its international division; new product added (Miller Malt Liquor); new advertising campaign; Texas and California breweries converted to aluminum cans; sales increased by 2.8 percent while operating income continued to decline.

1972:   Trade names and distribution network of Meister Brau acquired; Milwaukee Ale and Miller Ale introduced; several innovations in packaging; sales increased by 3 percent but operating income continued to decline.

1973:   Miller announced a $200 million dollar capital expenditure program to modernize, expand, and integrate plant and equipment; sales increased again but Miller had an operating loss.

1974:   A new can plant approved for construction at the Fort Worth installation; economies-of-scale began to pay off; Miller ran a $6.3 million profit.

1975:   Dollar revenues increased 63 percent; operating income increased 400 percent; Miller became the fourth largest U.S. brewer; Miller Lite Beer introduced along with a $10 million promotional campaign; Miller assumed exclusive U.S. distribution rights for Lowenbrau, a premium German beer.

1976:   Capacity again expanded; Miller moved into third position behind Schlitz.

Why did Heublein's strategy fail and PM's succeed? Their stated objectives were not entirely dissimilar. But PM, while looking to revise the marketing strategy of Miller, managed the acquired firm as a total business entity. The new Miller management team coordinated marketing innovations with the demands of manufacturing. PM's management, furthermore, displayed enough self-confidence to carry the burden of short-term losses until the new policies bore fruit.

The reader may properly remark that the real difference in the experience of Heublein and PM lay not in acquisition strategy *per se* but in the quality of management. Whatever Hamm's limitations, it was not destined to fail. A more perceptive management might have defined a market position which, after due attention to the manufacturing problem, would have enabled Hamm to operate profitably. The history of business combinations is crowded with illustrations of apparently well-suited acquisitions failing for lack of managerial skill. Equally, one can point to acquisitions, seemingly ill-suited, which prove successful because of strong, dynamic business leadership. In other words, an acquisition must be *doable*. No matter how attractive an acquisition strategy may be, it is doomed to failure unless the acquiring firm has the personnel, the will, and the means to execute the plan.

SUMMARY Proposals to merge relate to strategic planning and capital budgeting. Merger projects, therefore, have to meet the same criteria for acceptance established by the firm for inclusion in the capital budget. But, since acquisitions present unique problems, the analysis of merger projects merits the attention of an ongoing planning group, apart from the corporate staff normally engaged in capital project evaluation.

Acquisition strategy takes form in a general policy statement setting forth the objectives of the firm in making this type of investment. Broad policy is implemented by specifying criteria to guide the search for a suitable acquisition. These criteria refer to the type of combination sought (vertical, horizontal, etc.), the legal form of the combination, the optimal profile of the acquired firm, the preferred method of financing, and so on. This chapter briefly discussed the more obvious decision points to implement an acquisition strategy. Subsequent chapters provide a more complete discussion supported by reference to pertinent business experience.

NOTES 1. Clark, John J. and Pieter Elgers. "Merger Types and Shareholder Returns: Additional Evidence." *Financial Management*. Summer 1980.
2. Daughen, Joseph R. and Peter Binzen. *The Wreck of the Penn Central*. Boston: Little, Brown, and Company, 1971. pp. 90–128.
3. Eisen, Edward N. "Anatomy of a Merger." *The Philadelphia Evening Bulletin*. February 12–15, 1978.
4. Friendly, Fred. W. "McGraw-Hill and a Free Press." The *Wall Street Journal*. January 26, 1979.
5. Galbraith, John Kenneth. *The New Industrial State*. Boston: Houghton Mifflin Company, 1967. p. 221.
6. Gray, Ed. *Chrome Colossus: General Motors and Its Times*. New York: McGraw-Hill Book Company, 1980.
7. Hall, William K. "A Tale of Two Acquisitions." *Business Review*. University of Michigan, Graduate School of Business Administration, May 1977, pp. 1–8.
8. Louis, Arthur M. "The Bottom Line on Ten Big Mergers." *Fortune*. May 3, 1982. pp. 84–89. © 1982 Time Inc., All rights reserved.
9. Securities and Exchange Commission, *10K Reports*. Appropriate years prior to and after combination.
10. The *Wall Street Journal*. January 10, 1979; January 11, 1979; January 12, 1979; January 15, 1979; January 17, 1979; January 20, 1979; January 22, 1979; January 29, 1979; January 30, 1979; January 31, 1979; February 1, 1979; February 2, 1979; February 12, 1979; February 20, 1979; February 23, 1979; February 26, 1979.
11. Tincher, William R. "Yardsticks for Evaluating Corporate Acquisitions." *Management Review*. October 1964. pp. 33–45.

ACQUISITION STRATEGY
Financial Analysis

Assume that management has an established policy on acquisitions accompanied by specific criteria to measure the suitability of a merger partner. Assume, too, that on the basis of this acquisition strategy it has focused on certain industries that appear most likely to contain desirable candidates. The next step involves identifying individual firms within these industries which best fit the financial requirements, technology, and managerial talent of the acquiring firm.

Initially, the firm identification process centers on financial evaluation. Several techniques of evaluation are available, but their usefulness depends upon the objectives of the analyst. From our perspective, since acquisition projects are part of the firm's capital budget, there are two preferred methods of valuation: Net Present Value (NPV) and Capital Asset Pricing (CAP). Both rely on the projection of future benefits and costs; both treat value as the product of a trade-off between risks and return[5].

Before illustrating the use of NPV in assessing the feasibility of a prospective merger, it is useful to review some related concepts bearing on the management of debt and equity funding.

TERMINOLOGY OF FINANCIAL ANALYSIS

Cost of Capital: Exhibit 4–1 presents the balance sheet and supporting data of Electro Industry. The asset side shows the business capital of the firm as $20,000,000. How did Electro finance the acquisition of these assets?

In this respect, several terms circulate widely in financial literature but sometimes with careless regard for their content.

EXHIBIT 4–1
Electro Industry Balance Sheet
December 31, 198X

ASSETS

Current Assets

Cash	$ 515,000
Receivables	1,400,000
Inventories	1,000,000
Prepaid Interest	85,000

Long-Term Assets

Plant and Equipment,
at cost
Less: Accumulated
Depreciation
($2,000,000)   12,000,000
Investment in
Subsidiaries   5,000,000
Total $20,000,000

LIABILITIES

Current Liabilities

Accounts Payable[1]	$ 500,000
Notes Payable[2]	1,500,000

Long-Term Debt

Bonds Payable[3]	2,000,000

Net Worth

Preferred Stock[4]	2,000,000
Common Stock[5]	2,000,000
Capital in Excess of Par Value	5,000,000
Retained Earnings[6]	7,000,000
	$20,000,000

Notes
[1]Company policy is to take advantage of all trade discounts.
[2]Represents a continuing, long-established line of credit with Repo National Bank, discounted at 6 percent, for one year.
[3]Issued at par; coupon rate, twenty percent, paid semiannually; ten year maturity; the bond presently sells at a discount yielding 12 percent.
[4]Issued at $20 par; 100,000 shares issued with a stated dividend of $2 per share; preferred shares presently sell at $15.
[5]Common stock at par value of $2; one million shares outstanding; sold at $7 per share.
[6]Electro projects earnings per share (EPS) for 198X at $3.00 and plans to declare a $1.50 dividend. Dividends have been growing at the rate of 7 percent. The current market price approximates $16. Electro has a marginal tax rate (Federal and state) of 48 percent. To simplify matters, Electro has no transaction costs on the sale of existing or new securities.

Capitalization refers to the basic commitment of debt and equity funds evidenced by debt certificates with liabilities in excess of one year plus paid-in capital. The total traditionally excludes current liabilities and retained earnings. For Electro, the capitalization is $11,000,000.

Capital structure, on the other hand, includes long-term debt, paid-in capital, and retained earnings. This is sometimes referred to as invested capital. Current liabilities are again excluded. Electro's capital structure totals $18,000,000.

Financial structure includes the entire right-hand side of the balance sheet: current liabilities, long-term debt, and net worth. This figure equals the total assets of $20,000,000.

The normal order in which assets convert to cash suggests two categories of business capital:

Working capital assets or the total current assets normally expected to cycle through cash within one fiscal or operating period from the balance sheet date: cash on hand or on deposit, marketable securities, receivables, inventories, and prepaid expenses. Electro has $3,000,000 in working capital assets.

Long-term assets have a life of two or more fiscal periods; normally amortized against earnings over their life span: plant and equipment, goodwill, patents, and copyrights. Some long-term assets such as land and investments in subsidiaries are not typically amortized. Electro's long-term assets are $17,000,000.

Similarly, the sequence of maturities leads to a classification of the sources of funds:

Current liabilities usually mature within one fiscal year from the balance sheet date; for example, notes and accounts payable, taxes payable, and accrued expenses. These total $2,000,000 for Electro.

Long-term debts with maturities extending beyond a single fiscal period as bonds payable, deferred liability reserves, and so forth. Electro has $2,000,000 in bonds outstanding.

Paid-in capital represents sums paid to the corporation on the original issue of preferred and common stock including any excess over par or stated value. Preferred and common shareholders originally paid Electro $9,000,000.

The *excess* of total assets over creditor and ownership claims takes the form of *retained earnings*. Electro has accumulated $7,000,000 from past years' profits.

In most industrial companies, the capital structure will cover the total fixed assets and make some contribution to total current assets. This contribution equals net working capital, the excess of total current assets over current liabilities.

The cost of capital (K) refers to the weighted average cost of each of the different sources of capital represented on the right side of the balance sheet: short- and long-term debt, preferred stock, common stock, and retained earnings. *Each of these different sources of capital funds has a cost, implicit or explicit.* There is no such phenomenon as free capital. The cost of capital has several distinctive features:

1. It is composed of two elements: the risk-free rate of return (R_F) and a premium for risk (P). Thus, $K = R_F + P$. The risk-free rate of return is approximated by the yield on short-term U.S. Treasury securities. The premium for risk represents the *market's assessment* of the firm's risk posture—the number of points above the risk-free rate necessary to compensate the investor for committing his funds to the fortunes of the enterprise.

2. If the return on assets (ROA) falls short of the cost of capital (K), the market value of the firm's securities will decline until the yield is sufficient to cover the risk-free rate (R_F) plus the premium for risk (P) associated with the firm.

3. It follows that the firm should earn an *average* rate of return on new projects (including acquisitions) at least equal to or greater than its cost

EXHIBIT 4–2
Electro Industry Average Cost of Capital Book Weights

1	2	3	4	5 (3 × 4)
Source of Funds	*Amount*	*Proportion*	*Cost*	*Weighted Cost*
Notes Payable	$1,415,094	.0729	.0312[1]	.00227
Bonds Payable	2,000,000	.1030	.0771[2]	.00794
Preferred Stock	2,000,000	.1030	.1000[3]	.01030
Common Stock	7,000,000	.3605	.1638[4]	.11811
Retained Earnings	7,000,000	.3605		
Totals	$19,415,094	1.0000 (rounded)		
Weighted Average Cost of Capital (K)				.13862

Notes

[1]*Cost of Short-Term Debt* (K_c): The present value of $1,500,000 discounted for one year at 6 percent is $1,415,094. Therefore,

$$K_c = \frac{I}{P}(1 - T) \tag{1}$$

where,

K_c = Explicit cost of commercial credit
I = Interest deducted in advance ($1,500,000 − $1,415,094 = $84,906)
P = Present value of principal amount of debt
T = Marginal tax rate, 48%

Then,

$$K_c = \frac{\$84,906}{\$1,415,094}(1 - .48)$$
$$= .0312 \text{ or } 3.12\%$$

[2]*Cost of Long Term Debt* (K_d): The time adjusted cost of long-term debt is the rate (K_d) which equates the after tax interest payments $[I(1 - T)]$ and the principal at maturity (A) with the net proceeds of the issue (P). Hence,

$$P = \sum_{t=1}^{N} \frac{I(1 - T)}{(1 + K_b)^t} + \frac{A}{(1 + K_b)^N} \tag{2}$$

where t represents an interest payment period ($t = 1,2,3 \ldots 20$ for semiannual payments over 10 years) and N equals the number of years to maturity. Therefore,

$$\$2,000,000 = \sum_{t=1}^{20} \frac{\$200,000\,(1 - .48)}{(1 + K_b)^t} + \frac{\$2,000,000}{(1 + K_b)^{10}} \qquad K_d = .0771 \text{ or } 7.71\%$$

[3]*Cost of Preferred Stock* (K_{PS}): The cost of preferred stock (K_{PS}) relates the stated dividend per share (D_p) to the proceeds per share (P) representing the selling price less the flotation costs:

$$K_{PS} = \frac{D_p}{P} \tag{3}$$

In the absence of flotation costs,

$$K_{PS} = \frac{\$2}{\$20}$$
$$= .10 \text{ or } 10\%$$

[4]*Cost of Common Stock* (K_c): The cost of common is simply the current yield adjusted for the anticipated growth in dividends:

$$K_c = \frac{D_o}{P_o} + g \tag{4}$$

where

D_o = current period dividend
P_o = current market price
g = forecasted growth in dividends

Hence,

$$K_c = \frac{\$1.50}{\$16} + .07$$
$$= .1637 \text{ or } .1638$$

Since the book value of common stock includes retained earnings, K_c also represents the cost of retained earnings.

of capital. If it fails to do so, the market value of its securities will eventually decline. Therefore, assuming the firm continues to reinvest in projects related to present operations (no change in risk posture), the cost of capital tends to coincide with the firm's *reinvestment rate of return*.

4. It follows too that the cost of capital is the rate of return that will maintain the market value of the firm's outstanding securities and/or permit the enterprise to sell new securities at market value.

5. The cost of capital is not a static figure to be calculated and posted on the company bulletin board. It is a *dynamic* figure sensitive to changes in the money and capital markets as well as investor perceptions of the quality and trend of company earnings and financial plans.

Although the concept of cost of capital is easily grasped, in practice, the instability of the data allows only an approximate calculation. Exhibit 4–2 calculates Electro's cost of capital using nominal yields and book value weights. The resulting weighted average cost reflects the cost of incurred debt and the contemporary cost of equity capital. Book value weights have the advantages of stability and accessability especially in the case of small companies that infrequently resort to new financing and lack an active market for their securities. On the other hand, book values mirror the circumstances of prior periods—the financial and business risk of the firm and conditions in the money and capital markets at the time of original issue. However, the market value of common shares in a going concern will vary from the book value. Market values reflect current appraisals by investors of the firm's growth prospects and its financial policies, along with the state of the money and capital markets. Book values are static whereas market values are dynamic. In periods of business expansion, market values tend to exceed book values.

Exhibit 4–3 underscores two features of market value weights. When market values exceed book values, equity tends to make up a higher proportion of the capital structure. Since equity shares are also the more costly source of capital, the average cost based upon market weights will be higher. Hence, if the firm shapes future financing in the same proportions represented by market weights, the capital structure will evolve toward a higher proportion of equity financing when market values exceed book values.

While the case for using market weights is theoretically strong, it must be acknowledged that market values fluctuate more widely than book values. This means that Electro would have to utilize an average market value for each class of securities. For small companies, and those whose securities are sold sporadically at widely separated intervals, the questionable reliability of market averages undermines confidence in the calculated cost of capital. Whether book or market weights, the computation of K in Exhibits 4–2 and 4–3 is a compromise with the true notion of K.

EXHIBIT 4–3
Electro Industry
Average Cost of Capital
Market Weights

1	2	3	4	5 (3 × 4)
Source of Funds	*Amount*	*Proportion*	*Cost*	*Weighted Cost*
Notes Payable	$ 1,415,094[1]	.0660	.0314	.00207
Bonds Payable	2,000,000[2]	.0934	.0771	.00720
Preferred Stock	2,000,000[2]	.0934	.1000	.00934
Common Stock Retained Earnings	$16,000,000[3]	.7472	.1638	.12239
Total	$21,415,094	1.0000		
Weighted Average Cost of Capital (K)				.14100

Notes
[1] Net of prepaid interest on discounted note.
[2] Assume bonds and preferred stock are selling at their par value.
[3] One million shares at $16 per share. Market value of common also covers retained earnings.

As calculated above, K is basically historical. It may coincide with the firm's true cost of capital if (1) the firm raises new funds in the same proportions as the existing capital structure, (2) the earnings potential and risk posture of the enterprise are otherwise unaffected, and (3) fundamental forces shaping the structure of interest rates in the money and capital markets have not altered—not a highly probable confluence of events. *The true cost of capital is that return which meets the current expectations of investors.*

The *marginal cost of capital* (K_{mc}) most closely approximates the criteria set forth on pages 76–77. K_{mc} represents the weighted average cost of the *next* dollar of capital; a composite cost of new debt, new preferred, and new equity *weighted by the proportions intended by the company in new financing.* For example, assume Electro plans to obtain additional funds of $11,000,000: $4,000,000 in new common, $4,000,000 in retained earnings, $500,000 in new preferred, and $2,500,000 in long-term debt. The new financing represents a three-year plan to double the invested capital of Electro. Underwriters have advised the management that a coupon rate of 12 percent on long-term debt and 14 percent on preferred will be necessary to sell these securities at par. The new common will have to offer the prospect of a 20 percent yield. Exhibit 4–4 calculates Electro's marginal cost of capital.

Electro's marginal cost of capital (K_{mc}) exceeds the weighted average cost (K) whether computed with book or market weights. Electro will pay about 15.1 cents for each dollar of new financing composed of approximately one cent for long-term debt, one-half of a cent for preferred, thirteen cents for equity, and one-third of a cent for the continuing line of credit.

The actual cost of the next composite dollar of capital may be greater or less than the average cost (K). The risk attributes of net operating income may diminish or intensify over time; debt/equity ratios may change and the firm may seek additional funds in proportions different from the

EXHIBIT 4–4
Electro Industry
Marginal Cost of Capital

1	2	3	4	5 (3 × 4)
Source of Funds	*Amount*	*Proportion*	*Cost*	*Weighted Cost*
Notes Payable	$1,415,094[1]	.1139	.0314	.00358
Long-Term Debt	2,500,000	.2014	.0624[2]	.01257
Preferred Stock	500,000	.0403	.1400	.00564
Common Stock	4,000,000	.3222 ⎫		
Retained Earnings	4,000,000	.3222 ⎬	.2000	.12888
Totals	$12,415,094	1.0000		
Marginal Cost of Capital ($\overline{K}_{mc}$)				.15067

Notes:
[1]Line of credit with Repo National Bank continues unaffected by the new financing.
[2]Cost of debt is after-tax: $.12 \times (1 - .48) = .0624$.

existing capital structure; or fiscal and monetary policy may shift the structure of interest rates with perhaps unequal impact on short- and long-term financing arrangements. To these undeterminables must be added investor psychology. The expectations of investors, their risk–return trade-offs, fix the risk premium sought from investment in the company. Such perceptions fluctuate with prevailing moods of optimism or pessimism. In brief, neither K nor K_{mc} is a static figure, computed and enshrined. Alert financial management follows dynamic movements in the money and capital markets *to minimize the cost of capital.*

The rationale for a composite rate for the cost of capital rather than a single source—for example, K_e—rests upon explicit assumptions.

- All capital projects are financed by some bundle of debt and equity funds.
- As a corollary, it is not possible to identify a specific source of funds with a specific use. The company raises funds in the financial market which, in turn, support the whole group of business assets.
- The specific cost of each source of funds interacts with the proportion and cost of all other sources. Up to some point, the introduction of debt to the capital structure lowers the average cost of capital, but the continued increases in the debt/equity ratio eventually elevate the cost of capital by adding to the financial risk of the business.

The composite rate approach need not assume that the firm has already achieved an optimum capital structure and strives only to maintain the stated proportions. It will suffice that K_{mc} accurately measures the true cost of future financing. However, if the firm does not have an optimal capital structure, its decisions will also be suboptimal. The optimum capital structure and the valuation of the firm are discussed in the following sections. Finally, given that valuation of acquisition candidates depends primarily on the forecast of future cash flows, consistency dictates the use of K_{mc} in estimating net present value.

An important motivation in some conglomerate mergers of the 1960s lay in the enhanced debt capacity of the combination. This gave to management the opportunity to increase earnings per share and the market value of the firm without a comparable increase in the return on assets (ROA).

In arranging the capital structure, management seeks that the debt/equity ratio will minimize the firm's cost of capital. Common is the most costly source of capital, for it must compensate investors who accept the risk of a residual claim on the income stream. Hence, subject to qualification, the cost of capital to a firm financed solely by common stock will be higher than if some proportion of debt were inserted into the capital structure.

In the case of the all-equity firm, the *financial risk*—the variability of returns to common shareholders arising from the way the company is financed—would be zero. The risk to common shareholders orginates in the variability of the operating income stream, the *business risk*. As debt, lease commitments, and preferred stock are added to the capital structure, the financial risk to the common increases. Whether the price of the common declines in unison depends upon the earnings generated by the borrowed funds. Should these earnings offset the incremental risk to the common, the yield on the common (K_e) may not increase proportionately and the average cost of capital (K) may actually decline with the substitution of "cheaper" debt for common (Exhibit 4–5).

When a firm trades on the equity, it *de facto* pledges the net worth as security for the protection of creditors. Think of a firm with $100 in assets acquired by $60 of debt and $40 common. The assets would have to decline 40 percent before the position of the creditors is in jeopardy. Net worth acts as a cushion to absorb declines in the market value of

EXHIBIT 4–5
Leveraging and the Cost of Capital

1 *Percent Leverage Debt/Total Invested Capital*	*2* *Complement of Column (1)*	*3* *After-Tax Cost of Debt (T = .48)*	*4* *Yield on Stock Equity*	*5* *Weighted Average Cost [(1) × (3) + (2) × (4)]*
0	100%		.200	.200
10%	90%	.150 (1 − .48) = .078	.201	.189
20%	80%	.150 (1 − .48) = .078	.202	.177
30%	70%	.150 (1 − .48) = .078	.203	.166
40%	60%	.155 (1 − .48) = .081	.205	.155
50%	50%	.160 (1 − .48) = .083	.210	.147
60%	40%	.170 (1 − .48) = .088	.215	.139 ←
70%	30%	.200 (1 − .48) = .104	.225	.140
80%	20%	.230 (1 − .48) = .120	.260	.148

Note: Optimum capital structure comprises 40 percent equity and 60 percent debt and $K = .139$. Any other combination of debt and equity results in a higher cost of capital. For any given level of after-tax operating income, the lowest cost of capital will maximize the value of the outstanding securities.

assets below book values. The "pledge" of net worth is activated only in the extreme circumstance of liquidation.

More significant to current operations, trading on the equity gives rise to fixed charges (interest or debt service) and so creates a leverage factor—a greater proportionate increase (or decrease) in earnings before taxes (EBT) that follows an increase (or decrease) in earnings before interest and taxes (EBIT) when fixed charges are spread over a large number of units. Financial risk is measured by the degree of this financial leverage (DFL).

Exhibit 4–6 portrays four types of capital structures ranging from no debt (A) to a predominant debt position (D). In each instance, DFL is measured by:

$$DFL = \frac{EBIT}{EBT} \tag{5}$$

which, for capital structure B in Exhibit 4–6, Period 1, becomes

$$DFL = \frac{10.00}{7.50}$$
$$= 1.3$$

DFL is to be interpreted as a multiplier: for any given percent change in EBIT, from the Period 1 base year, the result will be a 1.3 times greater

---

EXHIBIT 4–6
Financial Leverage: Comparison of Four
Capital Structures

	A	B	C	D
Bonds[1]	0	$ 50	$100	$150
Stocks[2]	$200	150	100	50
Total	$200	$200	$200	$200
Period 1				
EBIT	$ 10	$ 10	$ 10	$ 10
Interest	0	2.50	5	7.50
EBT	$ 10	$ 7.50	$ 5	$ 2.50
EPS	.50	.50	.50	.50
Yield	5%	5%	5%	5%
Period 2				
EBIT	$ 20	$ 20	$ 20	$ 20
Interest	0	2.50	5	7.50
EBT	$ 20	$ 17.50	$ 15	$ 12.50
EPS	$ 1	$ 1.17	$ 1.50	$ 2.50
Yield	10%	11.6%	15%	25%
DFL (For Period 1)	1	1.3	2	4

For any level of EBIT, EPS will be larger as the DFL increases.
[1]Interest at 5%
[2]Issued at $10 par.

percent change in EBT. With each increment of debt in Exhibit 4–6, the
DFL increases bringing a proportionate increase in the variability of EBT.
Note too, for any given level of EBIT, the earnings per share increase
with the infusion of debt—the attractive side of leveraging to the common
shareholder at least on the way up. Between A and D, the EPS has
increased from 50¢ to $2.50 as the leverage factor rose from one to four.
The shareholder in D has more income and risk (what goes up can also
come down). Leverage works in both directions.

But leverage effects are not limited to the financial arrangements of
the company. The fixed costs found in the operating stream (depreciation,
factory overhead, fixed selling and administrative expenses) magnify the
variability of sales revenues. Operating leverage (DOL) relates to the
business risk and is measured by:

$$\text{DOL} = \frac{Q(S - V)}{Q(S - V) - F} \tag{6}$$

where Q is the number of units, S is the selling price per unit, F is the
total fixed costs, and V is the variable costs per unit. Similarly, DOL is
a multiplier: for any given percent change in sales, the change in EBIT
will be so many (DOL) times greater.

Operating and financial leverage combined (DOL $\times$ DFL) provide
a risk profile of the enterprise—the variability of returns to the common
stockholders arising from the business and financial risk. The income
statement in Exhibit 4–7 illustrates the calculations.

The variability of returns induced by leveraging can be quite substantial in particular industries. Air transport is such an industry. Typically, debt represents 60 percent of an airline's capital structure and
equity represents 40 percent. Operating revenues fluctuate with the number of passengers and the volume of cargo but operating expenses are
inflexible. Flight crews and ground crews are paid the same whether the
plane is empty or full; maintenance and depreciation vary little with traffic
carried. The overwhelming proportion of costs must be met regardless of
traffic density. It is estimated that once an airline reaches breakeven, 80–
90 percent of the additional revenues flow down to the pretax net. In the
prosperous sixties, United Airlines operating revenues advanced by 4.8
percent over the previous period (1962), while operating expenses advanced
2.8 percent but net income climbed 121 percent. In 1964, the respective
figures were 7.5 percent, 5 percent, and 86.8 percent. In the less wholesome
eighties, U.S. Air net operating revenues declined 12.49 percent (1981),
and income before taxes declined 36 percent. By way of further illustration,
1981 sales of RCA decreased 8 percent, expenses declined 2 percent, and
income before taxes decreased 81 percent. Fifty percent of the RCA capital
structure is represented by debt. The lessons are clear. Leveraging works
for and against the stockholder. Managing the capital structure (financial
risk) is not undertaken in isolation from the variability of the operational
characteristics (business risk).

EXHIBIT 4–7
Combined Financial and Operating Leverage
Industrial Company Income
Statement This Year

Net Sales		$200,000
Less:		
Cost of Sales		
Opening Inventory	$10,000	
Net Purchases	80,000	
Total	$90,000	
Closing Inventory	30,000	60,000
		$140,000
Gross Operating Income		
Less:		
Selling Expenses	$50,000	
Administrative Expenses	60,000	110,000
Net Operating Income (EBIT)		$ 30,000
Financial Charges		3,668
Net Income (EBT)		$ 26,332
Taxes		2,000
Net Income After Taxes (EAT)		$ 24,332

Added Data:	Selling Price (S)	$2.00
	Fixed Costs (F)	$100,000
	Variable Costs (V)	70¢ per unit
	Number of Units (Q)	100,000

Operating Leverage (DOL):

$$\frac{Q\,(S-V)}{Q\,(S-V)-F} \tag{6}$$

$$\frac{100{,}000\,(2-.70)}{100{,}000\,(2-.70)-\$100{,}000} = 4.3$$

Financial Leverage (DFL):

$$\frac{EBIT}{EBT} \tag{5}$$

$$\frac{30{,}000}{26{,}332} = 1.14$$

Combined Leverage:

DOL × DFL
4.3 × 1.14 = 4.9 or 5

Net Present Value

In NPV analysis, the *expected* benefits are the incremental cash flows resulting from the combination of previously independent firms. The cost of
the investment makes up search and negotiating costs plus the compensation paid to the shareholders of the acquired firm. NPV, the excess of
the incremental cash inflows over the investment cost, represents the
expected gain to the shareholders of the acquiring firm.

The dollar gain to shareholders of the acquired firm is the difference
between the value received for their shares and the preacquisition present **81**

value of the shares. The gain to the shareholders of the acquiring and acquired companies measures the economic effect (synergy) of the combinations. How this synergy is split depends upon the bargaining capacities of the parties to the transaction.

In one approach to assessing the NPV of a potential acquisition, the cash flow to the acquiring company—the stream of future dividends (D_1)—is projected and discounted at the acquirer's marginal cost of capital (K_{mc}) to obtain a *theoretical* market price (P_T) on the shares of the proposed acquisition. The theoretical price measures the value of the acquisition's stock in terms of the acquiring firm's criterion for new investment projects. The theoretical price may exceed or fall short of the actual market price (P_o).

Problem 1

Alpha ponders acquiring 100 percent of Delta's voting shares. Alpha's marginal cost of capital is 12 percent. Delta maintains a constant dividend payout ratio with the current dividend (D_o) at $1.00 per share. Delta's earnings are expected to grow(g) at 9 percent annually and Delta's shares currently sell at fifty-two. What is the theoretical price of Delta's shares to Alpha?

Solution

FUTURE DIVIDEND STREAM (D_1):

$$D_1 = D_o (1 + g)$$
$$= \$1 (1 + .09) \tag{7}$$
$$= \$1.09$$

THEORETICAL MARKET PRICE (P_T):

$$P_T = \frac{D_1}{K_{mc} - g}$$
$$= \frac{\$1.09}{.12 - .09} \tag{8}$$
$$= \$36$$

Since the theoretical price (the present value of the projected future dividends discounted in perpetuity) is less than the actual market price ($52), the investment in Delta would have a negative present value per share $(-\$15.67)$. In the absence of offsetting information or a downward shift in the market price of Delta shares, Alpha would not accept Delta as a merger partner. On the other hand, if Alpha's marginal cost of capital declined to 10 percent, the theoretical price would increase to $109 per share and Alpha's perspective on Delta might change significantly.

How would NPV apply to a firm which, over some interval, did not pay dividends? Growth companies, for example, frequently pay small or no dividends in favor of retaining funds for internal expansion. The bright prospects of the company are reflected in the market value of the common shares and capital gains to stockholders.

Problem 2

Hi-Tech, in 1984, has earnings per share of $2.00 and a projected growth rate of 20 percent. Hi-Tech pays no current dividend but corporate planning allows for a 50 percent payout ratio beginning in 1992. The reduction in retained earnings is anticipated to cut the growth rate after 1992 to 9 percent. Hi-Tech shares are valued on the exchange at $60. Delta is investigating Hi-Tech as a possible acquisition. What is the theoretical market price (1984) of Hi-Tech shares?

Solution

EARNING PER SHARE IN 1992:

$$EPS_{1992} = EPS_{1984} (1 + g)^N \tag{9}$$

where N = number of years to first dividend payment.
Therefore,

$$EPS_{1992} = \$2.00 (1 + .20)^8$$
$$= \$2.00 \times 4.2998$$
$$= \$8.60$$

DIVIDEND PER SHARE IN 1992:

$$\$8.60 \times .50 = \$4.30$$

PROJECTED DIVIDEND AFTER 1992:

$$\$4.30 (1 + g) = \$4.30 (1 + .09) = \$4.69 \text{ (rounded)}$$

PRESENT VALUE OF DIVIDEND STREAM AS OF 1992:

$$P_{1992} = \frac{D_1}{K_{mc} - g}$$

$$= \frac{\$4.69}{.12 - .09} \tag{8}$$

$$= \$156.33$$

DISCOUNTING PRESENT VALUE OF DIVIDEND STREAM
1992 TO 1982:

$$P_T = PV_{1992} \times \frac{1}{(1 + .12)^8}$$

$$= \$156.33 \times .403883$$

$$= \$63.14$$

The theoretical price exceeds the current market price of Hi-Tech shares and Delta might consider Hi-Tech worthy of further investigation.

However, the NPV is small ($3.14) and is dependent on the quality of long-term forecasting. Prudent management at Delta would carefully assess the margin of error before finalizing its strategy.

NPV analysis offers at best a point of departure for further investigation of the combination. Management should be aware of some warnings accompanying its use.

The reader will observe that in determining the theoretical price (P_T) in the illustrating problems, the projected dividend cash flow was discounted as a perpetuity. Common stock after all has no maturity date, and corporations are endowed by law with an indefinite life span. However, investors (including acquiring corporations) do not play the game forever. The marginal utility of money, limited resources, and technological shifts impose a time frame on common stock investment. This raises the concurrent issue of liquidation value on the investment.

Problem 3

Assume the facts as stated in our initial Alpha-Delta combination, but add that Alpha plans to impose a ten-year time horizon on the investment and estimates the liquidation value at $60 per share. What is the theoretical price and NPV of the proposed acquisition?

Solution

THEORETICAL PRICE:

$$P_T = \sum_{t=1}^{N} \frac{D_o(1 + g)^t}{(1 + K_{mc})^t} \tag{10}$$

where, N = number of periods (t) in the life of the investment, $N = 10$;

t = a given period as 1, 2, 3, . . . 10.

then,

$$P_t = \sum_{t=1}^{10} \frac{\$1(1 + .09)^t}{(1 + .12)^t}$$

$$= \$8.64$$

PRESENT VALUE OF LIQUIDATION PROCEEDS:

$$PV_L = \frac{L}{(1 + K_{mc})^N}$$

$$= \frac{\$60}{(1 + .12)^{10}} \tag{11}$$

$$= \$19.32$$

NET PRESENT VALUE (ten-year investment horizon):

Present Value of Dividend Stream	$ 8.64
Present Value of Liquidation Proceeds	19.32
Total	$27.96
Less:	
Current Market Price	52.00
Net Present Value	$(24.04)

Again Alpha would reject Delta as a merger partner.

Present value is a flexible tool and can be applied in a variety of ways as it would befit the circumstances of the acquisition. Problem 4 illustrates a variation in present value analysis involving a tender offer.

Problem 4

Metal Motors is considering a tender offer for 100 percent of General Plastics voting stock. General Plastics has an after-tax operating cash flow for 1982 of $500,000. This figure could grow at a rate of 10 percent annually for ten years if a $600,000 investment were made in the company. General Plastics does not have the resources to finance the required investment. Metal Motors' marginal cost of capital (K_{mc}) is 20 percent. General Plastics has 100,000 shares outstanding that presently sell at fifteen. However, to attract 100 percent of the shares, Metal Motors is advised that it will have to offer a 67 percent premium or an average cash tender offer of $25 per share.

Before going public with the offer, Metal Motors wishes to know: (a) the present value of General Plastics income stream; (b) the net present value of the investment at the tender offer price; and (c) the maximum price Metal Motors can offer for General Plastics.

Solution

GROWTH FACTOR:

Period	Growth Factor @ 10%
1	$(1 + .10)$ = 1.100
2	$(1 + .10)^2$ = 1.210
3	$(1 + .10)^3$ = 1.331
4	$(1 + .10)^4$ = 1.461
5	$(1 + .10)^5$ = 1.611
6	$(1 + .10)^6$ = 1.772
7	$(1 + .10)^7$ = 1.949
8	$(1 + .10)^8$ = 2.144
9	$(1 + .10)^9$ = 2.358
10	$(1 + .10)^{10}$ = 2.594

PROJECTED OPERATING CASH FLOWS OF GENERAL PLASTICS:

1	2	3	4 (2 × 3)
Period	Growth Factor	Cash Flow at Beginning of Period 1	Projected Operating Cash Flow
1	1.100	$500,000	$ 550,000
2	1.210	500,000	605,000
3	1.331	500,000	665,500
4	1.461	500,000	730,500
5	1.611	500,000	805,500
6	1.772	500,000	886,000
7	1.949	500,000	974,500
8	2.144	500,000	1,072,000
9	2.358	500,000	1,179,000
10	2.594	500,000	1,297,000

PRESENT VALUE OF GENERAL PLASTICS CASH:

1 Period	2 Projected Operating Cash Flow	3 Discount Factor $(K_{MC} = .20)$	4 (2 × 3) Present Value*
1	$ 550,000	$1/(1 + .20)$ = .833	$ 458,150
2	605,000	$1/(1 + .20)^2$ = .694	419,870
3	665,500	$1/(1 + .20)^3$ = .579	385,324
4	730,500	$1/(1 + .20)^4$ = .482	352,101
5	805,500	$1/(1 + .20)^5$ = .402	323,811
6	886,000	$1/(1 + .20)^6$ = .335	296,810
7	974,500	$1/(1 + .20)^7$ = .279	271,886
8	1,072,000	$1/(1 + .20)^8$ = .233	249,776
9	1,179,000	$1/(1 + .20)^9$ = .194	228,726
10	1,297,000	$1/(1 + .20)^{10}$ = .162	210,114
	Present Value of Operating Cash Flows		$3,196,568

Net Present Value of General Plastics Investment

Present Value of Operating Cash Flow $3,196,568*

Add

Present Value of Initial Investment at End of
   Period 10: 100,000 shares @ 25 × .162   405,000
                                     $3,601,568

Less

Initial Investment	$2,500,000	
Additional Investment	600,000	3,100,000
Net Present Value of General Plastics	.	$ 501,568*

MAXIMUM PRICE METAL MOTORS COULD PAY FOR A SHARE OF
GENERAL PLASTICS:

$$\frac{\text{Initial Investment + NPV}}{\text{Shares Outstanding}} = \frac{\$2,500,000 + \$501,568}{100,000} = \$30.02$$

*Rounded to nearest dollar.

Metal Motors could afford to pay $30.02 for a share of General
Plastics stock. At the maximum price, the NPV of General Plastics would
fall to zero. Metal Motors, if all turned out as projected, would then earn
the required 20 percent on its investment—there would be no excess or
net present value above the required return. Accordingly, since the business world does not move with mathematical precision, Metal Motors
should allow a margin of error and bargain down the size of the premium
on the market price of General Plastics stocks.

    Note that, in contrast to problems 1 and 2, a time frame (ten years)
was placed on the investment. For this reason, the discounted value of
the initial investment $405,000 ($2,500,000 × .162) was included as a
cash inflow for the tenth period. This assumes that should Metal Motors

chose to cut off General Plastics at the end of the tenth period, it would
at least regain the initial investment.

NPV analysis offers a point of departure for further investigation of the target firm. It has the following important advantages:

1. If the approach illustrated in problem 4 is used, NPV provides a means of determining value independent of the acquired firm's financial structure.

2. It gives full recognition to the fact that earnings received in future periods are less valuable than present earnings.

3. It allows for easy comparison with other projects in composing the firm's capital budget.

4. NPV can be estimated under different growth rates for the operating cash flows or the dividend stream of the acquired firm and a maximum offering price set for each assumed growth rate[4].

On the other hand, management should be aware of the limitations accompanying the application of NPV analysis.

1. Forecasting the future cash flows of the acquired firm (and subsequently of the combination) involves assessment of market forces, technological developments, labor and material costs, capital availability, competitive strategies, and so forth. With so many undeterminables, the one certainty about the forecast is that it will to some degree miss the mark. To hedge against the risks of forecasting, management might recast the cash flow estimates under a worst, most likely, and best set of scenarios with a present value of each alternative. Or, using probabilities, the forecast could be structured on expected present values with the variance used to quantify the inherent risks[2].

2. In projecting the cash flows from the acquired company, NPV analysis does not consider the covariance of these cash flows with those of the acquiring firm. Covariance refers to the pattern of movement in the cash flows of two firms over the course of the business cycle. If the cash flows of the two firms move in tandem as the economy expands and contracts, a *positive covariance* exists. If the cash flows move in opposite directions as the economy fluctuates, a *negative covariance* appears. Positive covariance intensifies the risk posture of the combination; as the cash flow patterns approach negative covariance, the combination achieves greater stability. The question of covariance is crucial to business combinations that seek to diversify their product line. Acquiring another firm that reacts similarly to economic fluctuations is not diversification; it can produce the opposite effect of intensifying risk.

3. Another critical issue in proposed mergers is the likelihood of synergy after the combination; that is, earnings and/or a growth rate in excess of the simple mathematical combination of premerger earnings and growth rates. The NPV analysis does not *per se* insure the subsequent emergence of synergism. Many other factors, quantitative and qualitative, influence the generation of synergism.

4. NPV implicitly assumes that the marginal cost of capital (K_{mc}) remains stable after the combination takes place. However, if the acquired firm is large (say 50 percent of the acquiring firm's assets) then the merger could radically alter the acquirer's risk–return characteristics, thereby changing marginal cost of capital and nullifying the conclusions reached in the initial evaluation. In this respect, it is a valuable addition to discount the cash flows from the potential acquisition by a rate which represents the risk–return posture of firms in the same industry and roughly comparable size. The resulting value can be compared to the price of the acquired firm's stock to ascertain whether the market is overvaluing or undervaluing its prospects.

5. Cash flow projections should incorporate adjustments to reflect the effect of inflation or deflation. Either way, it is probably unrealistic for the analysis to assume a stable price level. An alternative method of dealing with this problem lies in adjusting the firm's discount rate; for example, raising the discount rate to reflect the added risk of inflation.

CAPITAL ASSET PRICING MODEL (CAPM)

The focus of the CAPM in evaluating acquisitions centers on the security market line (SML). This measures the required return on a stock $E(R_j^0)$ in proportion to the market risk of the investment. The required return is expressed as:

$$E(R_j^e) = R_F + (E(R_M) - R_F)\beta_j \tag{12}$$

R_F = the risk-free rate of return, for example, the return on short-term Treasury securities;

$E(R_M)$ = the expected return on the market basket of risk securities frequently defined by the return on the Standard and Poor's 500 Index or the New York Stock Exchange Index;

$R_M - R_F$ = the premium paid by the market for assuming risk;

β_j = how the stock responds to changes in the stock market; or how the return on the stock *covaries* with movements in market returns. β_j is called the stock's Beta value.

Figure 4–1 depicts the Security Market Line and notes important underlying assumptions.

Problem 5

To illustrate the use of CAPM in evaluating merger candidates assume the following data:

Figure 4–1. Security Market Line (SML)

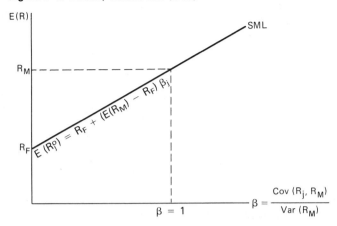

Notes:
[1]SML assumes a linear relationship between risk and return—the investor *expects* to be rewarded for assuming the market risk of investment.
[2]Beta is calculated from historical data on the relationship between the returns on a given stock and the market return over a given time frame. A beta value of one indicates the stock moves with the market. Beta values greater than one indicate stocks more volatile than the market which bears a heavier burden of risk and have a higher required return. Betas less than one identify defensive stocks, less volatile than the market and with lower returns on investment.
[3]The required return $E(R_j^0)$ sought by investors depends upon: the risk-free rate, the expected return and variance of the market portfolio, and the covariance of the stock's return with the market portfolio[6].

State of the Economy (S)	Probability of S (P_s)	Market Returns (R_M)
Revival (S_1)	.20	.10
Prosperity (S_2)	.60	.15
Recession (S_3)	.15	.08
Depression (S_4)	.05	.06
	1.00	

PROJECTED RETURNS ON FOUR MERGER PROSPECTS OVER THE BUSINESS CYCLE:

	Firm A	Firm B	Firm C	Firm D
S_1	.15	.10	.10	.25
S_2	.20	.15	.30	.15
S_3	.06	.10	.10	.08
S_4	.03	.08	.05	.06
$R_F = .06$				

The acquiring firm's cost of capital (K) is 12%.
Which firm(s) merits further investigation as a merger partner?

Solution

MARKET PARAMETERS:

	1	2	3(1 × 2)	4	5	6(1 × 5)
				d_M	(Col 4 Squared)	
	P_S	R_M	$E(R_M)$	$[R_M - E(R_M)]$	d_M^2	$d_M^2 P_S$
S_1	.20	.10	.020	− .025	.000625	.000125
S_2	.60	.15	.090	+ .025	.000625	.000375
S_3	.15	.08	.012	− .045	.002025	.000304
S_4	.05	.06	.003	− .065	.004225	.000211
			$E(R_M) = $ .125		Variance of R_M	= .001015

FIRM PARAMETERS:
FIRM A - Covariance (R_A, R_M) and B_A:

	1	2	3(1 × 2)	4	5	6(1 × 4 × 5)
				d_A		
	P_S	R_A	$E(R_A)$	$[R_A - E(R_A)]$	d_M	$(P_S)(d_A)(d_M)$
S_1	.20	.15	.0300	− .0105	− .025	+ .0000525
S_2	.60	.20	.1200	+ .0395	+ .025	+ .0005925
S_3	.15	.06	.0090	− .1005	− .045	+ .0006783
S_4	.05	.03	.0015	− .1305	− .065	+ .0004241
			$E(R_A) = $ .1605		Covariance (R_A, R_M)	= .0017474

$$B_A = \frac{\text{Covariance } (R_A, R_M)}{\text{Variance } R_M}$$

$$= \frac{.0017474}{.001015} \tag{13}$$

$$= 1.72$$

FIRM B - Covariance (R_B, R_M) and B_B:

	1	2	3(1 × 2)	4	5	6(1 × 4 × 5)
				d_B		
	P_S	R_B	$E(R_B)$	$[R_B - E(R_B)]$	d_M	$(P_S)(d_B)(d_M)$
S_1	.20	.10	.020	− .029	− .025	+ .0001450
S_2	.60	.15	.090	+ .021	+ .025	+ .0003150
S_3	.15	.10	.015	− .029	− .045	+ .0001957
S_4	.05	.08	.004	− .049	− .065	+ .0001592
			$E(R_B) = $ .129		Covariance (R_B, R_M)	= .0008149

$$B_B = \frac{\text{Covariance } (R_B, R_M)}{\text{Variance } R_M}$$

$$= \frac{.0008149}{.001015} \tag{13}$$

$$= .80$$

FIRM C - Covariance (R_C, R_M) and B_C:

	1	2	3(1×2)	4	5	6$(1 \times 4 \times 5)$
				$\dfrac{d_C}{[R_C - E(R_C)]}$		
	P_S	R_C	$E(R_C)$	$[R_C - E(R_C)]$	d_M	$(P_S)(d_C)(d_M)$
S_1	.20	.10	.0200	− .1175	− .025	+ .0005875
S_2	.60	.30	.1800	+ .0825	+ .025	+ .0012375
S_3	.15	.10	.0150	− .1175	− .045	+ .0007931
S_4	.05	.05	.0025	− .1675	− .065	+ .0005443
			$E(R_C) = $ .2175		Covariance (R_C, R_M)	= .0031624

$$B_C = \frac{\text{Covariance } (R_C, R_M)}{\text{Variance } R_M}$$

$$= \frac{.0031624}{.001015} \tag{13}$$

$$= 3.1$$

FIRM D - Covariance (R_D, R_M) and B_D:

	1	2	3	4	5	6$(1 \times 4 \times 5)$
				$\dfrac{d_D}{[R_D - E(R_D)]}$		
	P_S	R_D	$E(R_D)$	$[R_D - E(R_D)]$	d_M	$(P_S)(d_D)(d_M)$
S_1	.20	.25	.050	+ .095	− .025	− .0004750
S_2	.60	.15	.090	− .005	+ .025	− .0000750
S_3	.15	.08	.012	− .075	− .045	+ .0005062
S_4	.05	.06	.003	− .095	− .065	+ .0003087
			$E(R_D) = $ .155		Covariance (R_D, R_M)	= .0002649

$$B_D = \frac{\text{Covariance } (R_D, R_M)}{\text{Variance } R_M}$$

$$= \frac{.0002649}{.001015} \tag{13}$$

$$= .261$$

REQUIRED RETURNS $[E(R_j^0) = R_F + (E(R_M - R_F)\beta_j]$:

Firm A $= E(R_A^0) = .06 + (.125 - .06)\ 1.72 = .172$
Firm B $= E(R_B^0) = .06 + (.125 - .06)\ .80 = .112$
Firm C $= E(R_C^0) = .06 + (.125 - .06)\ 3.1 = .262$
Firm D $= E(R_D^0) = .06 + (.125 - .06)\ .261 = .007$

Comparison of Required Returns E(R_j^0) and Estimated Returns E(R_j^0):

Under the CAPM approach, if the expected return equals or exceeds the required return $[E(R) \geq E(R_j^0)]$, the prospect merits further investigation.

	Estimated Return	Required Return	Decision
Firm A	.161	.172	Reject
Firm B	.129	.112	Accept
Firm C	.218	.262	Reject
Firm D	.155	.077	Accept

The reader will observe that under NPV criteria the acquiring firm would have accepted all the candidates for further investigation since the expected returns from each project exceeded the cost of capital ($K = .12$)[2].

Observations on the Use of CAPM

Several features of the CAPM technique in the valuation of acquired firms warrant comment.

1. The states of the economy must be forecasted over a reasonable time horizon. The probabilities related to different phases of the economic cycle can be derived from historical data or by simulation. Importantly, the method forces the analyst to assess the effect of foreseeable economic fluctuations on the investment in the proposed acquisition.

2. The beta value of the potential acquisition is derived from the historical relationship between the return on its common stock and the return on the market index—the S & P 500 Index or the NYSE Index. Actually, beta values on listed firms are readily obtained from the financial services as well as from brokerage and investment banking houses. The availability of the data [beta, the risk-free rate (the rate on Treasury bills), and the return on the market basket of risk securities (the return on the S & P 500 or the NYSE Indices)] permits quick calculation of the required return on the potential acquisition.

3. All acquisition candidates are valued against the same standard of performance—the market index. Beta measures the covariance of each candidates stock with the market index.

4. The required return represents a risk adjusted yield reflecting the market risk of the acquisition's stock. Since the acquiring firm will accept investments only if the expected return $[E(R_j)]$ exceeds the required return (R_j^0), the problem of diversification does not arise. Each acquisition can be evaluated without reference to the acquiring firm's existing risk–return posture.

5. CAPM can be integrated with the NPV approach. If we know the beta of the acquiring firm, then the cost of common stock equity capital can be defined using expression 12:

$$K_e = E(R_j^0) = R_F + [E(R_M) - R_F]\beta_j$$

The cost of equity so determined can be used in calculating the acquiring firm's average cost of capital (K_{MC}) or inserted directly as the discount factor in problems 1 to 4.

All the same, CAPM has not resolved many issues attending the valuation of business organizations. The technique rests upon many assumptions concerning investor behavior and market characteristics which lie largely beyond the scope of the present discussion. However, we may profitably note that CAPM assumes the market is efficient and promptly discounts all publicly available information. Thus, the market risk expressed in the beta value captures the underlying business and financial risks of the firm.

Moreover, while concentrating on market risk, CAPM further assumes that the cost of insolvency or bankruptcy is zero; that is, in the event of bankruptcy the economic value of the assets is realized. Under real world conditions, the assets in a bankruptcy are sold at distress prices and accompanied by selling costs, legal fees, and other opportunity costs of a cumbersome legal system. Given these circumstances investors are not able to diversify risks as CAPM assumes. Accordingly, when bankruptcy costs are significant and potential, the financial manager may be well advised to keep an eye on total risks and not exclusively on market risk.

Yet despite these limitations and others not discussed,* CAPM makes a useful contribution to the handling of valuation in merger analysis. Stockholders do benefit by the knowledge of how their investment behaves in relation to movements in the market index. The question, "Does the forecasted return from the investment adequately compensate for the market's perception of the associated risk?" is of single importance to every investor.

INTEGRATING NPV AND CAP ANALYSIS

NPV analysis and CAP can be joined in a single evaluation using the required return $E(R_j^0)$ as the discount factor in the calculation of present value. To illustrate the procedure, let us return to Problem 1 as Alpha ponders acquiring 100 percent of Delta's voting shares. Alpha's marginal cost of capital (K_{MC}) is 12 percent. Delta maintains a constant dividend payout ratio with the current dividend (D_o) at $1.00 per share. Delta's earnings are expected to grow (g) at 9 percent annually. Delta's shares sell at fifty-two and the company has a Beta value (β_j) of .8. The risk-free rate (R_F) is 9 percent and the market return on risk securities is 15 percent. Compare the theoretical market price (P_T) with the actual price (P_o).

---

*A complete discussion of the assumptions underlying CAPM can be found in John J. Clark, Thomas J. Hindelang, and Robert E. Pritchard, *Capital Budgeting*, cited in the notes to this chapter.

Solution

The NPV analysis from pages 82–83 gives a theoretical price of $36. Since $P_T < P_o$, the investment in Delta would have a negative market price and not merit further investigation.

Combining NPV and CAP analysis we have:

REQUIRED RETURN ON DELTA STOCK:

$$K_e = E(R_j^0) = R_F + (E(R_M) - R_F)\, \beta_j$$

$$= .09 + (.15 - .09)\, .8 \qquad\qquad (12)$$

$$= .138$$

THEORETICAL PRICE (P_R):

$$P_T = \frac{D_1}{K_e - g}$$

$$= \frac{\$1.09}{.138 - .09} \qquad\qquad (14)$$

$$= \$22.71$$

Since $P_T < P_o$, Alpha would once again reject Delta as a potential merger partner.

The risk adjusted return on the *acquired firm's* common stock (K_e), which is synonymous with the return required by the riskiness of the investment $E(R_j^0)$, takes the place of the average cost of capital (K_{MC}) of the *acquiring firm*.

Divestiture

Acquisitions are a method by which the marketplace induces the transfer of assets into the hands of more efficient managers. It does not work to perfection, for men do not always accomplish what they intend. Nevertheless, a mechanism to reshuffle corporate assets can work to the benefit of society and the parties concerned. It follows that divestiture, the other side of the acquisition coin, deserves the same meticulous attention given acquisition projects.

The decision to dispose of a subsidiary or sell off a division rests upon the same financial criteria applied to evaluate acquisitions. If a division or subsidiary does not yield a return on assets sufficient to cover or exceed the firm's marginal cost of capital, it is a candidate for divestment. Similarly, if a division or subsidiary has a required return $(E(R_j^0)$ greater than the expected return on assets, it too is a candidate for divestment. Whatever reason, another firm may manage the division or subsidiary to better economic effect.

Apart from these internal criteria pointing to divestment, stock price trends may suggest a realignment of corporate investment strategy. The widely known Q-ratio explains how the level of stock market prices affects capital spending. The Q-ratio relates the market value of a company's physical assets to the cost of replacing those assets. If the Q-ratio is greater than one, the stock market values one dollar of company assets at more than one dollar. In this case, the company has a greater incentive to invest in new plants and equipment because the market values direct each investment dollar at more than one dollar.

Conversely, when the Q-ratio falls below one, each dollar invested in new plants and equipment adds less to the market value of the stock because of the returns it can generate. At a Q-ratio less than one, firms may find it cheaper to acquire physical assets by combination rather than by direct investment. Similarly, companies with a low Q-ratio might improve their position by ridding themselves of divisions or subsidiaries which fail to earn a return in proportion to their market risk.

As a final comment, with reference to the discussion on direct and indirect investment in Chapter 1, companies with high Q-ratios tend to have significantly higher levels of direct and indirect investment than companies with low Q-ratios[1].

SUMMARY

Financial analysis alone cannot dictate the decision to merge. However, faulty financial analysis may lead management to acquire a poor company or pay so much for a good one that it cannot hope to earn an acceptable return on the investment.

This chapter has presented two approaches to evaluate merger candidates that are not mutually exclusive. Each has a story to tell based upon a particular perspective. The prudent financial manager uses both approaches. When the recommendations conflict, further investigation is undertaken to explain the differences.

In all events, both NPV and CAPM are only initial steps to more extensive investigation of the merger candidate. The remaining steps in the process involve the gathering of additional data and the establishment of a bargaining area to set the parameters for negotiation.

NOTES

1. *Business Week*. (August 24, 1981).
2. Clark, John J., Thomas J. Hindelang, and Robert E. Pritchard. *Capital Budgeting*. Englewood Cliffs, New Jersey: Prentice-Hall, 1979. See Section 2 for a discussion of risk management in planning capital expenditures.
3. Halpern, Paul. "Corporate Acquisitions: A Theory of Special Cases? A Review of Event Studies Applied to Acquisitions." *The Journal of Finance*. May 1983, pp. 297–317.
4. MacDougal, Gary E., and Fred V. Malek. "Master Plan for Merger Negotiations." *Harvard Business Review*. January–February, 1970. pp. 71–82.
5. Von Bauer, Enc E. "Meaningful Risk and Return Criteria for Strategic Investment Decisions." *Mergers and Acquisitions*. Winter 1981. pp. 5–16.
6. Weston, J. Fred. "Investment Decision Using the Capital Assets Pricing Model." *Financial Management*. Spring 1973. pp. 25–33.

Bargaining Area

5

After the identification of one or more merger prospects, investigation can proceed in earnest to estimate a bargaining area which defines the boundaries of negotiation. This entails in-depth research into the history and current operations of the would-be acquisition. On the basis of the investigation results, the acquiring firm projects before negotiation the maximum exchange ratio acceptable to its stockholders and the minimum exchange ratio likely acceptable to the shareholders of the acquired firm. For this purpose, Larson and Gonedes offer a framework for estimation[1].

BARGAINING AREA

The L & G technique make the following assumptions about the firms entering the combination and their shareholders:

- The objective of the combination is to enhance the market value of the common shares.
- The shareholders will not approve of the combination unless it promises to maintain or increase their wealth position measured by the market value of their holdings.
- The P/E ratio of the shares captures the risk–return characteristics of the merging firms. In other words, security prices indicate a consensus of opinion regarding the risk and future returns of investment in the merging firms.
- The shares are publicly traded in a reasonably active market. (The problem of infrequently traded shares is discussed below.)
- No synergism from increased earnings will appear in the first year of the combination. As a practical matter, *problems attending reorganization make it difficult* for the combination to realize the anticipated benefits at least for the year following the transaction.

The process of estimation involves determining the preacquisition wealth position (W) of the shareholders in each company, the estimated market value of the combination (W_{AB}), the postacquisition wealth position of all shareholders, and the anticipated synergism from the combination and the sharing of the synergism between the stockholders of the acquiring and acquired firms.

Problem

Assume the following data relate to firms looking into the prospects of combination:

	Acquiring Firm (A)	Acquired Firm (B)
	National Oil	M & M Mining
EPS	$2.87	$1.65
Dividend	1.80	1.00
Dividend growth Rate	6%	7%
Book Value per share	$26.50	$33
Market Price per share	$43	$52
Number of shares	3,000,000	1,000,000
P/E	15	31.5
Total Earnings	$8,610,000	$1,650,000
Total stockholder wealth	$129,000,000	$52,000,000

Projected P/E (θ) of the combination: 25
Combination will be affected by a stock swap.

Solution

PREACQUISITION WEALTH POSITION (W):
ACQUIRING SHAREHOLDERS:

$$W_A = (\text{EPS}) \times (\text{P/E})$$

$$= \$2.87 \times 15 \qquad\qquad (1)$$

$$= \$43 \text{ (rounded)}$$

ACQUIRED SHAREHOLDERS:

$$W_B = \$1.65 \times 31.5$$
$$= \$52 \text{ (rounded)}$$

POSTACQUISITION VALUE OF THE COMBINATION (W_{AB}):

$$W_{AB} = \theta\,(Y_A + Y_B) \times \left(\frac{1}{S_A + (\text{ER})S_B} \right) \qquad\qquad (2)$$

where,

$\qquad\qquad W_{AB} =$ expected price per share of stock after the combination.

$\qquad\qquad\quad \theta =$ the expected P/E ratio after combination.

$\quad Y_A \text{ and } Y_B =$ total first period earnings after combination assuming no synergism. Thus $Y_A + Y_B$ equals the sum of the preceding period earnings for the acquiring company (A) and the acquired company (B).

S_A = number of shares of the acquiring company (A) prior to the combination

S_B = number of shares of the acquired company (B) prior to the combination.

ER = exchange ratio; assume 1.2 shares of A = 1 share of B as a tentative exchange ratio.

Then,

$$W_{AB} = \frac{25\ (\$8,610,000\ +\ \$1,650,000)}{3,000,000\ +\ (1.2)(1,000,000)}$$

$$= \frac{256,500,000}{4,200,000}$$

$$= \$61.07$$

POSTACQUISITION WEALTH POSITION OF THE SHAREHOLDERS:

Acquiring shareholders:

The shareholders of A will support the combination if $W_{AB} \geq W_A$. Since $\$61.07 > \$43$, the acquiring shareholders have improved their wealth position.

Shareholders of the Acquired Company:

The shareholders of B will support the combination if $W_{AB} > W_B$ $(1/ER)$. Thus, $W_B\ (1/ER) = \$52\ (1/1.2) = \$43.33$. Since $\$61.07 > \$43.33$, the shareholders of the acquired companies would support the combination as improving their wealth position. *Note* that the wealth position of the shareholders in the acquired firm is calculated after adjustment for the exchange rates.

MAXIMUM EXCHANGE RATIO ACCEPTABLE TO THE ACQUIRING COMPANY (ER_A):

$$ER_A = \frac{\theta\ (Y_A\ +\ Y_B)\ -\ (P/E_A)(Y_A)}{(P/E_A)(Y_A)\ (1/S_A)(S_B)}$$

$$= \frac{25\ (\$8,610,000\ +\ \$1,650,000)\ -\ (15)(\$8,610,000)}{(15)(\$8,610,000)\ +\ (1/3,000,000)(1,000,000)}$$

$$= \frac{\$256,500,000\ -\ \$129,150,000}{(\$129,150,000)\ (.33)}$$

$$= 3\ \text{(rounded)}$$

(3)

The maximum exchange ratio is 3 shares of A for 1 share of B. It represents an exchange ratio which will maintain the wealth position of the acquiring firm's shareholders. A higher ratio transfers wealth to the shareholders of the acquired firm. Consequently the acquiring firm will attempt to bargain down from the maximum exchange ratio; that is, seek a lower exchange ratio.

$$ER_B = \frac{(P/E_B)(Y_B/S_B)(S_A)}{\theta(Y_A + Y_B) - (P/E_B)(Y_B)}$$

$$= \frac{(31.5)(\$1,650,000/1,000,000)(3,000,000)}{25(\$8,610,000 + \$1,650,000) - (31.5)(\$1,650,000)} \qquad (4)$$

$$= \frac{\$155,925,000}{\$256,500,000 - \$51,975,000}$$

$$= .76$$

The minimum exchange ratio acceptable to the shareholders of the acquired company is .76 shares of A for 1 share of B. Similarly, the minimum ratio represents a price that will maintain the wealth position of the acquired firm's shareholders. A lower ratio transfers wealth to the shareholders of the acquiring firm. Thus, the acquired firm will bargain for a higher exchange ratio.

Postcombination synergism:

Value of the enterprise after combination:	
$61.07 × 4,200,000	$256,494,000
Less	
Value of enterprises before combination:	
A = $43 × 3,000,000 plus B = $52 × 1,000,000	181,000,000
Total Synergism	$ 75,494,000
Less	
Share of synergism to stockholders of A:	
$61.07 − $43 × 3,000,000	54,210,000
Share to B stockholders	$ 21,284,000

The synergism results from the higher projected P/E ratio for the combination, not from any increase in earnings. However, if the circumstances of the combination pointed to an increase in first year earnings post combination, Y_A and Y_B could properly reflect the projections. Synergism, in this case, would measure both the projected improved earnings and the projected P/E ratio (θ) for the combination.

Several features of the analysis merit further comment and illustration.

1. The analysis is carried through on a per share basis.
2. The wealth position of stockholders (W), is defined by the market value of their shares before and after the combination.
3. The value of the firm(s) before and after combination is simply the product of the market value per share and the number of common shares outstanding. Observe that the valuation process centers on the common shares and does not incorporate other outstanding securities in the capital structure.

4. The data in the analysis comprises known and readily accessible information: P/E ratios, total earnings (Y), shares outstanding (S), earnings per share (EPS), and market value per share (W). The key forecasted variable is the P/E ratio of the combination (θ, theta).

5. In expression 2, for any given value of theta (θ), there is a corresponding exchange ratio (ER). If theta is increased, the exchange ratio can be raised. Accordingly, negotiations on the exchange ratio focus on the projected P/E ratio for the combination.

6. Hence, in expression 3, the maximum exchange ratio acceptable to the acquiring company (ER_A) increases with the value of the combination's P/E ratio. If the reader will envision a series of possible thetas, the bargaining line for the acquiring firm is depicted in Figure 5–1. For each theta on the line ER_A, there is a corresponding maximum exchange ratio. If the acquiring firm settles for a higher exchange ratio, the wealth position of its common stockholders is reduced; wealth is transferred to the stockholders of the acquired firm. *It follows that the acquiring firm will strive to negotiate lower exchange ratios.*

7. Similarly, in expression 4, the minimum acceptable exchange ratio (ER_B) diminishes as the P/E ratio of the combination increases (Figure 5–2). Exchange ratios below these minima will decrease the wealth position of the shareholders—transfer wealth to the stockholders of the acquiring firm. *It follows that the acquired firm will negotiate for higher exchange ratios.*

8. The bargaining area is defined by combining Figures 5–1 and 5–2.

Figure 5–1. Maximum Exchange Ratio
Acquiring Firm

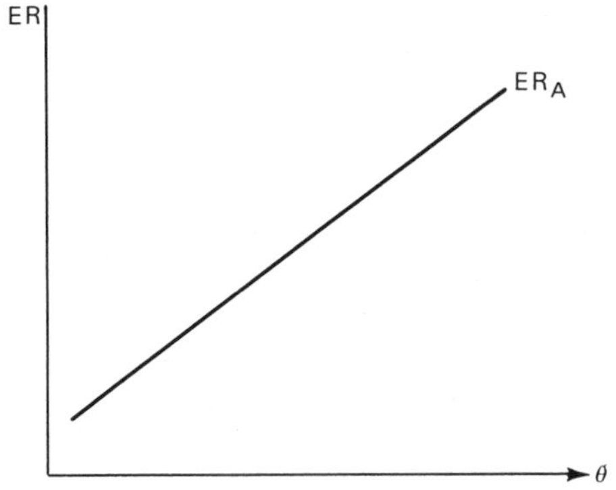

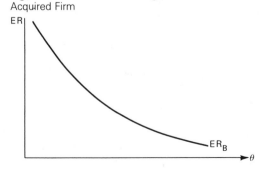

Figure 5–2. Minimum Exchange Ratio
Acquired Firm

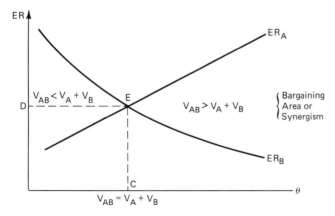

Figure 5–3. Bargaining Area

In Figure 5–3

V_{AB} = the market value of the combination:
  W_{AB} × the number of shares outsanding (S_{AB}).
V_A = the market value of the acquiring firm before combination:
  W_A × number of shares outstanding (S_A).

V_B = the market value of the acquired firm before combination:
  W_B × number of shares outstanding (S_B).

In the area to the left of point E, the combination would not take place; the precombination values of the two firms would exceed their combined value and the wealth position of one or both groups of shareholders would suffer adversely. At point E, the combined value of the firms equals their precombination values. To the right of point E, the market value of the combination exceeds the precombination values of the independent firms. The area $ER_A - E - ER_B$, therefore, measures the amount of potential synergism and defines the bargaining area.

Consider the exchange ratio at point D and the P/E ratio at point C. The exchange ratio at D equals the ratio of W_B/W_A, the market values of the two stocks. The P/E ratio at C represents a weighted average of the P/E ratios of the acquiring and acquired companies.

1 Company	*2* P/E Ratio	*3* Total Earnings	*4* Weights	*5 (2 × 4)* Weighted Average
National Oil	15	$ 8,610,000	.839	12.58
M & M Mining	31.5	1,650,000	.161	5.07
		$10,260,000	1.000	
		P/E Ratio at Point C		17.65

How is the potential synergism within the bargaining area divided and how do the parties benefit *proportionately*? If the final exchange ratio equals W_B/W_A, the parties share the synergism in proportion to their **101** preacquisition wealth positions. If the final exchange ratio exceeds W_B/W_A, the shareholders of the acquired firm do proportionately better. If the final exchange ratio is less than W_B/W_A, the shareholders of the acquiring firm improve their relative position.

For purposes of the preceding analysis, the discussion assumed that the stocks of the two firms entering the combination were actively traded and the transaction was completed by an exchange of stock. These assumptions are not imperative. If the stocks involved are not actively traded, the necessary data can be approximated by appraisal values or by references to the stock values of companies in the same industry of similar size and risk posture. If the consideration involves cash, bonds, or preferred stock in addition to common stock, the exchange ratio can be recast by expressing these alternative forms of consideration in terms of stock values.

Illustrating Case: The merger of Raytheon Company and Beech Aircraft Corporation, completed on September 30, 1979, is used to illustrate the construction of the bargaining area and the anticipated synergism from the combination[3]. The pertinent data include the following:

	Raytheon (A)	Beech (B)
Market price of common (W) (average of four quarters prior to merger)	$48.81	$27.53
Earnings per share (fully diluted)	4.71	3.26
P/E ratio	10.36	8.44
Number of Shares (S)	31,668,000	12,884,000
Total Earnings (Y)	$149,156,000	$42,001,000
Total Wealth [(W) × (S)]	$1,545,715,000	$354,696,520

The first step in application requires determination of the equilibrium point: $V_{AB} = V_A + V_B$. The exchange ratio at the equilibrium position becomes:

$$W_B/W_A = \$27.53/48.81 = .564$$

and the P/E ratio represents a weighted average of the respective P/E ratios of Raytheon and Beech:

1 *Company*	*2* *P/E Ratio*	*3* *Total Earnings*	*4* *Weights*	*5 (2 × 4)* *Weighted Average*
Raytheon	10.36	$149,156,000	.780	8.08
Beech	8.44	42,001,000	.220	1.86
		$191,157,000	1.000	
P/E ratio at equilibrium position				9.94

The second step concerns the projection of the P/E ratio of the combination (θ), which is the critical variable in the negotiation. In the estimation of theta, management will input all known information on the companies, assumptions concerning postcombination environmental factors (the state of the economy and the industry), the financial market reaction to the merger, the effects of the accounting method used to record the merger, tax consequences, the combination's risk posture, and so forth. Using these inputs, a series of possible P/E ratios (θ) is projected, and the maximum (ER_A) and minimum (ER_B) exchange ratios for each possible θ are calculated using expressions 5–3 and 5–4. Starting from the equilibrium point, $\theta = 9.94$, we project the possible thetas and corresponding exchange ratios as follows:

θ	ER_A	ER_B
10	.582	.560
11	.886	.499
12	1.190	.450
13	1.494	.409
14	1.798	.376
15	2.102	.347
16	2.405	.322

For example, using 12 as the P/E ratio of the combination,

$$ER_A = \frac{12\,(149{,}156 + 42{,}001) - 10.36\,(149{,}156)}{(10.36)(149{,}156)(12{,}884/31{,}668)}$$

$$= \frac{2{,}293{,}884 - 1{,}545{,}256}{1{,}545{,}256\,(.4068)} \tag{3}$$

$$= \frac{748{,}628}{628{,}610}$$

$$= 1.190$$

and

$$ER_B = \frac{(8.44)(42{,}001/12{,}884)(31{,}668)}{12\,(149{,}156 + 42{,}001) - (8.44)(42{,}001)}$$

$$= \frac{(27.53)(31{,}668)}{2{,}293{,}884 - 354{,}488} \tag{4}$$

$$= \frac{871{,}308}{1{,}939{,}396}$$

$$= .450$$

The series of projected P/E ratios and maximum–minimum exchange ratios are plotted in Figure 5–4. This defines the bargaining area for Raytheon and Beech. The parties actually negotiated a final exchange ratio of one share of Beech equal to .775 shares of Raytheon. This exchange ratio implied a projected P/E ratio (θ) of about 12.5. After the combi-

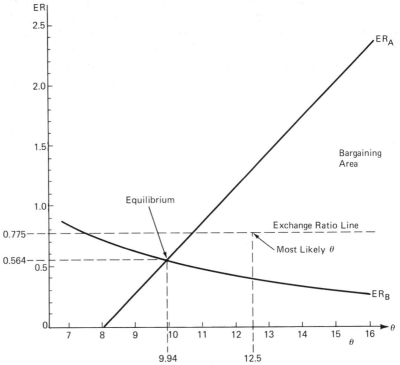

Figure 5–4. Bargaining Area
Raytheon Company and Beech Aircraft

nation, Beech shareholders would hold about 25 percent of the outstanding Raytheon shares (assuming conversion of the Raytheon debentures).

As to synergism, with $\theta = 12.5$, we have:

Wealth Position	Raytheon	Beech	Total
Postacquisition	$1,816,793,000	$572,670,000	$2,389,463,000
Preacquisition	1,545,715,000	354,696,520	1,900,411,520
Synergism	$ 271,078,000	$217,973,480	$ 489,051,480

Assuming that 41,653,100 shares were outstanding after the combination, the postacquisition wealth position of the shareholders—$2,389,463,000—implied an expected market price of $57.36. Although Beech Aircraft was 23 percent of the size of Raytheon, its shareholders were allocated 44.6 percent of the estimated synergism. The .775 exchange ratio in effect valued Beech common at $37.83 compared to an average preacquisition value of $27.53—a premium of 37 percent.

For the record, by November 1982, Raytheon stock traded in an annual range of $28.25 to $49.87. The realization of anticipated synergism is manifestly sensitive to the time frame of the calculation. At that time, the synergism implicit in the .775 exchange ratio had not been realized as the business recession already underway in 1980 continued to deepen.

The previous chapter addressed the issue of identifying possible merger partners. This chapter concentrates on setting the parameters for subsequent merger negotiation. In both cases, the analysis centers on the valuation of the acquired firm by forecasting future cash flows from the investment. Yet the derived accounting data and financial ratios influence the perceptions of managers and investors if only for their informational content (See Chapter 8).

The presentation of accounting data permits the exercise of options that influence the bottom line and the firm's cash flow. Accordingly, it is usually necessary to normalize accounting numbers for purposes of comparing the financial position of the acquired and acquiring firms.

Whatever the strategy of the acquiring firm, therefore, it should include *ab initio* a purchase audit. Negotiations often turn on projected earnings and key financial ratios. The parties have to agree on the content of accounting income, and the seller's data should be recast to agree with the accounting principles employed by the acquiring corporation.* The purchase audit, performed by a public accountant retained by the buyer, develops a set of comparable income figures for prior periods to facilitate earning comparisons and projections. It is a confidential report to the buyer and is not for public consumption.

In a purchase audit, the accountant reviews the financial statements, tax return, and records of the seller to form an estimate of the current worth of the assets—as opposed to their book values—and to assess the reliability of prior earnings as a basis for prediction. In relation to the seller's assets, a partial audit checklist involves the following:

- Validation of cash balances.
- Validation of receivables including age, turnover, bad debt experience, and the possible existence of liens.
- Inventory and the method of valuation. For example, in a period of sustained price increases, LIFO will generally result in undervaluing inventories (the closing inventory is valued at an earlier, lower set of prices). Also, it is necessary to check if the accounting system captures all the costs of producing goods for inventory.
- Regarding fixed assets, how realistic is the estimate of useful life? How realistic is the estimate of salvage value? Under accelerated depreciation or ACRS, the asset amortization might exceed the real loss in economic value. What is the seller's policy in distinguishing a capital investment from an expense item? Is this similar to the buyer's policy? Have maintenance expenditures been charged to capital accounts?
- What are the current values of real estate holdings?
- How well do the buyers and sellers fit together as a tax-reporting entity? What is the status of pending litigation?

---

*Accepted accounting practice does not require that all components of a business uniformly follow the same accounting method; the critical point is that financial managers realize the effect of the accounting options chosen on reported earnings.

- What obligations does the seller have arising from product warranties, pension plans, and so on?
- Are there debtor-creditor agreements that restrict future financing?

Purchase audits assist management in evaluating the suitability of the merger candidate. Thus, the objectives of the merger specify the client's instructions to the auditor. There are a number of illustrations. If the objective of the combination were risk reduction, the acquiring firm would look hard at the variability of the operating cash flows, flexibility in reorganizing the capital structure, unused financial leverage, and so forth. If the objective were market penetration, does the seller have the distribution facilities, contractual arrangements, and personnel to handle the product line? If the objective were enhanced liquidity position, in addition to a working capital analysis, the buyer would seek information on capital budget commitments, long-term debt maturities and lease obligations, credit lines, and any restrictive covenants on the use of funds. The auditor has the task to marshal the internal evidence in response to his client's need to know.

There are two warnings regarding purchase audits. First, not all assets show up on a balance sheet. Management skills, loyal clientele, favorable locations, good labor relations, and superior technical personnel do not appear directly on a balance sheet, although they may explain above average earnings. However, such intangibles figure in with the ultimate terms of purchase.

Second, purchase audits are normally not as extensive as end-of-year audits leading to the release of certified statements. Purchase audits provide some knowledge and, sometimes, more comfort than is warranted. The buyer may yet have a few surprises awaiting him after completion of the deal.

The 1954 Studebaker-Packard merger makes the point. Both companies were marginal producers at best. Studebaker's net sales did not cover manufacturing costs and while Packard had better control of costs, it too came up red on the bottom line. Yet the parties saw the merger as the road back to profitability. The union would permit marketing a full line of cars to match the GM and Ford product mix. Sales and costs were projected on this basis. It soon became evident that Studebaker's costs had been seriously underestimated. Losses mounted and creditors refused new financing. By 1957, plans for a full line of cars were shelved. The merger had failed. The reason: Packard simply did not look hard enough at the Studebaker situation prior to the combination.

Similar experiences have led some companies to insert in the purchase agreement a provision for a full audit after closing with adjustments to the purchase price (exchange ratio) based upon audit results.

Obviously, the purchase audit assumes a friendly merger. In the event of a hostile takeover, financial analysts following the companies in question can provide valuable insights into the worth of a company in terms of assets and sustainable earning power.

The bargaining area can set the limits to negotiation in the form of maximum and minimum exchange ratios, but the establishment of a final exchange ratio also demands a complete set of data on the acquired company. The acquisition team must literally write the "book" on the acquired firm. In skeleton form, the principal sections would include:

I. *Financial Data*, for some relevant period but not less than five years, include:
  A. Balance Sheet
    1. Gross and Net Working Capital.
    2. Cash and Marketable Securities as a percent of current assets.
    3. Notes and Accounts Receivable by amount, percent of working capital, turnover, age, and bad debt experience.
    4. Inventory classified as raw materials, goods in process, and finished goods; inventory turnover and method of valuation.
    5. Size and nature of Prepaid Expenses.
    6. Fixed Assets (plant, property, and equipment); if owned, the dates of acquisition, accumulated depreciation, and residual values; if leased, by type of lease under FASB 13, details of lease agreement, and the method of capitalization.
    7. Long-Term Investments in subsidiary corporations; the extent of stock ownership, the method of valuation (cost or equity), and nature of intercompany transactions.
    8. Intangible Assets as patents, copyrights, goodwill, and the methods of amortization.
    9. Accounts Payable as a percent of current liabilities with a schedule of due dates.
    10. Notes Payable as a percent of current liabilities and classified by lender, interest rate, and due dates.
    11. Other current liabilities as serial bond redemptions and sinking fund obligations.
    12. Unrecorded and contingent liabilities.
    13. Capitalized value of remaining lease payments.
    14. Long-Term Debt classified by amount, interest rates, and due dates. Are there particular indenture clauses which bear adversely on the combination? Is long-term debt wholly or partially convertible? Are the bonds callable?
    15. Funded and unfunded liabilities; such as, pension plans.
    16. Preferred stock and stated dividend. Is the preferred cumulative, participating, convertible, and/or redeemable?
    17. Common stock and retained earnings, company dividend policy and payout ratio, and regularity of dividends.
  B. Profit and Loss Statement (preferably based upon direct costing)
    1. Sales by product line.
    2. Variable materials, labor, and overhead costs by product line.
    3. Fixed factory, selling, and administrative costs.
    4. Contribution margin by product line.
    5. Other Income (interest, rents, royalties), amount, and stability.
    6. Other Deductions (interest and expensing of R & D costs).
    7. Tax credits, losses, and carryovers.
  C. Statement of Surplus
    1. Adjustments applicable to prior periods.
    2. Direct write-offs against net worth, especially those bearing on asset valuations.
  D. Statement of Sources and Uses of Funds

107

II. Product Line Data

A. Product Characteristics

1. Volume of each product line over the relevant time period.
2. The trend of demand for each product line. What is the growth potential?
3. Estimated future life span of each product item.
4. Probable line of technological development to maintain competitive position of each product.
5. Competition from substitute products.
6. Behavior of product line demand over the course of the business cycle. Are the product lines equally affected by business fluctuations?
7. Is the product line supported by patents and licenses which confer a degree of distinction?
8. Are there auxiliary services accompanying product line sales as repair and maintenance contracts? Is there a secondary market for the renovating and selling of used items?
9. How is the research and development budget distributed over the product lines?

B. Technological Characteristics

1. Technology of production for each product line.
2. Are there commonalities in the technologies employed?
3. Are the technologies in place transferable to the production of other consumer or industrial outputs?
4. Are the technologies in place compatible with those of the acquiring firm? To what extent are economies-of-scale enhanced by the acquisition?
5. Can the existing capacity meet the anticipated growth in demand? Is additional investment needed to meet the anticipated demand and/ or update the production process?

C. Competition

1. What is the market share of each product line and how is the market defined?
2. Does the firm primarily service a regional, national, or international market?
3. Who are the principal competitors? Do any of the competitions enjoy inherent advantages in terms of access to or ownership of particular factors of production?
4. Vis-à-vis the competition, what are the strengths and weaknesses of each product line?
5. How sensitive is the product line to advertising expenditures, price changes, and other promotional strategies?
6. How accurate is the firm's short and long forecasting of sales and earnings? Is forecasting done in-house and/or with the assistance of consultants? Are data processing techniques adequate to the objectives of the company? Is data processing, a possible source of improved management decision making?

D. Distribution

1. What is the type and location of the firm's distribution facilities: warehouses, service offices, and so on?
2. What are the channels of distribution?
3. Are the acquired firms, distribution facilities, and channels compatible to those of the acquiring firm?
4. Would the proposed combination generate economies in product distribution?

E. Product Promotion
  1. What is the mode(s) of advertising employed by the company? Does it compare to the promotional efforts of principal competitors?
  2. Are the lines of advertising compatible with those of the acquiring firm? Are there possible economies in this area through combination?
  3. What is the advertising budget by product line?
  4. How is the advertising budget monitored to assure the cost effectiveness of the expenditure? Would shifting expenditures among the product lines and modes of advertising produce a better mix to enhance the ratio of sales to advertising dollars?

III. Human Resource Development
  A. Top Management
    1. List the names, ages, experience, and other pertinent information on executive officers and directors.
    2. How do the personalities and philosophies of the management team match those of the acquiring firm? Where are the likely points of conflict? Is the combination an ego trip or a viable economic transaction?
    3. How is the problem of redundant management personnel to be addressed?
    4. What are the direct compensation and fringe benefits paid to executive management? Are there "golden parachute" contracts in place to cover the executives of the acquired company?
    5. What package seems essential to assure the support of the acquired firm's management for the combination?
  B. Stockholders
    1. How is the outstanding stock of the acquired firm distributed among individuals and institutions?
    2. List the names of the principal individual stockholders.
    3. Do family interests create a bond among a segment of individual stockholders?
    4. What percentage of the outstanding stock will assure *de facto* control?
    5. What package appears best to meet the needs of the individual and institutional stockholders to gain the required support for the combination?
  C. Professional Personnel
    1. List the key professional employees (engineering, chemists, accounting, and legal) by department and product line.
    2. How are professional personnel compensated?
    3. Do they have stock options?
    4. Are there economies and/or new horizons in research as a result of the combination?
    5. Are there potential points of friction among the professional personnel?
    6. Is there potential redundancy? How is this issue affected by individual or union contracts?
  D. Labor Force
    1. Size, age, sex, length of service, and wage distributions of labor force.
    2. Breakdown of labor costs by product line and department.
    3. Labor turnover by product line and department.
    4. Classification of employees by nature of compensation: semimonthly and weekly payment; hourly or piecework ratio.
    5. Type and cost of fringe benefits.
    6. How does scale of compensation compare to the competition?
    7. Is there a union contract and what are the specific provisions of the contract?
    8. Is the union independent or nationally affiliated? If the latter, what

are the policies and history of the national organization that bear on the combination?

9. What is the acquired firm's history of labor relations?
10. What are the major sources of labor recruitment?
11. What is the routine of recruitment: application, interviewing, testing, and so forth?
12. How will the labor force be affected by the combination?

IV. History of the Acquired Firm
   A. Origin of the firm and date of incorporation; state of incorporation.
   B. Evolution of the corporate structure; decentralized or centralized management control.
   C. Growth of company and direction of expansion (horizontal, vertical, market extension, and so forth).
   D. Method of financing and special connections within the financial community.
   E. Special legal problems affecting the company's future.
   F. Philosophy of management and the behavioral style of the organization.

Despite the scope of the research into the potential acquisition, the pressure of circumstances may dictate completion with dispatch lest the opportunity slip away. But pressure or no, painstaking effort is demanding; superficial analysis will not withstand the scrutiny of the opposition.

In 1975, Joseph S. Graziano was president of Tyco Laboratories when the firm purchased Grinnell Fire Protection Systems from ITT. Grinnell sales were three times higher than Tyco's. Many members of the Tyco board felt the firm was biting off more than it could chew with small prospect of ongoing gains.

> However, in presenting the case to the Tyco board, Mr. Graziano "had learned every single, solitary thing about Grinnell and about the future of fire protection business in this country." One board member remarked, "I'll never forget that presentation; it was the best I'd ever seen." The board approved the deal.

Tyco paid $14 million in cash and agreed to future payments equal to 40 percent of Grinnell's earnings over the succeeding ten years[2].

Finally, from the display of information marshalled in the "book," the areas of compatibility and incompatibility, as well as the likely postcombination points of friction, merit particular emphasis as alerts to top management pondering the acquisition.

SOURCES OF DATA

Mature appreciation of the acquired firm's worth does not arise spontaneously from the written word. Informal sources have much to contribute even in the nature of anecdotal evidence. Informal sources include: former employees of the acquired firm, current suppliers, and contacts with colleagues in the business and financial community. Obviously, in collecting this information discretion will acknowledge the ethical and legal boundaries to investigation. All the same, an established firm leaves a trail of "folklore" well within the public domain.

Sources of formal information include:

- Articles in *The Wall Street Journal, Barron's, Fortune, Business Week*, and similar publications.
- Reports to the Securities and Exchange Commission:

10-K.	Annual report of the company's business and financial condition.
13-D.	Listing of stockholders with ownership of 5 percent or more of the outstanding shares.
14-D1.	Report covering tender offers to the stockholders of a desired acquisition.
10-Q.	Quarterly report on financial condition.
8-K.	Report on significant current changes in financial condition.
6-K.	Report on stock sales by foreign companies.
11-K.	Covering annual reports of employee stock purchase plans.

  (For a definitive listing of SEC reporting requirements, see Commerce Clearing House. *Accountants SEC Practice Manual*, latest edition.)
- Standard and Poor's Corporation:
  - Stock reports
  - Corporation records
  - Corporations, directors, and executives
  - Industry Surveys
  - Current statistics
  - Outlook
  - Computer credit analysis
- Moody's Investors Services:
  - Industrial Manual
  - Transportation
  - Utilities
  - Banking and Finance
- Dun & Bradstreet:
  - Reference Book of Corporation Management
  - Reference Book of Manufacturers
  - Metalworking Directory
  - Million-Dollar Directory
  - Principal International Business
  - Credit reports, individual companies
- Value Line Investment Survey:
  - Individual company analysis
- Federal Trade Commission:
  - Annual Report on Mergers and Acquisitions
- U.S. Department of Commerce.
- "Mergers and Acquisitions." *The Journal of Corporate Venture*. Published six times per year.
- W. T. Grimm & Co., Chicago, publishes statistics on merger.

Banks, brokerage houses, investment banking houses, consultants and universities have aggregated a substantial quantity of computerized data. Tapes can generally be rented or purchased. Although the tapes mostly reproduce the output of government agencies and other public sources, the format facilitates the use of financial models in evaluating the worth of an enterprise and in making intra- and inter-industry comparisons.

SUMMARY   Chapter 4 dealt with the identification and evaluation of merger prospects. This chapter took the process a step further by proposing a technique for establishing a bargaining area and a framework for negotiation. Simultaneous with the calculation of the bargaining parameters, the acquiring firm would write the "book" on the potential acquisition using all available qualitative and quantitative information. While the "book" stresses the points of compatibility and conflict in the proposed merger, the perception of the data and the weight given to particular items of information depends upon the acquisition strategy of the acquiring firm. The following chapter treats the negotiation of an exchange ratio in a friendly merger or the preparation of a tender offer in a takeover operation. Attention at this stage focuses on the isolation of strategic variables from the quantity of information gathered about the target company.

NOTES   1. Larson, Kermit O., and Nicolas J. Gonedes. "Business Combinations: An Exchange Ratio Determination Model." *The Accounting Review*. October 1969. pp. 720–728.

2. Lynch, Mitchell C. "Takeover Tactics: Tyco's Wily Methods in Acquisitions Cause Jitters at Many Firms." The *Wall Street Journal*. May 18, 1978.

3. Raytheon Company and Beech Aircraft Corporation. 10K reports to Securities and Exchange Commission for 1978, 1979, and 1980; annual reports for 1978, 1979, and 1980.

Negotiating the Terms of Acquisition

Based upon the knowledge provided by the premerger investigation, the specific terms of acquisition are negotiated within the parameters of the bargaining area. From the accumulated data on the acquired firm, negotiations eventually narrow to certain key variables. What is a significant variable in turn depends upon the acquisition strategy and motivations of the acquiring firm.

Here is a possible pitfall. Motivations often color perceptions of data. The "urge to merge" can generate an optimism which perceives the benefits of combination but glosses over weaknesses. Culminating negotiations in the Penn-Central merger, for example, leave the impression that despite the extended nature of the talks, the participants overestimated the gains from consolidation and gave lesser weight to the problems of implementation[7]. Good bargaining does not allow enthusiasm to overtake realistic appreciation.

In this respect, when a merger negotiation begins, it tends to develop an internal dynamic pushing inevitably toward completion. Frequently, in a merger transaction, both the acquiring and acquired corporations are represented by an investment-banking firm. In major transactions, a single advisory fee can amount to six or seven figures. Eventually, law firms, public relations people, market consultants, public accountants, officers and directors become entangled in the process. These may have much to gain from the successful outcome of the negotiation. Pressures build with time and it becomes difficult to call off the wedding as the bride walks down the aisle.

113

SOME KEY VARIABLES IN MERGER NEGOTIATIONS

The following is a list—by no means definitive—of significant variables which have played a role in effecting particular combinations. However, the mention of a given variable(s) does not rule out other considerations.

Liquidity.   In the McDonnell-Douglas merger, for example, Douglas had important contracts but suffered working capital problems. McDonnell had the liquidity to rectify the deficiency, and this became an important element in fashioning the combination. It is worth recalling that the primary cause of business failures in the 1970s among larger firms had been inadequate working capital.

Financial problems also figured in the Standard Oil Company (Ohio) acquisition of Kennecott Corporation in June 1981. Although Kennecott had been an active participant in the merger arena, it had fallen on hard times primarily due to low copper prices, costly litigation, and expropriations which eroded profits and drained cash during the 1970s. Kennecott's 1978 acquisition of Carborundum Co. added to the disappointments of Kennecott management. As the nation's largest copper producer, Kennecott lacked the huge sums needed to modernize facilities and develop new deposits. Kennecott achieved the dubious distinction of being the highest cost producer in the U.S. copper industry.

SOHIO and its subsidiaries are primarily an integrated domestic petroleum company engaged in all phases of the petroleum business: exploration and production of crude oil and natural gas; transportation, refining, and marketing of crude oil products. As a result of its Prudhoe Bay operations, SOHIO had $3.8 billion in cash available for investment and was actively seeking a significant position in coal and petrochemicals.

The acquisition, therefore, met the stated objectives of both companies. Kennecott gained a source of badly needed capital for a modernization program. SOHIO broadened its base in hard minerals, primarily copper[21].

Special Assets: One party may possess research facilities, raw materials, special plant and equipment, patents, and so on that enhance its bargaining power. The decade of the 1970s witnessed growing awareness that the stability and progress of industrialized societies depended upon access to a wide spectrum of raw materials not simply cheap oil. Against this background, the shareowners of the General Electric Company and Utah International overwhelmingly cast their votes on December 15, 1976 to make Utah a wholly owned subsidiary of GE[10–20].

Utah held large reserves of iron ore, copper, uranium, and precious metals in several countries. Particularly impressive were the huge reserves of coking coal in Utah's Australian holdings. *Quid pro quo*, merging with Utah would help GE achieve its objective of becoming a worldwide operation. Eighty-three percent of Utah's gross profits and other income from operations originated in Australia, Brazil, Canada, New Zealand and Peru.

114   The DuPont acquisition of Conoco (August 1981) further illustrates the search for raw materials control. Before the Conoco acquisition, DuPont strategy sought out companies which would broaden its market base within existing business segments. The Conoco acquisition marked a shift in the DuPont acquisition strategy from horizontal to vertical integration. Conoco was engaged in four principal business segments: petroleum exploration, production and refining; coal mining; minerals; and high-volume low-technology chemical production. In a letter to shareholders (*Annual Report.* 1980), DuPont confirmed the company's intention to guarantee a supply of raw materials [3,7,17].

Management Capabilities: If one firm possesses a particularly strong management team, it may figure prominently in assessing the future prospects of the combination. For example, the securities industry itself experienced a wave of mergers in the 1970s. The assets of the securities industry comprised mainly capital and people. The low profit margins of the 1970s and the unfixing of commissions (May 1, 1975) raised the prospect of scale economies in an industry marked by relatively small, closely-owned firms. Given these ingredients, the combinations which took place while differing in particulars shared a common feature in their people orientation. Some houses sought to build their retail base by acquiring other firms with a strong retail following. Successful retail salesmen tend to take their accounts with them wherever they go. Other houses sought to strengthen their research capabilities by the merger route. A research department is little more than the people who staff it. Also, acquiring another firm's personnel and financing expertise can provide access to that firm's investment-banking clients. Still other firms, primarily engaged in the retail and institutional distribution of securities, sought to gain a foothold in the origination of securities via the merger route[19].

Dayco Corporation produced tires and auto parts but lacked managerial depth, complicated by a serious problem of succession. Cadillac Plastics had managerial talent but could not provide the opportunities to take full advantage of this human resource. When Dayco acquired Cadillac, it acquired a new source of profits and opened up advancement opportunities for Cadillac personnel[15].

Diversification Effects: In 1972, the United Technologies Corporation (UTC) moved to reduce its dependency on aerospace activities that accounted for 75 to 80 percent of annual revenues. Four major areas were identified as sources of diversification: energy, transportation, electronics, and telecommunications. Under the program, nine acquisitions and three divestitures were made by 1982. Among these, the UTC acquired the Mostek Corporation in 1979. Mostek had a strong position in the semiconductor field but needed additional capital to continue its rapid growth. The UTC, as part of the acquisition agreement, invested $200 million in Mostek to meet the company's capital equipment requirements. With the acquisition of Mostek, the UTC became an established factor in the electronics industry[5].

Product Line Reinforcement: In the following cases, the acquiring firm generally sought to strengthen an existing product line. Biomedical products, for example, is one of DuPont's eight principal business segments. In December 1980, DuPont acquired New England Nuclear Corporation (NEN), the largest manufacturer of radioactive drugs used as tracers in medical research and diagnosis. The acquisition of the NEN, positioned to play an important role in commercializing advances in the life sciences, bolsters DuPont's budding program in recombinant-DNA research. The DuPont-NEN merger also illustrates the case of special assets discussed above[8].

The food line provides many illustrations of combinations designed to reinforce product lines. The matching point here, however, is not so much technology as in the DuPont-NEN case but in the utilization of common distribution channels and compatible management talents. In 1978, The Campbell Soup Company acquired Vlasic Foods. Vlasic processed and merchandised vegetable products (pickles, relishes, peppers, and sauerkraut). Vlasic's strengths were in marketing and finance; Campbell's managerial skills centered on production and engineering. The combination added depth to the Campbell product line and satisfied the organizational needs of each entity[4].

In July 1981, Nabisco and Standard Brands Inc. consolidated their enterprises. Nabisco manufactured, processed, and distributed cookies, crackers, snack products, and related items under a variety of brand names for an international market. Standard Brands functioned similarly over a wider range of food products. The combination promised to enhance the stability of Standard Brand earnings and implement the concentric diversification strategies of both companies—to bring together a wide diversity of product lines which share the same channels of distribution[16].

This same strategy inspired the acquisition of Mrs. Smith's Pies Company by the Kellogg Company in 1976. Kellogg primarily manufactured over twenty different ready to eat breakfast cereals; Mrs. Smith's Pies Company produced and distributed frozen pies, crepes, and waffles in the United States[12]. Although other factors also influenced the decision, we see the same pattern in The Pillsbury Company's acquisition of the Green Giant Company in 1979. Green Giant, a major international company in food processing and restaurant chains, ranked 430th among *Fortune's* 500 largest industrial corporations. Pillsbury, with a similar orientation, ranked 129th in the *Fortune* listing. The merger enabled Pillsbury to broaden its product line and solidify its hold in the supermarket area. Green Giant's food processing segment of canned and frozen prepared vegetables complemented Pillsbury's consumer foods segment of desserts and flour related items[22].

Compatible Technology: Emhart Corporation, formerly American Hardware Corp., operated in four product areas: hardware, machinery, stove equipment, and firearms. The company also had interests in electronic security systems and vinyl-coated fabrics. In 1975, Emhart acquired

USM (United Shoe Machinery Corp.) which produced shoe machines; machines for manufacturing plastic and rubber goods; production and sale of industrial adhesives, sealants, blind rivets, and brushes. Emhart's strategy was to diversify into a relatively new field sharing some of the same technologies[9].

Miehle-Gross-Dexter manufactures heavy printing equipment. The firm needed an electronics capability to maintain its competitive position in the industry. The acquisition of MGD by North American Rockwell provided the needed technical expertise and simultaneously gave Rockwell the advantage of diversification[14].

Tax Loss Carryovers: Under a tax-free exchange, tax losses carry over to the acquiring corporation, but the purpose of the acquisition cannot look strictly to tax benefits. Assuming a legitimate business objective, however, tax loss carryovers are attractive when the acquiring firm has a high marginal tax rate and lacks comparable deductions. Net operating losses in effect reduce the costs of acquisition. In a taxable exchange, the loss remains with the selling firm and may be applied against the gains from the sale of assets.

Reproduction Costs: In an era of sustained price level increases, it may be more economical to acquire assets through combination than by new construction. This factor has motivated combinations based upon the acquisition of fixed assets. Thus, in the oil industry, finding costs for U.S. domestic oil tripled in the period 1977–82 with only a modest offset in drilling costs. Consequently, oil companies found it cheaper to buy existing reserves than to spend funds on discovering new reserves since the reproduction values of the desired assists exceeded their market values.

Interest Rate: Rising interest rates, all things equal, tend to discourage acquisitions by reducing the present value of future cash flows. Declining interest rates provide an incentive to merge by raising the present value of projected revenues. The 1982 bull market in equities, triggered by the prospect of lower interest rates, illustrates this point. Beyond the question of valuation, interest rate trends influence the structure of the deal. In the early 1980s, lowering interest rates encouraged leveraged buyouts. These deals entailed the purchase by private investors of publicly held shares with the purchase price financed by money borrowed against the assets acquired.

The reader can, of course, cite other variables in other combinations that affected the agreed purchase price: growth rates, P/E ratios, accounting methodology, and so on. In this respect, Louis Perlmutter of Lazard Freres & Co., speaking on the trend of merger activity in the 1980s, notes:

> More important considerations now are the business fit—how the acquisition fits into the long-range strategic plan of the company and where the company wants to be five years or ten years out. As a result, acquiring firms are willing to incur earnings dilution. At some point there is a presumed

crossover point, and there will be a contribution to earnings, either because of the company's inherent growth or because of what the combined companies can do together. There is also a concept by managers of going into a business and creating strings of earnings; even though there is some initial earnings dilution, they think the quality of earnings is higher, with the result that stockholders possibly will become richer through shares receiving a higher price earnings ratio[13].

To summarize, the acquisition team of the acquiring company has prepared a "book" of quantitative and qualitative information about the acquired firm and outlined a bargaining area. The negotiating process, by a series of trade-offs, eventually clues in on key variables at the core of the acquiring firm's strategy and motivations. These variables have a predominant influence on the bargaining power of the parties and the ultimate terms of purchase.

However, as previously noted, negotiations once undertaken develop a momentum of their own. The participants on both sides strive to conclude an agreement. In this atmosphere, each party may begin negotiations with an initial offer and a fall-back position. Often the initial offer is quickly compromised to the fall-back position and the negotiations either break off or go beyond the fall-back position. Unless the parties have carefully determined their strategy and disciplined the negotiating teams, the latter is a likely outcome. Pressure of circumstance can impel either party to accept an agreement beyond that deemed feasible by prior analysis. The merger of Allied Corporation and Bendix Corporation may be a case in point. Premerger negotiations developed in heated controversy and the glare of publicity. After the announcement of the agreement, Allied Corp.'s stock fell on the Exchange. Allied had agreed to pay an amount equal to about twenty times Bendix yearly earnings. The stock market typically valued Bendix at only five or six times earnings. Martin-Marietta Corp., another contender in the Bendix battle, was so weakened financially by the struggle that observers anticipated a sell off of assets to regain losses. The case is discussed in Chapter 11[23].

Finally, the variables discussed above should not be confused with *ex post* macroanalyses of mergers by academicians (economists, sociologists, political scientists, etc.) who attribute causation to a merger or to a wave of mergers. By way of illustration, some economists explained the number of conglomerate type mergers in the 1960s and after by the 1950 Cellar-Kefauver Amendment to the Clayton Act. The amendment enabled the Department of Justice to successfully challenge large horizontal and vertical acquisitions. With familiar types of combinations increasingly amenable to antitrust prosecution, the business community, the argument states, turned to the conglomerate form. Other researchers prefer alternative hypotheses to explain the emergence of conglomerates. Our comments by contrast look to the micro characteristics of particular mergers—an *ex ante* analyses based upon current assessments and declared intentions of management. The latter may anticipate or diverge from the *ex post* analyses of events.

Chapter 4 addressed the problem of valuing a proposed acquisition. The accepted methodology discounts the future revenues from the investment to obtain the present value of the anticipated cash flows. Although the value of the estimate depends upon the accuracy of the projected cash flows and the discount factor applied, it provides management with an estimate of the proposed acquisition's worth. Rational management would not pay a price exceeding the worth of the acquired enterprise. In an efficient securities market, the market value of the shares theoretically approximate the present worth of the company.

On the other hand, existing studies suggest that premiums of more than 30 percent may be commonly paid to acquire another firm. A survey by *Barron's* (July 19, 1982) of fifty tender offers in the preceding year showed premiums of 20 to 40 percent above market value. One bid carried a 75 percent premium and two bids exceeded 100 percent. Bradley's survey of 161 successful bids indicated:

> . . . bidding firms paid target stockholders an average premium of 49 percent for the shares they purchased. This premium is calculated relative to the closing price of a target share two months prior to the announcement of the offer. The average appreciation of the target shares through one month subsequent to the execution of the offer was 36 percent, relative to this same benchmark. In sum, target stockholders realized a 49 percent capital gain on the shares purchased by acquiring firms and a 36 percent capital gain on the shares they retained. Thus, bidding firms suffered a 13 percent loss on the target shares they purchased. However, these same acquiring firms realized an average 9 percent increase in the market value of their own shares as a result of the offer[2].

The apparent contradictory behavior of acquiring firms may be attributable to several phenomena:

• The securities market may have undervalued the stock of the acquired firm, at least in the opinion of the acquisitor's management. In fact, some observers cited the premiums paid in effecting combinations as evidence of a general undervaluation of common stocks in the era of double digit inflation. Inflation casts doubt on the quality and credibility of earnings per share calculated from accounting numbers. If accounting numbers do influence stock prices, an acquiring firm in a period of inflation could find it cheaper to buy all the stock of the acquired firm rather than purchase all its assets. Exhibit 6–1 portrays the generally inverse relationship between P/E ratios and the premiums paid in merger transactions.

• Corollary to the above, the reproduction costs of the assets may exceed their market values. If market values are less than reproduction costs, then the acquiring firm would do better to purchase the stock rather than invest directly in the desired assets. The source of the premium arises from the spread between reproduction costs and market values.

• The acquiring firm's analysis might reflect the synergistic effects of the combination not wholly envisioned by the market. The premium **119**

EXHIBIT 6–1
Average Price Earnings Multiples Paid in
Merger and Acquisitions Transactions and
Average Premium Paid Over Market 1970–1983

Year	Average P/E Paid	Average Premium Paid Over Market	Year	Average P/E Paid	Average Premium Paid Over Market
1970	23.1	33.4	1977	13.8	40.9
1971	24.3	33.1	1978	14.3	46.2
1972	21.4	33.8	1979	14.3	49.9
1973	18.9	44.5	1980	15.2	49.9
1974	13.5	50.1	1981	15.6	48.0
1975	13.3	41.4	1982	13.9	47.4
1976	15.1	40.4	1983	16.7	37.7

Source: W. T. Grimm & Co., *Mergerstat Review*, 1983, pp. 99–100.

tendered in this case represents a draw down on the future benefits of combination.

• Combination may offer the prospect of increased debt capacity and the opportunity to further leverage the common stock.

• The number of bidders for the stock of the target firm may, in the heat of battle, push up the amount of the premium.

Empirical studies on the source and amount of the premiums offered in merger negotiations are altogether inconclusive. Without being specific as to a particular source, we can generalize that premiums originate in differing valuations of income producing assets between the securities market and the acquiring firm(s). However, putting aside the urge to win, *rational* management should not pay more than the present or anticipated worth of the acquisition or put an offer on the table outside the upper limits of its bargaining area.

One study by Donald M. Boesel, based upon a limited sample of thirty combinations, merits further investigation. Boesel's survey covered the period from January 1973 through August 1974 and selected acquiring firms from the 1973 *Fortune* 500 groups. The combinations were classified as:

Negotiated Mergers.
Contested Tender Offers.
Uncontested Tender Offers.

Premiums were calculated using four different methods:

1. Premium based on the target firm's common stock (CS) trading price on the day of the merger announcement.
2. Premium based on the target firm's CS trading price six months prior to the merger announcement.

120

3. The "Austin Premium," which reflects a CS trading price two weeks prior to the offer announcement.

4. Premium based on a CS trading price taken six months prior to the merger offer announcement, then adjusted forward to the date of the offer in accordance with the general market behavior over that six month period.

Boesel's conclusions were:

1. Tender offers were more likely to be made by larger firms while negotiated mergers were more common among smaller firms.

2. Premiums paid in tender offer combinations are less than or equal to those paid in negotiated combinations. (This tends to run counter to popular wisdom.)

3. Tender offer premiums are higher in contested combinations than in uncontested deals[1].

STOCK PRICE MOVEMENTS IN ANTICIPATION OF MERGER

Premature price increases in the stock of a prospective acquisition can upset the effect of the acquiring firm's bid and/or adversely affect negotiations. For this reason, most firms intending to enter upon a merger take great pains to keep their plans secret. Information on the proposed deal is kept within a closed circle on a need to know basis; code names are assigned to the acquired companies, negotiations are held at locations off the beaten path, and so on.

Despite these precautions, premerger price movements remain an almost inevitable complication with which management(s) must contend. *The Wall Street Journal* (July 12, 1978) surveyed thirty publicly traded stocks in April and May which were subject to first-time merger attempts. Of the thirty stocks, twenty-seven rose in price two weeks preceding any announcements and twelve rose 20 percent or more over their initial market values. A follow-up on a survey by *Barron's* (July 19, 1982), after the SEC intervention in 1980, showed that out of fifty stocks involved in merger activity, 75 percent showed price increases prior to public announcements. On the other hand, the largest increases occurred after the announcements.

The persistence of leaks and use of inside information is caused by one or more of the following factors:

• The relatively large number of people brought into the planning of a merger. Not only officers, directors, lawyers, accountants, economists, and others, but secretaries and the personnel of other firms who prepare the required reports for regulatory agencies also get into the act. Murphy's Law states that the probability of a leak increases geometrically with the number of persons in the know. In 1974, for example, three employees of Sorg Printing Company (N.Y.) were charged with trading in stocks of several tender-offer candidates on the basis of information obtained while preparing documents for the offers. In 1978, Vincent Chiarella, a printer for Pandick Press (N.Y.), was sentenced on Federal criminal charges stemming from his purchases of stocks in five companies that were takeover targets of Pandick clients. (Mr. Chiarella's conviction was subsequently overturned by the U.S. Supreme Court in 1980. The case, however, led to the publication of rule 14e-3 by the SEC relating to nonpublic information on a tender offer.)

• Many acquiring companies themselves discreetly try to establish a position in the target firm's shares before going public with an announcement. This operation can start the price moving upward. Holdings under 5 percent need not be reported to SEC.

• The price of the stock may move up due to random factors operating in the market. This may set off rumors of the merger and further price increases without any insider influence.

• Analysts focusing on trends in merger activity may correctly identify a takeover target without access to inside information.

• It is difficult to prove the use of insider information. The alleged culprit may have a well conceived cover story, may deal through relatives, or resort to the use of Swiss banks which do not disclose the names of purchasers they represent. The latter is an element of growing importance with the increase of foreign investment in U.S. concerns.

The actual evidence on the extent and effect of insider trading is ambiguous at best. If insiders do, indeed, transact profitably, their activities make the securities markets less than "fair game" for other "noninformed" investors, which causes such investors to earn smaller profits (or absorb larger losses) than would otherwise be the case with equal access to information. Keon and Pinkertown examined 194 mergers between 1975 and 1978. Concentrating on *registered* insiders (officers, directors, and beneficial holders), they reported that 76 percent of the target firms had no open market transactions by insiders during the *one* month prior to announcement; in 12 percent of the firms, insider net purchases were made during this one month. But the survey did show excessive trading in the target firm stocks three weeks prior to the announcement. Obviously, the limited scope of the survey excludes the activities of agents for registered insiders and others in gaining access to inside information[14].

Oppenheimer and Dielman investigated sixty-seven target firms and 3,700 transactions for the period 1962–1978. They found that corporate officers were net purchases throughout the two-year preannouncement period and especially so during the three months prior to the announcement. Twenty-five percent of the firms showed significant increases in officers' purchases during this period. On the other hand, there was little direct evidence of directors or beneficial owners increasing purchases prior to the merger announcement. The evidence on officer-directors is mixed with some indication of increased activity during the month prior to announcement. Paradoxically, insiders did not appear to generate returns in excess of those of a nonknowledgeable individual. An interesting question arises: Do insiders really profit by their information[16]?

For the record, Rule 14e-3 of SEC (1980) prohibits trading in a security by any person in possession of material, nonpublic information relating to a tender offer which was acquired from the bidder or from the subject company. The ultimate effect of the rule rests upon the compliance of the investment community and judicial determinations. Managements seeking confidentiality can only exercise the utmost discretion and trust to good fortune.

THE CONSIDERATION MIX

The purchase price of the acquired firm has to be parceled among specific forms of consideration: cash, bonds, preferred stock, and common stock. The particular mix in a given case results from the interaction of internal and external factors: the objectives of the acquired and the acquiring firms, the state of the economy and the level of interest rates, the tax status of the parties in interest, the accounting options chosen to record the transaction (purchase or pooling), and the preferences of the financial markets.

Cash: Over 50 percent of the merger transactions in 1979 constituted cash deals. Cash acquisition deals were supported at this time by low P/E ratios on the stock market, increased liquidity among business firms, rising interest rates, and the fear of double-digit inflation. High interest rates lowered the market values of common shares while double-digit inflation raised the specter of a serious recession. On the other side, inflation cheapened the value of money (added to the money stock) and made the existing burden of indebtedness easier to carry.

At the firm level, a solely cash acquisition reduces the complexity of negotiations, minimizes valuation problems and probably postcombination headaches. If the shares of the acquired corporation are completely bought up by the acquiring firm, the political complexion of the acquiring firm remains unchanged. A cash transaction also avoids the underwriting fees associated with a public distribution of new securities. On the other hand, the purely cash transaction drains off working capital, can lower the firm's growth rate, and create tax problems for the selling stockholders. Moreover, the number of acquisitions affected by the cash route is necessarily limited, since each deal constitutes a substitution of assets on the balance sheet of the acquiring company. A firm cannot create cash but can create a substitute for cash by issuance of new stock.

SOHIO's acquisition of Kennecott illustrates the pure cash transaction. Under the terms of the merger, holders of Kennecott common received $62 in cash for each share held. Since the weighted average cost of SOHIO's stock was $69, the final exchange ratio was the equivalent of .9 shares of SOHIO for each Kennecott share. Thus, the holders of Kennecott stock would have an interest in SOHIO only if they purchased SOHIO's shares on the open market. The deal did not qualify as a tax-free exchange and any net advantage to Kennecott shareholders would fall under the capital gains provisions of the IRS code[21].

Exchange of Common Stock: Merger by stock swap prevailed in the 1960s (in 1968, 60 percent of the combinations were effected by an exchange of stock). Stock swaps were encouraged by an optimistic stock market and high P/E ratios, a rising economy, and liberal accounting rules. Market values per share tended to exceed book values; hence, it was cheaper to acquire assets by an exchange of stock rather than to purchase outstanding shares for cash. Relatively low interest rates also reduced the costs of acquisition.

An exchange of stock offered other advantages too: it conserved working capital; it more easily qualified as a tax-free exchange; and assets could be carried over at book values thereby minimizing charges against revenues and maximizing accounting earnings. The stock-swap route facilitated participation in the P/E game. If a large company of substantial reputation takes over a smaller firm with good earnings but a lower P/E ratio, the market tends to apply the former's P/E ratio to the latter's earnings. The effect creates instant wealth by raising the value of the acquired firm's earnings. If the transaction is also recorded as a pooling, the acquiring firm picks up the entire income of the acquired firm in the fiscal year of the acquisition. Thus, unless the new stock issued is disproportionately large relative to the acquired earnings, the transaction generates an instant increase in EPS for the acquiring corporation. The GE-Utah International merger illustrates these elements.

> Effective the date of the merger (December 20, 1976), GE issued 1.3 shares of common for each share of Utah International outstanding. Utah's earnings grew at an annual rate of 47.8 percent from 1966, compared to GE's growth rate of 5.25 percent. Both GE and Utah shares hovered around $47 but GE had a P/E ratio of sixteen and Utah eleven. GE recorded the transaction as a pooling and increased EPS by five cents; GE stock increased to $48.62[10].

Similarly, DuPont acquired NEN in a stock swap which qualified as a tax-free exchange and recorded as a pooling of interests[8]. In both these cases, the acquiring firm exchanged paper for paper as consideration in a contract that conferred control over real assets. Working capital remained intact. The companies had only to avoid overissuing stock and thereby diluting earnings.

Preferred Stock: As with the exchange of common stock, the issuance of preferred stock conserves working capital. For this reason, in the 1960s and 1970s, growth companies effected combinations by issuing convertible preferred stock. Buttressed by a high P/E ratio on the common, the convertible preferred reinforced the growth company policy of low dividend payout and plowback of earnings. At the same time, it gave the investor an opportunity to share in the capital gains of the common by conversion or by allowing the preferred to ride the market with the common.

Convertible preferred has been used to adjust dividend policies. If the acquired firm has a higher dividend rate than the acquiring firm, the new entity may have to increase the dividend payout on all outstanding common or face unhappy stockholders. The solution could lie in giving the shareholders of the acquired firm convertible preferred with an appropriate yield.

Preferred stock is often used in combination with other forms of consideration. For example, on October 18, 1978, Johns-Manville announced a tender offer of $65 per share for 49 percent of Olinkraft common. The remaining 51 percent was to be acquired with nonconvertible cumulative preferred carrying a $5.40 dividend[11].

Preferred stock is also a convenient device for neutralizing the controlling interests of the acquired firm. The issuance of a nonconvertible preferred for the common stock of the acquired firm deprives the selling shareholders of voting rights in the reorganized entity.

The use of preferred stock in business combinations suffers some drawbacks, however. First, the financial statements must reflect the effect of preferred conversion on earnings per share; that is, the firm must report EPS on a fully diluted basis. Second, the dividends on preferred stock do not qualify for tax deductions.

Convertible Bonds: The issuance of converts has the same rationale as the convertible preferred. However, the interest charge against earnings is offset by the tax shield. Thus, the cash flow may look better than by issuing preferred. As with preferred, the financial statements must show the effects of conversion.

The various forms of consideration can be used jointly to fit the particular circumstances of the combination. Exhibit 6–2 portrays the proportions of the different types of consideration paid over the period 1970–1983.

Assuming the acquiring firm has arrived at a valuation (purchase price) of the acquired firm, it must then calculate the year-by-year effect on earnings per share of alternate combinations of cash, bonds, preferred and common stock. For example, at a given purchase price, what is the dilution effect of increasing the cash portion from 10 to 20 percent? Similarly, if the acquiring firm has stipulated an acquisition criterion that any dilution must be overcome within a specified period, what consideration package will achieve the goal? High growth rates in acquired firm earnings will more quickly offset dilution effects and encourage stock

EXHIBIT 6–2
Dollar Value Paid and Form of Consideration (%) in
Mergers and Acquisitions 1970–1983

Year	Value Paid (1)	Cash	Stock	Combi-nation	Debt	Year	Value Paid (1)	Cash	Stock	Combi-nation	Debt
1970	$16.4	29%	52%	16%	3%	1977	$21.9	54%	26%	18%	2%
1971	12.6	32	49	17	2	1978	34.2	46	30	23	1
1972	16.6	34	51	14	1	1979	43.5	53	26	20	1
1973	16.7	41	44	14	1	1980	44.3	47	31	21	1
1974	12.5	48	33	16	3	1981	82.6	42	34	23	1
1975	11.8	48	27	23	2	1982	53.8	37	29	31	2
1976	20.0	52	26	20	2	1983	73.1	32	35	33	–

(1) Billions of Dollars

Source: W. T. Grimm & Co., *Mergerstat Review*, 1983, pp. 99–100.

swaps. These financial considerations must be balanced against the problem of corporate control. The acquiring firm's control position improves as the percentage of cash, bonds in the package, or preferred is increased.

NEGOTIATED COMBINATION

In a negotiated merger, the burden of selling the combination falls upon the acquiring firm. This requires an in-depth, candid appraisal of the prospects and pitfalls which lie ahead. Executives of the acquired company should in turn be asked to contribute their ideas on the scenario. MacDougal and Malek suggest the development of a "combined growth plan" to facilitate successful negotiation. This would include the following:

1. A statement of corporate goals for the new enterprise.
2. A joint marketing program.
3. A tentative program for further acquisitions in the same or allied fields.
4. A substantive organizational philosophy.

An imaginative growth plan, demonstrating the potential for increased earnings per share and the synergistic effects of the combination, can be crucial in a situation when the target company is not for sale and financial inducements are of secondary concern to its management[15].

SUMMARY

In this chapter, we described selected variables that figure prominently in calculating exchange ratios in particular combinations. These were chosen to illustrate how a magnitude of information negotiations will eventually center on a few variables at the core of each party's objectives.

Merger negotiations have a strong psychological content, which places a premium on successful completion of the talks—at times running contrary to the interests of one party. The internal pressures of merger negotiations account for the questionable premiums over market value paid in some cases. Experience proves that the quality of negotiations is noticeably enhanced by the formation of disciplined negotiating teams supported by carefully prepared instructions that reflect the objectives of the parties.

Each combination is an amalgam of exogenuous and endogenuous factors. Broad socioeconomic factors (the state of the economy, the politics of the period, the prevailing uncertainties that mark business activity, tax and regulatory postures) set the stage for the parties to play out their drama. Factors inherent in the relationship of the parties determine their specific arrangements. These include corporate acquisition strategies and the personal motivations of the management and stockholder groups concerned. Personal self-interest is perhaps most clearly evident in arranging the consideration package and in provisions bearing on the continuity of management personnel.

NOTES

1. Boesel, Donald M. *A Comparison of Premium Payments in Negotiated Vs. Tender Offer Payments.* Drexel University, College of Business and Administration, seminar paper, 1983.

2. Bradley, Michael. "Interfirm Tender Offers and the Market for Corporate Control." In Michael Keenan and Lawrence J. White. *Mergers and Acquisitions*. Massachusetts: Lexington Books, 1981. p. 267.

3. "DuPont's Costly Bet on Conoco." *Business Week*. July 20, 1981.

4. Campbell Soup Company, and Vlasic Foods. 10K reports to Securities and Exchange Commission for 1977, 1978, and 1979. Annual reports for 1977, 1978, and 1979.

5. Curtiss, Richard B., "Implementation of the Mergers and Acquisitions Program at United Technologies Corporation." in Michael Keenan and Lawrence J. White. *Mergers and Acquisitions*. Massachusetts: Lexington Books, pp. 349–355.

6. Daughen, Joseph R., and Peter Binzen. *The Wreck of the Penn Central*. Little, Brown and Co., 1971.

7. E. I. DuPont de Nemours & Company, and Conoco. 10K reports to Securities Exchange Commission for 1980, 1981, and 1982. Annual reports for 1980, 1981, and 1982.

8. E. I. DuPont De Nemours & Company, and New England Nuclear. 10K reports to Securities and Exchange Commission for 1979, 1980, and 1981. Annual reports for 1979, 1980, and 1981; DuPont *News*. June 1981; *Chemical Week*. December 17, 1980.

9. Emhart Corporation, and USM. 10K reports to Securities and Exchange Commission for 1974, 1975, and 1976. Annual reports for 1974, 1975, and 1976.

10. General Electric Company, and Utah International. 10K reports to Securities Exchange Commission for 1975, 1976, and 1977. Annual reports for 1975, 1976, and 1977.

11. Johns-Manville Corporation, and Olinkraft. 10K reports to Securities and Exchange Commission for 1977, 1978, and 1979. Annual reports for 1977, 1978, and 1979.

12. Kellogg Company, and Mrs. Smith's Pies Company. 10K reports to Securities and Exchange Commission for 1975, 1976, and 1977. Annual reports for 1975, 1976, 1977.

13. Keenan, Michael, and Lawrence J. White. *Mergers and Acquisitions*. Massachusetts: Lexington Books, 1981. p. 306.

14. Keon, A., and J. Pinkertown. "Merger Announcements and Insider Trading Activity." *Journal of Finance*. September 1981. pp. 855–869.

15. MacDougal, Gary E., and Fred V. Malek. "Master Plan for Merger Negotiations." *Harvard Business Review*. January–February 1970. pp. 71–82.

16. Nabisco and Standard Brands. 10K reports to Securities and Exchange Commission for 1980, 1981, and 1982. Annual reports for 1980, 1981, and 1982. Proxy statement of Nabisco Brands for 1982 annual meeting.

17. "The New Urge to Merge." *Newsweek*. July 27, 1981.

18. Oppenheimer, Henry R., and Terry E. Dielman. "On Mergers, Tender Offers, Competitive Bidding and Insider Transactions: Some Direct Evidence." *Working Paper #8*. Texas Christian University, 1982–83 Series.

19. Schaefer, Jeffrey M. "Comment; Mergers and the Securities Industry." In Michael Keenan and Lawrence J. White. *Mergers and Acquisitions*. Massachusetts: Lexington Books, 1981, pp. 301–304.

20. Standard and Poor's *Industry Surveys*. "Electronics-Electrical Current Analysis," p. E1 and "Steel-Coal Current Analysis," p. 535.

21. Standard Oil Company (Ohio), and Kennecott Corporation. 10K reports to Securities Exchange Commission for 1980, 1981, and 1982. Annual reports

for 1980, 1981, and 1982. *The Wall Street Journal*. April 6, 24; May 6 and 12; and November 23, 1981.

22. The Pillsbury Company, and Green Giant Company. 10K reports to Securities and Exchange Commission for 1978, 1979, and 1980. Annual reports for 1978, 1979, and 1980.

23. The *Wall Street Journal*. October 5, 1982.

Behavioral Component

7

Fairchild Camera and Instrument Corp., formerly one of the premier semiconductor manufacturers, had fallen on hard times when acquired by Schlumberger Ltd. in 1979. The latter was a leader in the oil field services industry and, in the view of some, "one of the best managed companies in any industry." This managerial finesse was hardly evident when a Schlumberger executive told Fairchild employees: "You're all frogs, and we're going to see if you can learn to be princes." The frogs have yet to become princes, but the king may have lost his shirt. Fairchild's market share continued to dwindle. In 1982, the company lost $100 million as sales fell 20 percent compared to a 2 percent decline for the industry. Remodeled plant and equipment remains largely underutilized. But more important, the exodus of Fairchild managers, complaining of Schlumberger's arrogant behavior, casts doubt on the ability of Fairchild to sustain any revitalization program[10]. Schlumberger did show the business community how not to undertake a merger reorganization.

Successful completion of acquisition of a firm does not guarantee automatic achievement of the economic and strategic objectives of the acquisition. There are many factors that management of the acquiring firm must control and influence to have the acquisition pay off. In this chapter we will discuss some of the managerial and the behavioral elements that hinder successful management of an acquisition.

ACQUISITION OBJECTIVES

Preacquisition objectives and the motivations behind a specific acquisition are important factors in determining how the acquired unit is going to perform in the postacquisition period. The reasons for acquisition vary

This chapter was written by Alok K. Chakrabarti.

from company to company and from one acquisition to another one. Whatever the reason and motivation, the management of the acquiring company must have a clear understanding of the strategic objectives and determine the extent to which the objectives will be met by the acquisition.

IBH Holding Co. in West Germany bought the money-losing construction equipment division of General Motors, Terex, through a cash and equity mix. Horst Esch, the Chief Executive of IBH Holding, announced that the motivation for Terex acquisition was to have a strong presence in the United States in the construction machinery industry. Esch cut one-third of the salaried personnel, consolidated six regional offices, and demanded reliable forecasts from the dealers. Although it is too soon to say whether Esch has succeeded, the pattern is similar to what he had done with his acquisitions of Hanomag (German manufacturer of loaders and bulldozers) and Hymac (British maker of excavators), both losing money at the time of acquisition[3].

It should be noted here that IBH Co. had determined the strategic objectives for its acquisitions and could then take appropriate actions for managing the acquisitions. Consider the case of American Can Company, which acquired the Pickwick International, a manufacturer and distributor of records, and Sam Goody, the record chain company. American Can was attempting a diversification through these acquisitions. However, the company executives knew little about running the music business and therefore properly controlling them. The record business was later found to be involved in illegal activities for which American Can was held responsible[3]. The evidence suggests that American Can knew very little about integrating an entertainment business with their other lines of business.

For a successful acquisition, management must conduct an analysis outlining the fit between the proposed acquisition and the existing business. In particular, there must exist a clear understanding of the specific steps necessary to make the acquisition profitable. To cite an earlier example, when Pan Am bought National for $394 million, it seemed to be motivated to acquire a modern fleet of aircrafts at a bargain price. It also appeared that National would feed Pan Am's international traffic. Subsequent experience revealed that National's route structure was not conducive to feeding Pan Am's international traffic. Poor integration and rapid turnover of National employees destabilized the entire organization. Preoccupation with the National merger diverted Pan Am's attention from its own international business.

In our National Science Foundation study of corporate acquisitions, we encountered the case of an air conditioning equipment manufacturer who acquired a small motor and fan manufacturer. The acquiring company was inspired by the thought that it would be a vertical integration, as the air conditioning equipment needs fans and motors. In the postacquisition period, the management learned the following:

1. The acquired company was a manufacturer of specialized fans and was not an efficient manufacturer of high-volume standardized products; it could not become a supplier.

2. The acquiring company was not very knowledgeable about custom fan business; their strength lies in high-volume products.

3. The technological capabilities of the acquiring company were not high enough for an effective transfer of technology from the acquiring company to the acquired unit.

From our interviews with various executives in the acquiring company, it appeared that there was an inadequate analysis of the strategic fit between the two companies. After losing money for several years, the management employees of the acquired company bought it from the parent[12].

MacDougal and Malek note:

**MANAGING
HUMAN
RESOURCES
IN
THE
POST-
ACQUISITION
PERIOD**

> Even when all business interests interlock and the financial terms are acceptable, a surprising number of acquisitions fail to mature because the buying company overlooks the importance of the "personal touch." Particularly when large corporations are involved, it is easy to think that the financial terms, the compelling logic of a sound plan, and the business advantages are all that count. Yet there are enough examples from recent years, when the success or failure of the negotiations depended on personal relationships, for even the most rigidly analytical manager to take them into account[9].

The management of the human resources in the postacquisition period involves several elements: (1) retention of competent staff in managerial and technical structures, (2) reduction of incompetent and redundant staff, (3) motivating for better performance, and (4) institution of appropriate control mechanisms for performance evaluation.

Retention of competent people in the managerial and technical structures depends in part upon the preacquisition environment. Managing the merger process itself can foster retention or aggravate unrest. For example, when Esmark won its takeover battle for Norton Simon, a certain unrest quickly surfaced among the employees of both organizations. The president of Esmark, Donald P. Kelley, had remarked that layoffs could come at either organization. Rumors were widespread that Norton Simon's New York headquarters would close; that product lines would be shuffled between Hunt-Wesson foods (Esmark) and Swift (Norton Simon), putting their respective executives in an adversarial position; that the Norton Simon management style (central control) would necessarily give way to the Esmark style (decentralization); and that the Max Factor division of Norton Simon would be reorganized under an Esmark executive. Mr. Kelley's subsequent statements aimed at allaying these fears did not entirely succeed[10]. Studies in the United States and Europe show that a strong preacquisition selling job, and subsequent involvement of the employees of the acquired firm in postmerger planning and implementation, mitigates the fear of change.

Retention of the management and key technical people is of special importance when the acquired company is an entrepreneurial firm founded by one or a few people. When a larger company buys an entrepreneurial company, it is very important that the founder-manager stay with the company to ensure a smooth transition. The reasons for this are:

1. The founder-manager is often the key technical person. The technical information associated with the product and the production processes often remains as an art mastered by this individual. Until a suitable successor is found and trained, it is necessary that the founder continue his employment.

2. The key people in the company know the details about the business and might have developed personal contacts with the key customers. It takes time to transfer this marketing know-how to other people, if the acquiring company chooses to do so. Often such people have detailed knowledge about the specific market niches in which small companies do well. This specialized knowledge is generally not put in any formalized information system. People are the information systems in small organizations.

3. Employees in a small organization often identify themselves with the founder and his/her key managers in a family type of environment. It takes time to get adjusted to the culture of a larger organization. If one does not allow a smooth cultural transition, the morale of the employees may be negatively affected.

4. Large-scale turnover in any organization creates a great deal of uncertainty and morale problem.

What determines the turnover of management personnel in an acquired company after the acquisition? Hayes & Hoag gave some answers to this question based upon interview studies. Their conclusions, summarized here, are:

1. *Managerial autonomy and control* is the most important factor in determining the turnover rate. Interference by the parent company has been cited as the major reason for leaving the company after the acquisition. When executives perceive a satisfactory degree of autonomy in their position, they tend to remain with the company. Autonomy does not, however, imply complete freedom for division management. The division is subjected to close supervision for performance and budgetary control, but the division management has meaningful discretion with respect to the operational decisions on a day-to-day basis.

2. *The performance of the acquired company* is related to the turnover of the management after acquisition. However, the causality is not clear from the interviews conducted by Hayes and Hoag.

3. *Reduction in pay* is a factor often mentioned in turnover. However, the data showed that actual reduction was not as important as the manner in which the pay reduction was handled.

4. *Financial independence* of the executives is not a factor in leaving the acquired unit[5].

How can one minimize the retention problems? There are several steps that the acquiring company should take to alleviate the problem. In the preacquisition period, be candid with the manager to dispel, as far as possible, any myths and misunderstandings. The acquired executive then will not feel that he/she has been mistreated or ignored. On the other hand, complete impartiality is often difficult for the acquiring company, since the primary job is to sell the merger. In any event, care must be taken not to make promises that clearly cannot be kept after the acquisition.

The acquired executives should be granted reasonable autonomy in practice and not just on paper. The emphasis here is on the word "reasonable." It is expected that the parent company will exert budgetary and other types of control. But the acquired executive should be allowed significant latitude in running the business on a day-to-day basis. It must be remembered that executives are conditioned to exercise authority, and managerial style cannot be changed abruptly.

Reporting systems should be reasonable. The parent company should examine the rationale for all reports. The purpose of reporting is to help manage the company. To that extent reports are necessary. If the acquired executive has to spend a substantial part of his/her time writing trivial reports to the parent company, then relationships will be strained.

Relationships between the middle level managers in the staff departments with the acquired executives should be treated delicately. Constant interference from the corporate staff is a factor which should be avoided at all costs. The staff analysts must recognize the fact that the top management of the acquired companies, particularly those who owned the company, are often wealthy and independent minded individuals. Many of them started their own companies to escape the plodding routines of large bureaucracies.

ORGANIZATIONAL LINKAGE

How should an acquired company be structured into a large company? We have noticed generally three practices followed in this regard. The first and very prevalent practice is to keep the acquired company as a separate division reporting to some top executive of the parent. The advantage of such an organization arrangement is that the acquired unit maintains a separate identity and function as a semiautonomous entity. If it becomes necessary to sell that business, it can easily be done without much disturbance to the total organization. The second type of organizational arrangement is to set up the acquired unit as a part of an existing division. This is done when the acquired company is closely related with the business of the division. This helps in developing a close relationship with the two related business entities. The third organizational arrangement is the total integration of the acquired unit by disassociating its organizational structure and absorbing the functions of the various subunits into existing departments of the parent. The acquired company loses its separate identity altogether. This arrangement is the least frequent choice among the organizational options.

Whether or not an acquired company should be made part of an existing division depends on a number of factors. If the acquired company closely resembles an existing division, then the natural choice is to link it with the latter. On the other hand, if the acquisition is a true diversification removed from the existing lines of business, then it should be left as a separate entity. The criteria for matching an acquisition with the existing line of business or with an existing division can be defined in terms of market characteristics, environmental uncertainties, technological changes, as well as the fit between the strategic objectives of the acquired company and the division in question. Lorsch & Allen have provided some excellent guidelines for developing organizational structures to assist differentiation or integration among divisions and functional units. Environmental diversity faced by the divisional entities dictates the degree of required differentiation. The organizational structure should be such that the complex interdependencies will be contained within the divisional units[8]. Lawrence & Lorsch have shown that the members in different functional units develop different styles of interpersonal orientations, levels of formalization, time orientation and goal orientation based on the environmental uncertainties, dominant competitive issues, and time span for feedback. A division's long-term performance is dependent on the proper fit of differentiation and environmental requirements[7].

According to Lorsch & Allen, the degree of differentiation between the headquarters and the divisions depends on the:

1. Cognitive limits of individuals and groups within headquarters and divisional units which that define the upper limit of differentiation.
2. Degree of diversity between the demands posed by the division's industrial environment and demands posed by headquarters' total environment which determines the lower limit of differentiation.
3. Diversity of the firm's total environment[8].

Once we recognize the need for differentiation among the various organizational subunits, we need to understand the needs for interdependence between and among them and design appropriate integration mechanisms. The three types of interdependence are: pooled, sequential, and reciprocal. Under pooled interdependence, the subunits work independently, render a discrete contribution to the whole organization, and in turn are supported by the whole organization. Sequential interdependence is a direct asymmetrical relationship between two organizational units, where output of one is the input for the other. In reciprocal interdependence, outputs of each unit represent inputs for the other units. The complexity of the required interdependence determines the complexity of integrative devices used to achieve the required integration[11].

Hansen, in his book on the history of the "Silicon Valley" firms in the West Coast area, has given several examples of failures of the semiconductor companies after they were acquired by other companies from the petroleum and other industries. Bureaucratic red tape stifled the innovative spirit of the companies. The acquiring companies did not understand the required differentiation essential to these rapidly changing, technologically oriented firms. The strategic objectives of the firm and the divisions did not mesh to their mutual benefit, since the dominant competitive issues were quite different. For example, in one case, the semiconductor unit was making a handsome profit and it needed to plow back the profit for further development in technology. The parent company thought otherwise in terms of its strategy for the overall organization and diverted the cash from the semiconductor unit to other units. Needless to say, the semiconductor company lost its competitive edge[4].

The ultimate success in effectively and efficiently running an acquired unit depends upon the communication and control mechanisms. According to Lorsch & Allen, organizations with appropriate types of differentiation and integration have high quality information systems between the divisions and the headquarters. They further found that properly differentiated and integrated organizations do the following:

COMMUNICATION AND CONTROL

- Use confrontation or problem solving as their method of conflict resolution.
- Distribute the influence over decision making literally and hierarchically to coincide with the location of relevant information.
- Develop divisional performance evaluation systems consistent with the overall uncertainty and the patterns of diversity and interdependence characterizing their environment[8].

In our NSF study of sixteen acquired firms, we noted that the planning and control system imposed on the acquired firm may be very beneficial to the acquired unit under certain situations. Often a small growing firm lacks a strict financial control and planning mechanism. The headquarters of the acquiring company can impose these necessary disciplines on the acquired firm to the mutual benefit of parent and subsidiary.

Technology and innovation has motivated many mergers and acquisitions. Kitching observed that 14 percent of acquisitions were technology related[6]. Ansoff observed that technology is the second most important dimension from which corporations sought synergy through acquisition. Technology was an important factor in the acquisition of Reliance Electric by Exxon, Beckman Instrument by Smith Kline, Zilog by Exxon, and so on. Gould, Harris Corporation, Intermedics, Agfa Gevaert, Motorola, United Technology, and others have acquired firms for technological reasons. Ansoff found that only 12 percent of those who sought technological synergy actually obtained it[1]. Kitching observed that the failure rate of the technology related mergers was highest[6]. Biggadike reported poor financial performance for the *technology entrant* type diversifications. It is, therefore, prudent to explore some of the contingencies for successful technological innovation in postmerger organizations[2].

Technological innovation in postmerger organization depends upon

TECHNOLOGICAL INNOVATION IN POST-MERGER ORGANIZATION

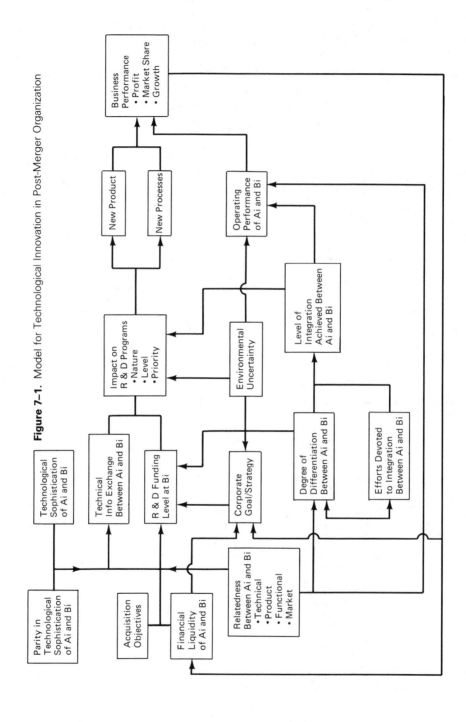

Figure 7–1. Model for Technological Innovation in Post-Merger Organization

the complex interactions of various factors as shown in Figure 7–1. The
acquired unit (Bi) can perform better on the technology dimension in several ways:

- Through better technology transfer from the parent.
- Through better technical information exchange.
- Availability of dollars for its R & D program and product introduction programs.
- Through changes in nature, direction, and sophistication of R & D programs.
- Through its own better operational performance, it can improve its R & D programs and budgets.

The extent to which the acquiring company (Ai) can help the acquired unit in its technological pursuit depends on a number of factors such as:

- The acquisition objectives.
- Financial position of the company before and after the acquisition.
- Parity of technological sophistication of the pair.
- Technological base of the parent.
- Organizational integration.
- Environmental uncertainties.

These factors are interrelated. A proper understanding of these factors and controlling them will enhance the chances of success.

THE CEO

The chief executive officer of the acquiring company has the burden of creating an atmosphere wherein effective personal contacts can be made between the managements of the acquiring and acquired companies. The personnel of the acquiring company take their cues from the CEO. This requires that the CEO maintain close contact with negotiations in the preacquisition stage to demonstrate his intentions and the importance of the selling company to the buyer. If the CEO remains aloof, on the other hand, negotiations will tend to exhibit a rigid formality without the support of desirable informal contacts. This potential adversary relationship will carry over to the postcombination environment. If the parent is a frequent acquirer, the CEO might follow the practice of introducing the executives of the proposed acquisition to the satisfied executives of previously acquired companies. Another desirable practice is for the CEO to keep in weekly contact with his counterpart. This tends to mitigate the possible development of deadlocks in the negotiations[9]. In short, the behavior of the CEO will define the quality of the relationship between the acquiring and acquired firms.

The failure of the Bendix bid to take over Martin Marietta is in no small part attributable to the tactics of William Agee, chairman of Bendix. Thomas G. Pownall, chairman of Martin Marietta, describes his reactions to the Bendix maneuvers:

The chances are fifty-fifty that if this were to have taken three months instead of one, it might have turned out differently. Agee did not pay any attention to us. If he had, he would have sensed how indignant we were right off. He never came to see me. His letter announcing the tender offer was a gun at my head.

We were behind the power curve. Everywhere we turned they were there. They had signed up Hill & Knowlton and Bob Gray's public relations firms. They had called the generals and admirals for whom we do work . . . They had called our aluminum customers. It was amazing[12].

SUMMARY

Managing a successful business combination is not a question of "frogs" and "princes." Perhaps, more than any major business decision, it requires a sensitivity to human needs and aspirations. This does not mean that the acquiring management has to be all things to all people. It does mean that management foster the type of relationships essential to achieve the strategic objectives of the merger. If management remains blissfully unaware of the human content of its acquisition strategy, then it had better not play the merger game.

NOTES

1. Ansoff, H. Igor, Richard G. Brandenburg, Fred E. Portner, and Raymond Radosevich. *Acquisition Behavior of U.S. Manufacturing Firms, 1946–1965*. Nashville: Vanderbilt University Press, 1971.

2. Biggadike, E. Ralph. *Corporate Diversification: Entry, Strategy and Performance*. Cambridge, Massachusetts: Harvard University Press, 1976.

3. *Business Week*. March 24, 1980, April 30, 1981, June 22, 1981.

4. Hansen, Dirk. *The New Alchemists: Silicon Valley and the Microelectronics Revolution*. Boston: Little, Brown and Company, 1982.

5. Hayes, Robert H., and Gerald H. Hoag. "Post Acquisition Retention of Top Management: A Research Study." *Mergers & Acquisitions*. Vol. 9, No. 1, Spring 1974. pp. 8–18.

6. Kitching, John. "Why Mergers Miscarry?" *Harvard Business Review*. November–December 1967. pp. 84–101.

7. Lawrence, Paul R., and Jay W. Lorsch. *Organization and Environment: Managing Differentiation and Integration*. Boston: Division of Research, Harvard Business School, 1967.

8. Lorsch, Jay W., and Stephen A. Allen III. *Managing Diversity and Interdependence: An Organizational Study of Multidivisional Firms*. Boston: Division of Research, Harvard Business School, 1973.

9. MacDougal, Gary E., and Fred V. Malek. "Master Plan for Merger Negotiation." *Harvard Business Review*. January–February 1970, pp. 71–82.

10. The *Wall Street Journal*. July 27, 1983, August 26, 1983.

11. Thompson, James D. *Organizations in Action*. New York: McGraw-Hill, 1967.

12. *Time*. April 25, 1983.

13. Work in this area has been supported by a grant from the Division of Industrial Science and Technological Innovation, National Science Foundation to Drexel University, Grant #83–10116. Alok K. Chakrabarti, Principal Investigator.

ACQUISITION STRATEGY
Accounting Options

8

Copeland and Wojdak stated the essence of the accounting decision in business combinations:

> The manipulative quality of the purchase-pooling decision rule derives from the fact that acquired assets may be valued differently under the two methods. If a merger is accounted for as a purchase, acquired assets are recorded at the fair value of the consideration given by the acquiring company; however, under the pooling method they are valued at their preacquisition book values . . . *The method that minimizes asset values usually maximizes profits* (Italics added)[8].

Minimizing asset values on the books reduces future charges against income. Hence, if book values exceed market values, the decision rule dictates a purchase treatment. When this condition is reversed, the pooling of interest is the appropriate treatment. But two assumptions underlie the rule: (1) that management seeks to maximize future accounting incomes, and (2) accounting numbers determine the market value of the common shares—the value of the combination.

Empirical evidence supports the first assumption. Gagnon investigated a sample of 500 mergers from the New York Stock Exchange listing applications for the period 1955–1958. He found approximately 51 percent followed the proposed decision rule[13]. Copeland-Wojdak showed a much higher incidence of maximizing behavior in the period 1966–1967. They concluded:

> There had been a trend toward pooling since 1958 . . . and the results strongly support the hypothesis that firms record mergers by the method that maximizes reported income[8].

139

A study by Anderson and Louderback covered the period 1967–1974. They found about 86 percent of the surveyed firms followed the decision rule[3]. Their findings seemingly lend support to an observation of Wyatt:

> ... accounting for a combination is commonly decided in advance of completion of the transaction. That is, *the accounting treatment is one of the variables that must be firmed up before the final price (in terms of exchange ratios) is determined* (Italics added) [3].

Or, to restate the proposition, the accounting methodology is one component of an overall acquisition strategy.

As to the second assumption—that accounting numbers influence the market value of the combination—the evidence is less conclusive and we shall postpone the discussion to the end of the chapter. For the present, assume that managers and investors believe accounting numbers influence market valuation and that rising earnings per share signify high share prices. Actually, those who hold the contrary—that security markets pierce the veil of accounting statements and discount "efficiently" all that is known about the size and variability of the cash flows—concede that in some cases accounting numbers do influence the time distribution of the cash flows. Accounting numbers may affect market values in two respects: accounting numbers can directly affect the firm's cash flows (for example, the basis of accountability for tax purposes will determine tax liabilities, compliance with restrictive accounting ratios stipulated in bond indentures may be sensitive to changes in accepted accounting practice, or the amount of retained earnings available for shareholders' dividends may reflect accounting calculations). The accounting numbers may *indirectly* affect the firm's cash flow by altering the cost of capital, investor assessments of firm riskiness, or the amount of future cash flows shaped, in part, by accounting numbers.

Since optimists make mergers, pressures mount for instant payoffs in market prices and per share earnings to justify the design. Delay ignites shareholder unrest. To the shareholder, the pertinent questions raised in our chapter remains: "Is my wealth position at current values more or less than before the merger?"

PURCHASE VERSUS POOLING

When one corporation acquires a voting interest in another corporation, it may elect—depending upon the degree of ownership and other material circumstances—to treat the selling corporation as a subsidiary or nonsubsidiary. If the former, it may opt to retain the legal entity of the subsidiary or to liquidate the acquired corporation. If the legal entity is maintained, the corporation may prepare consolidated statements or simply carry the investment on its unconsolidated financial statements. The criteria relating to these options are defined by Generally Accepted Accounting Practice (GAAP).

Basically, a merger may take form as a purchase or a pooling. Not unexpectedly, given the issues at stake, much controversy surrounds the accounting standards that some authorities contend have opened the door to corporate abuse. Before probing these questions, it will be necessary to define and illustrate each approach.

Purchase: Accounting Principles Board (APB) Opinion No 16, *Business Combinations,* defines a purchase as a "business combination of two or more corporations in which an important part of the ownership interest in the acquired corporation or corporations is eliminated"[1]. The notion is one of discontinuity in voting participation, financial structure, and accountability. The characteristics of a purchase transaction follow from the definition:

1. The acquiring corporation views the transaction as an investment; if the value of the consideration (cash and/or securities) exceeds the *appraised* value of the assets acquired, the excess may be recorded as goodwill. APB Opinion No. 17 requires that the portion of the excess recorded as goodwill be amortized against earnings over some reasonable period not to exceed forty years. The charge against earnings, on the other hand, while lowering accounting net-income does not qualify as a tax deduction[1]. Other things equal, taxable income exceeds accounting income.

2. The surviving firm records the acquired assets at their cost (i.e., current value) not the book value to the selling corporation. A new basis of accountability is established, possibly resulting in higher depreciation charges against income with consequent effects on the bottom line.

3. Consideration may take the form of debt securities, stock, and/or cash. Securities issued by the acquiring corporation are deemed to have been issued at current market values. Debt securities and cash are frequently used to reduce the participation of the acquired firm's shareholders in the management of the surviving corporation. If the surviving corporation had acquired its own voting stock (Treasury stock) in contemplation of the combination, the transaction must be recorded as a purchase.

4. Liabilities of the seller corporation become the obligations of the surviving firm. However, the retained earnings of the seller are not added to those of the surviving firm. Purchase accounting in effect capitalizes the retained earnings of the seller. The basic notion is that one company cannot increase its retained earnings by buying another company.

The nature of the purchase option suffers several disadvantages—fatal impediments perhaps to a management seeking to demonstrate the wisdom of the combination quickly:

1. Given the presence of goodwill and/or a higher basis of accountability on depreciable assets, net income will be lower than if the transaction were completed as a pooling.

2. There are negotiation problems. If the consideration includes cash, the seller may incur substantial taxable gains and demand a higher price to offset the tax bite. Or, the acquiring firm may wish the purchase price allocated to assets, which can be amortized to reduce taxable income, while seller may seek to allocate purchase price against assets that reduce his taxable gains. The sets may not match.

3. The investor corporation requires earnings projections on the seller under a variety of purchase terms. This implies an understanding of the accounting methods adopted by the seller in calculating net income and an estimate of the current value of the seller's assets.

Exhibits 8–1 through 8–4 contrast purchase and pooling accounting for the acquisition by Alpha of Delta. The basic facts on each company are:

	Alpha	Delta
Total Market Value of Outstanding Shares	$150,000	$100,000
Net Book Value (Assets less Liabilities)	100,000	30,000
Net Income	7,500	12,000
Shares Outstanding ($50 par)	1,000	1,000
Earnings Per Share	7.50	12
P/E Ratio	20	4.17
		(rounded)

(A) The exchange ratio is 1 share Alpha for 2 shares Delta and 100 percent of Delta is acquired.
(B) The higher current yield on Delta shares is attributable to the risk posture of the firm.
(C) The merger takes place on January 1, 1984 and Alpha picks up all Delta earnings for the subsequent year.
(D) In the first case (Exhibit 2), Alpha has chosen to issue 500 shares of *nonvoting*, Class B Common. Since this alters the managerial control structure, purchase accounting is thus mandatory. In the latter case (Exhibit 3), the transaction was effected by an exchange of *voting stock* at book values. This makes pooling the required procedure.

EXHIBIT 8–1
Balance Sheet
December 31, 1983
(Precombination)

	Alpha	Delta
Assets:		
Current Assets	$120,000	$20,000
Fixed Assets	80,000	30,000
Total	$200,000	$50,000
Current Liabilities	$ 40,000	$20,000
Shareholder Equity:		
Capital Stock ($50 par)	$ 50,000	$10,000
Excess Over Par	50,000	10,000
Retained Earnings	60,000	10,000
Total	$200,000	$50,000

EXHIBIT 8–1

continued

Income Statement
December 31, 1983
(Precombination)

		Alpha		Delta
Sales Revenues		$ 20,000		$40,000
Less				
Expenses	$7,500		$20,000	
Income Tax (40%)	5,000	12,500	8,000	28,000
Net Income		$ 7,500		$12,000
EPS		$7.50		$12.00

EXHIBIT 8–2
Balance Sheet
Alpha-Delta
December 31, 1984
(Postcombination)

Assets		*Equities*	
Current Assets	$140,000	Current Liabilities	$ 60,000
Fixed Assets[1]	120,000	Shareholders Equity:	
Goodwill[1]	10,000	Capital Stock[2]	75,000
		Excess Over Par	75,000
		Retained Earnings	60,000
Total	$270,000		$270,000

[1]Alpha issued shares having a total market value of $50,000 and assumed Delta's liabilities of $20,000 so that the total purchase price of Delta's gross assets is $70,000. An appraisal of Delta's assets reveals that the current assets are recorded at approximately their current value, but the fixed assets have an estimated value of $40,000. Accordingly, the purchase price is allocated as follows:

Delta's Current Assets	$20,000
Delta's Fixed Assets	40,000
Goodwill	10,000
Total Purchase Price	$70,000

[2]Alpha's Paid-in-Capital has increased by $50,000 to reflect the fair market value of the additional shares.

Note: The entry to record the combination on Alpha's books was:

Current Assets	$20,000	
Fixed Assets	40,000	
Goodwill	10,000	
Current Liabilities		$20,000
Capital Stock		25,000
Excess Over Par		25,000

EXHIBIT 8–2
continued

Income Statement
Alpha-Delta
December 31, 1984
(Postcombination)

Sales Revenues		$60,000
Less		
Expenses[3]	$30,500	
Income Tax	$11,800	42,300
Net Income[4]		$17,700

[3]The depreciable base of the fixed assets has increased by $10,000; assuming a five-year life, the annual depreciation charge increases by $2,000. Also, the goodwill must be amortized over a reasonable life; assuming 10 years, the annual charge is $1,000. While the additional depreciation is tax deductible, the goodwill amortization is not. Total expenses are computed as follows:

Alpha's Continuing Expenses	$ 7,500	
Delta's Continuing Expenses	20,000	
Additional Depreciation	2,000	
Total Tax Deductible Expenses	$29,500	(Tax Shield: 40% or $11,800)[5]
Goodwill Amortization	1,000	
Total Expenses	$30,500	
EPS	$11.80	

[4]Management may structure the transaction as a purchase or pooling. However, a purchase or a pooling is not an alternative interpretation. Either the transaction qualifies as a pooling or it must be treated as a purchase.

[5]The existence or nonexistence of tax shields can be of significance in the choice of accounting methodologies. Thus, under Purchase Accounting, the firm may show a lower EPS but enjoy a higher cash flow due to the tax shields accruing from the revalued tax basis of the acquired assets.

An important limitation of the purchase option should be mentioned at this point. Under purchase, the acquiring corporation includes all assets and liabilities of the seller in its consolidated statement, *no matter when during the fiscal period the transaction was consummated.* However, on the consolidated income statement, it picks up only the income of the seller applicable to the period between the transaction date and the end of the fiscal period.

The choice between purchase or pooling depends upon the state of the economy, earning capacity of the combining firms, their financial structures, and the objectives of the ownership interests. In general, focusing only on the accounting numbers, purchase is the choice if the book value of the acquired assets exceeds their fair market value and the effective yield on the financing used is less than the ROA for the acquired company. This situation prevails frequently in prolonged periods of declining business activity. Conversely, in a period of expansion, market values tend to exceed book values and pooling may seem to be the attractive option.

The firm can structure a transaction to qualify for either treatment.
The merger of International Nickel and ESB could have been accomplished as a pooling. But the parties chose to structure the combination as a purchase. INCO issued approximately 5.5 million shares valued at $233,794,000 to cover the total purchase price including fees, commissions, and expenses. ESB's net assets at acquisition were transferred to INCO's books at their fair value of $189,639,000. The difference of $44,155,000 was set up in an account "Cost in Excess of Fair Value" to be amortized on a straight-line basis over fifteen years.

Mobil's acquisition of Marcor (the fifth largest general merchandise retailer in the U.S. and the largest producer of paper-board packaging worldwide) illustrates the mix of accounting treatment and acquisition strategy. In the year prior to the announced tender offer, Mobil had acquired on the open market 4.1 percent of Marcor at a cost of $27 million. In 1974, Mobil made the following offer to acquire voting control:

1. To purchase 17,250,000 equivalent voting shares of Marcor common (one vote per share) at $35 or its Series A, $200 cumulative convertible preferred (two votes per share) at $70; and
2. To issue 8,000,000 shares of a new Mobil preferred for $25 (one vote per share). The new preferred represented an effort to satisfy Marcor's need for cash.

The offer would give Mobil 50.5 percent of Marcor's voting shares. Mobil eventually purchased 13,430,788 shares of common and 1,933,975 shares of Series A preferred for a total of $605,455,830. The new preferred cost was $200,000,000. Mobil accounted for the transaction as a purchase. The excess of the consideration over the value of the assets received was allocated among the assets of Marcor with no goodwill resulting. Marcor is operated as a separate profit center. Mobil made no changes in the personnel or management structure other than to place members on Marcor's Board of Directors.

Pooling: The APB Opinion No. 16 describes pooling as a business combination in which the holders of substantially all of the ownership interest in the constituent corporations become the owners of a single corporation which owns the assets and businesses of the constituent corporations[1]. *Continuity* of voting participation and operations is the core of a pooling arrangement. From this flows the specific features of the accounting treatment:

1. The acquisition is not viewed as an investment; rather, the two predecessor corporations combine into a single entity.
2. The original accounts—assets and liabilities—are carried over to the combined entity at book values. The transaction does not create a new basis of accountability or generate goodwill.
3. A pooling must be accomplished by an exchange of voting stock between previously independent companies. Bond and preferred stocks that alter the structure of ownership may not form part of the consideration. For the same reason, cash is ruled out along with Treasury Stock acquired in contemplation of the merger.

4. Since assets and liabilities carry over at book values, the retained earnings of the seller corporation carry over to the combination.

The par or *stated* capital of the pooled companies may be greater or less than the total capital of the individual units. If the former, the excess is deducted first from the total of any other contributed capital and then from the consolidated retained earnings. If the latter, the difference is reported on the consolidated balance sheet as excess over par.

Distinct advantages can accrue to management through executing a pooling-of-interests:

1. The transaction may qualify as a tax-free exchange if it also meets Internal Revenue criteria.
2. The transaction does not drain liquid assets nor increase the debt/equity ratio of the combination.
3. All things equal, pooling results in a higher net income due to the absence of goodwill and no change in the basis of accountability.
4. Regardless of market values, the postcombination entity bears responsibility only for the dollar amounts that existed prior to the combination. Hence, if synergism results, pooling can create "instant growth" earnings. As a general rule, pooling is desirable if the assets of the acquired company at book are undervalued in relation to actual or potential earning power.
5. Retention of retained earnings may permit the combination to write-off any deficit on the books of the acquiring firm.
6. In contrast to the purchase transaction, the combination may pick up not only the assets and liabilities of the constituents but their *full income* irrespective of the transaction date—even after the close of the fiscal year or before the auditors arrive.

Exhibit 8–3 uses the same basic data to record the accounting for a pooling of interests. The Pooling concept envisions the blending of two enterprises into a single unit without substantial change in management or operations; it creates a common ownership over two previously independent organizations. The accounting procedure, therefore, is a simple additive process.

Exhibit 8–4 displays the comparative advantage of purchase and pooling under the assumed conditions. For Alpha EPS is lower then before the merger. Whether or not the market price of the postcombination shares matches the precombination performance depends upon the P/E ratio; that is, Alpha shareholders are hopefully trading EPS for capital gains. In this instance, the quality of the earnings—the risk posture of the combination after the merger and growth of earnings—would principally determine whether the P/E ratio increases sufficiently to improve the wealth position of all shareholders. In other respects, the comparative advantage in accounting numbers rests with pooling: lower asset base and expense items; higher net income. The lower asset base has the potential for gains on disposal; the larger retained earnings may allow a higher dividend payout. Conversely, tax shields could generate a better cash flow

EXHIBIT 8–3
Balance Sheet
Alpha-Delta
December 31, 1984[1] (Postcombination)

Assets		Equities	
Current Assets	$140,000	Current Liabilities	$ 60,000
Fixed Assets	110,000	Shareholders Equity	
		Capital Stock-Alpha	75,000
		Excess Over Par-Alpha	45,000
		Retained Earnings	70,000[2]
Total	$250,000		$250,000

Income Statement
Alpha-Delta
December 31, 1984
(Postcombination)

Sales Revenues		$60,000
Less		
Expenses	$27,500	
Income Tax	13,000	40,500
Net Income		$19,500
EPS		$13.00

[1]Entry to record pooling on Alpha's books:

Current Assets-Delta	$20,000	
Fixed Assets-Delta	30,000	
Excess Over Par-Delta	15,000	
Current Liabilities		$20,000
Capital Stock		25,000
Excess Over Par		10,000
Retained Earnings		10,000

[2]Ordinarily, under Pooling, the Retained Earnings of Alpha and Delta would simply be added together for a total of $70,000. However, consider the position of Delta which paid 500 shares with a *stated value* of $50 per share and assumed $20,000 in liabilities—*de facto* exchanging $25,000 in stated capital for $10,000. Following the rule, this deficit is accounted for by the debit to Excess Over Par. The stated Capital on the Postcombination Balance Sheet comprises the following elements:

Alpha's Stated Capital Before Combination:	
1,000 shares @ $50 =	$50,000
Plus	
Delta's Stated Capital Before Combination:	
200 shares @ $50 =	$ 1,000
Plus	
500 new shares of Alpha to acquire Delta =	$25,000
Less	
Cancellation of Delta Old Shares	$1,000
Total Post Combination Stated Capital	$75,000

See APB Opinion No. 16 quoted on page 254.

under purchase accounting due to the tax write-offs from the higher asset base.

The advantages to pooling are easily demonstrated in a situation where all variables are basically similar except the choice of accounting method as in Exhibits 8–1 to 8–3. The real world, on the other hand, shows few instances affording such simple laboratory comparisons. Instead, the relative advantage to pooling will depend upon the specific terms of the combination: the asset values, type and amounts of consideration, presence of goodwill, and so on. Earnings per share could be higher under purchase accounting depending upon the consideration mix and asset values. This complicates the researchers' problem of assessing whether security markets ignore accounting numbers in pricing the common shares of a business combination. The accounting effects may be clouded by the presence of other variables. More on this topic later.

ABUSES AND MISINTERPRETATIONS UNDER ACCOUNTING RESEARCH BULLETIN NO. 48

Since the issuance of the Ten Commandments, mankind has learned to interpret guidelines in the light of self-interest. So far, accounting rules have not been immune to the process. Of course, interpretation colored by self-interest is both necessary and legitimate. Wise regulation anticipates elasticity in application. However, carried to extremes, it vitiates the original intent of the guidelines and so calls forth a restatement. Such is the origin of Accounting Principles Board (APB) Opinion Nos. 16 and 18. More and more liberal interpretation of the pooling requirements in the 1960s gradually eroded the criteria for pooling until almost any combination could be considered a pooling-of-interests. The abuses stemmed from the ambiguities of Accounting Research Bulletin (ARB) No. 48[2]. In the following discussion, the major abuses under ARB No. 48 are numbered and the present practice is indicated.

1. Consistent with ARB No. 48, some combinations allocated a large part of the acquisition cost to goodwill but did not amortize the intangible asset against income. Although this did not affect cash flow, the omission overstated accounting income. If the asset base were not otherwise affected, the failure to amortize goodwill made the reported earnings the same as though pooling-of-interests accounting had been applied.

APB Opinion No. 17, *Accounting for Goodwill*, now requires that goodwill arising in business combinations be recognized and reported as an asset. The goodwill must then be amortized by systematic charges to income over the periods estimated to be benefited but not to exceed forty years[1].

2. Some companies credited negative "goodwill" (the book value of the assets acquired exceeded the consideration paid) to income over short periods rather than applying it to a reduction in the book value of non-current assets. This increases accounting income and would in some degree offset future losses by the affiliate.

Negative "goodwill" must now be applied first to reduce the carrying value of the identifiable depreciable assets with impaired earning power and the balance amortized over a period not to exceed forty years.

3. Others created instant earnings following a pooling by disposing of nonoperating assets or investments at low book values. For example, suppose Buyer paid $144,000 for Seller. The latter's assets consist of $16,000 in cash and patents of $2,000. Buyer subsequently sells the patents for $98,000 and records a $96,000 profit. Actually, the cost of the patents is $128,000 ($144,000 − $16,000 cash) and Seller should have reported a loss of $30,000. If the goodwill had been assigned to the patents (the only earning asset), the result would have better reflected the true situation.

The issue here is *continuity* of operations presupposed by the Pooling concept. If the assets disposed of *materially* alter the nature of the business, their disposition may violate the pooling criteria of APB Opinion No. 16. Conversely, Opinion No. 16 does not tie the hands of management *in perpetuum* simply because the combination qualifies as a pooling. The APB stipulates a two-year holding requirement on pooled assets.

4. Firms gave retroactive effects to pooling arrangements after the close of the fiscal year. Depending on the terms of the agreement, this also created "instant earnings" and increased returns on assets.

This practice persists, however, justified by the view that failure to report on the transaction ignores material information important to the shareholders and the need for comparability between financial statements.

5. To minimize the dilution effects of the exchange of stock under pooling-of-interests and, in some instances, to modify voting arrangements, some firms issued convertible preferred stock or a special class of common in exchange for the seller's voting shares. Others made disproportionately favorable distributions of common to one class or group of shareholders, thus altering the structure of participation in management.

As an example of the former practice, in 1968, Sun Oil and Sunray DX Oil Company entered upon a pooling arrangement subject to the following terms, as summarized here:

    A. Sun Oil will be the surviving corporation and will continue to be governed by the laws of New Jersey.

B. Sun Oil will succeed to the rights, properties, and assets of Sunray and will be subject to and responsible for the debts and liabilities of Sunray.

C. Sun Oil will issue a new class of common stock, $1 par value, with an initial authorization of 100,000,000 shares. These shares will be exchanged at par, one-for-one for Sunray common. Current authorized capital of Sun Oil is 35,000,000 shares, no par value common.

D. Sun Oil will issue a new class of $2.25 cumulative, convertible preferred stock, no par value, authorization 19,000,000 shares. The preferred will exchange for Sunray common stock, $1 par value, on a one-for-one basis.

E. A maximum of 18,556,735 shares of preferred stock will be issued and 12,061,878 shares of Sun common stock, $1 par value, will be reserved for issue upon conversion of the preferred shares.

F. Each share of new preferred stock will be entitled to one-quarter of one vote and each share of new common stock will be entitled to one full vote.

G. Each share of preferred stock will be entitled to a cumulative $2.25 annual dividend, payable quarterly, in preference to the common stock.

H. Each share of preferred stock will be immediately convertible into 0.65 of a share of common stock; and on and after June 1, 1975 will be redeemable in whole or in part, at Sun's option, at $60 per share from June 1, 1975 through May 31, 1976; at $59 from June 1, 1977 through May 31, 1978; and at $57 on and after June 1, 1978 in each case plus accrued dividends.

APB Opinion No. 16 now permits the acquiring corporation to issue only voting common stock with rights identical to the majority of voting shares outstanding.

6. Contingent payments keyed to some future event violated the pooling criteria. In a genuine pooling there would be no unresolved contingencies with respect to the exchange rates. Contingent payments arose when the parties failed to agree on the value of the companies or their future earning power. Their contract then provided for the issuance of additional securities if earnings achieved a stipulated level or if the market value of the common shares hit a specified price range.

APB Opinion No. 16 now rules out contingent payments in a pooling agreement but not in a purchase transaction.

7. More complex was the part-purchase, part-pooling situation. For example, the Buyer owned 30 percent of the Seller's voting stock acquired several years previously. Buyer then acquired the remaining 70 percent in exchange for his voting stock. Would the transaction qualify as a 30 percent purchase and 70 percent pooling? Under the old rules many combinations of this type were recorded as hybrid transactions. If so, only the appropriate portion of the goodwill (30 percent) and retained earnings (70 percent) would be reflected on the books.

The APB now requires that the combination be effected in a single transaction or completed in accordance with a specific plan within one year after the plan is initiated.

8. *Bailouts*—In many pooling-type mergers, former stockholders of the acquired company disposed of their shares in the acquiring company immediately after the merger. In some instances, the acquiring company arranged the sale with its own investment bankers or sold the securities in conjunction with a new security issue at a guaranteed price.

Under APB Opinion No. 16 the investor corporation may not agree to reacquire voting shares issued to effect the combination.

9. A method employed to avoid the dilution of EPS under pooling was the cash acquisition of Treasury Stock and its subsequent issuance for the shares of the investee corporation. *De facto*, the combination was accomplished by a cash consideration, not by previously unissued stock.

Current practice prohibits the acquisition of Treasury Stock in contemplation of the merger or for other than normal business purposes between the dates of initiation and completion of the plan.

APB Opinion Nos. 16 and 18 have alleviated the more flagrant "abuses" or misinterpretations under ARB No. 48. However, they have not resolved the essential accounting issue in all business combinations: recording the economic substance of a combination on a basis which permits comparison of pre- and post-combination results and together facilitates predicting future performance. Consider the following cases:

U.S. Home Corporation: By the end of Fiscal 1971, U.S. Home had *pooled* five separate operations. To acquire these companies, U.S. Home gave up 671,063 common shares. The average market of these shares was $25 per share; the total cost of the five companies to U. S. Home being $16.8 million. Of this sum, U. S. Home credited its books as follows:

Preferred Stock	$ 20,000
Common Stock	122,879
Earned Surplus	1,150,053
Capital Surplus	20,453
TOTAL	$1,313,385

Thus, for acquisitions costing $16.8 million U. S. Home added only $1.3 million to book values. The full cost of these assets at current values will never appear on the books. Moreover, subsequent disposals of so conservatively valued assets may provide the basis for inflated earnings performance in the future.

U. S. Home also used the purchase method of accounting to its advantage. In November 1970, the firm acquired Thompson Construction Company for $12 million: $5 million paid immediately and $7 million contingently payable over the succeeding five years. U. S. Home recorded the transaction as a $5 million purchase. Several benefits accrued to the firm from this tactic: (1) as a purchase, U. S. Home picks up Thompson's postacquisition sales and profits without requiring restatement of the earlier years' operations. This allows U. S. Home earnings trend to show better growth than would otherwise be the case; (2) In addition, U.S. Home escapes the burden of amortizing, *initially*, the full cost of the purchase, yet reaps the full income advantage[5].

McDonald's Corporation: In 1973, McDonald's acquired 90 restaurants and accounted for these acquisitions as a pooling-of-interest. A summary of the results of these ninety restaurants for the four years 1969–1972 follows:

	Net Income	*Return on Sales*
1969	$1,252,000	6.4%
1970	525,000	2.5%
1971	$1,053,000	3.5%
1972	844,000	2.3%

For the above income stream, averaging less than $1 million per year, McDonald's paid out $50 million in stock. Yet McDonald's stated, in the listing applications filed with the New York Stock Exchange, that "the purchase price agreed upon was based upon the underlying value of the assets and earning power of the acquired business."

As to the underlying values, the composite balance sheet of the ninety acquired companies showed: the ninety restaurants had a working capital deficit of $2.8 million; $10.7 million in depreciated plants and $1.5 million in miscellaneous assets, for a total value of $9.3 million. Long-term debt amounted to $3.5 million, leaving an equity position of just $5,840,000, for which McDonald's paid $50 million.

Undoubtedly, McDonald's realized that the land, buildings, and inventories had a market value of at least $50 million or more. Here lies the major point. McDonald's books did not show a $50 million outlay for the restaurants. The accounting entries recorded only $5,840,000 as the cost. McDonald's had acquired property worth $50 million and need depreciate only $5,840,000 against future operations.

If the acquired companies produce aggregate earnings of less than $1 million per year, not much effect would be felt on McDonald's financial statement and the user would not be misled. However, the real objective was apparently disposal and not operation of the restaurants. If the restaurants could be sold in the future for $50 million or more, McDonald's could *book profits* of about $45 million on disposal of land and buildings. If, on the other hand, the land and buildings were recorded at market values, the book profit might disappear altogether.

There is reason to suppose that McDonald's management had this in mind. The 1970–1974 profits from property dispositions were as follows:

1970: $1,704,000
1971: $1,800,000
1972: $3,408,000
1973: $5,553,000
1974: $3,667,000 (first 3 months 1974) [5]

From a management perspective, the accounting distinction between purchase and pooling seems quite clear. Not so readily discernible is which
method better reflects investor needs, the economic substance of the transaction, and conveys information accurately to the user of the financial
statements. *Is the predictive ability of financial reports enhanced by the inclusion
of goodwill*; specifically, do the financial ratios used for credit scoring, for
risk prediction, for profitability measures, bankruptcy prediction, and so
on become more or less reliable as goodwill is included (or omitted) in
the calculations? Does management's choice of a goodwill amortization
schedule provide information about the firm's cash-generating ability? Is
the firm's tax burden, debt capacity, or other wealth related variables
affected by management's goodwill policy?

Whenever a *group of assets* is purchased, the goodwill problem arises.
Some writers think of goodwill as the excess of the amount paid for a
business as a whole over the fair value assigned to its tangible and identifiable intangible assets less liabilities assumed; others see it as the value
attributed by the purchaser to the earning power of a going concern in
excess of a "normal" return on the investment in the net assets other than
goodwill. APB Opinion No. 16, *Business Combinations*, states that in allocating the cost of an acquisition:

> First, all identifiable assets acquired . . . should be assigned a portion of the
> cost of the acquired company, normally equal to their fair values at date
> of acquisition. Second, the excess of the cost of the acquired company over
> the sum of the amounts assigned to identifiable assets acquired . . . should
> be recorded as goodwill[1].

The opposite situation—the book values of the investee's assets exceed
their market values—results in a deferred credit, sometimes termed, "Negative Goodwill." Both positive and negative goodwill are to be amortized
over the period benefited, not to exceed forty years.

The goodwill of a business was initially perceived to emanate from
the quality of the proprietor's relationship with his customers, which
constituted the advantage over his competitors. This conception, mainly
applicable to small business, has today been replaced by the notion that
goodwill consists of everything that might contribute to the advantages
that a business possesses.

The reader will observe from Exhibit 1 that purchase accounting
explicitly recognizes goodwill on the financial statements. However, under
pooling-of-interests (Exhibit 2), the accounting treatment *de facto* charges
off either to paid-in-surplus or to retained earnings, the amount that would
have been recorded as goodwill if the transaction had been accounted for
by the purchase method. Hence, the problem of purchase v. pooling is
closely linked to the issue of goodwill. The knot can be unraveled only by
taking apart the distinguishing features of goodwill:

• The overall value of the enterprise may be determined by a number
of different methods, such as the market value of the company's securities

or present value of the anticipated earnings. In any event, regardless of the approach used, the value assigned to goodwill has no reliable relationship to the costs that may have been incurred in its creation. The various individual factors that contribute to goodwill cannot be valued separately.

• Goodwill attaches to the business as a whole, does not exist apart from the business, and has no specified term of existence.

• The actual value usually fluctuates widely with investor opinion about the firm's earning power.

• Economic resources (assets) are consumed in production and properly charged against income. *But goodwill is not consumed or used in the production of earnings; it is the result of earnings or the expectation of earnings and its value fluctuates with these expectations.*

• Goodwill is an element of value tracing directly to the investor or owner of the enterprise.

• A group of assets (a firm) produces (in the general case) a joint stream of income. The firm also includes people, goals, attitudes, and so on. It is an open *system* responding to its environment. As a system, there is no way under conditions of certainty or uncertainty to itemize the market value and apply the values unambiguously to the separate assets and call any excess goodwill. To attempt the allocation is a purely arbitrary exercise. This would not apply, of course, to project valuation in capital budgeting where the analysis deals with incremental income and expense traceable to the project, which would disappear if the project were rejected.

• Actually, *goodwill arises whenever a firm accepts any project (or revision of financial policy) having a positive net present value.* But the accountant records goodwill only when it is purchased in a business combination.

• The amortization of purchased goodwill includes in the determination of income an amount unrelated to the operations of the period. If positive goodwill, the charge reduces income; if negative goodwill, the charge increases income.

Yet the question remains of what to do with goodwill and the reader who, familiar with the literature regarding efficiency of the market with respect to publicly available information, may query whether there is any point to the argument at all. The trend of accounting literature points to several options:

1. *Carry goodwill as an unamortized asset:* Generally, assets are written off when their anticipated earnings no longer justify their book values. This school, accordingly, would retain the amount allocated to goodwill at its initial level so long as the related earnings are maintained at or above the level projected when the original value was placed on goodwill. Goodwill, therefore, would be written off only if earnings fell below the anticipated level for the combination—at some indefinite point in the future.

2. *Amortized goodwill:* Goodwill here is assumed to have limited life and like any other asset should be charged against cost in an orderly manner. As we have seen, this position demands an arbitrary decision on the amortization period as well as the amount of goodwill. Also, the rule of consistency would suggest that if earnings subsequently exceed the anticipated level of real value, goodwill should be increased—and this is never done.

3. *Elimination of goodwill at date of acquisition:* If goodwill were immediately charged against the Excess Over Par (Paid-in Capital) or Retained Earnings, it would at least conform to the pooling-of-interest treatment. The procedure would further clearly recognize that the goodwill of the absorbed company has no continuing, separate, and measurable existence after the combination. It consequently lacks the key characteristics of an economic resource: separability and exchangeability, depending solely on the fortunes of a particular enterprise.

The write-off of goodwill swings earnings per share in favor of purchase due to the dilution effects of the extra shares under the pooling-of-interest approach. The higher asset values (actually a disadvantage under the Copeland-Wodjak decision rule) of the purchase method now directly relate to the revaluation of the acquired economic resources devoted to the production of income. Conversely, where dilution effects can be avoided, pooling will continue to enjoy basic advantages for those who accept accounting numbers at face value.

However, assuming a semistrong efficient market, the argument over goodwill may add up to "much ado about nothing." The real issue is disclosure so that security prices can reflect publicly available information. The investors (including especially professional analysts) need to know the terms of the combination. Armed with this information, they can project the cash flow consequences of the merger, and the accounting decisions relating to goodwill or purchase v. pooling become matters of secondary interest.

ACCOUNTING METHODOLOGY AND SECURITY PRICES

Combination by purchase or pooling-of-interests can result in significant differences in earning per share. Do security prices reflect these differences? Will the market price of the common shares be higher if the combination is effected as a pooling rather than purchase? Does the accounting treatment convey important information to the user of financial statements? To this point, we have assumed that managements believe in the importance of accounting numbers in shaping security prices. They are not alone. It is also widely believed by business writers that stockholders of companies using pooling make abnormal gains from higher stock prices as a direct consequence of reporting relatively higher earnings.

From the arguments on purchase v. pooling, two competing approaches to accounting policy emerge. The first, traditional in accounting literature, attempts to establish the merits of accounting methods by demonstrating their consistency with some underlying economic theory. Statements of financial position are examined in light of economic concepts of capital and value, and business earnings are evaluated against the content of economic income. The second approach regards accounting data as one part of an information set reaching security market partici-pants. Here, the structure of relative security prices is determined by investors' assessments of the probability distribution of rates of return based upon the total information set. Any nontrivial alteration in the information set reaching investors, by definition, causes a change in market values. This alters the terms (revises the cost) by which a given firm may raise funds as well as affecting investor wealth levels. In addition, investor perceptions of systematic risk may respond to the choice of accounting alternatives, and these, in total, can influence the level of savings and investment.

Given the framework of the debate, it is premature to attempt a resolution of the controversy or, for that matter, to evaluate any other method proposed by accountants for dealing with business combinations. Of course, one can easily assert a preference for pooling, since the cor-porate partners "simply join hands"; it is equally easy to counter that one firm "obviously" buys out the other. Different sets of assumptions lead to normative conclusions where neither side can challenge the premises of the other. On the other hand, the second approach to accounting policy (based upon the total information set) generates empirical studies that are, in principle, capable of disproving hypotheses about the purported effects of accounting alternatives. The following pages survey some mar-ket-based research pertinent to the purchase v. pooling decision.

For example, Copeland and Wojdak sampled 160 poolings and esti-mated that earnings were overstated by 3 percent to 98.15 percent[8]. Lintner agrees that companies that manipulate accounting numbers in mergers successfully mislead shareholders and raise the aggregate value of the combination even in a perfect securities market[18]. Mosich gives a theoretical estimate of a 60 percent increase in stock price of a typical merging company choosing pooling instead of purchase accounting[21].

On the significance of the accounting treatment for the user of finan-cial statements, the Financial Accounting Standards Board (FASB) sur-veyed analysts using financial statements in making investment and credit decisions. Most respondents expressed a greater need for appropriate disclosures about a combination rather than preference for a particular accounting method. With better disclosure, the analyst can adjust the statement amounts to reflect the economic and financial effect of the combination[11]. Burton surveyed 210 financial analysts and found them evenly split as to whether purchase or pooling presented data more mean-ingfully[7]. Yet a survey of sixty-four financial analysts by Bullard showed a marked preference for purchase accounting[6]. In general, these and other surveys show no unanimity among users of financial statements regarding a preference for a particular accounting treatment nor do they provide much information about the preference rationale of users of par-ticular accounting treatments. Implicitly the evidence points to a general conclusion; namely, *analysts are alert to the effect on earnings of recording the combination as a purchase or pooling*. It would seem that they would allow for these effects in evaluating the combination.

Recent studies have looked at the informational content of alternative accounting methods and their effects on stock prices. These studies report that accounting manipulations *not related to real economic events* (cash flows) have no statistically significant effect on stock prices. Apparently, the presence of alternative sources of information on corporate performance enables investors to look beyond the accounting numbers in assessing equity securities. Therefore, if the market is efficient, it will respond to the real economic consequences of the combination and not be affected by the particular method used to record the combination. Kaplan and Roll, Sunder, and Ball report that differences in accounting methodology have no statistically significant effect on security prices. Accounting data are but one element in the total supply of information.

A study by Hong, Kaplan, and Mandelker typifies the methodology of investigations into whether the market is efficient and able to distinguish between the higher earnings caused by using pooling-of-interests from higher earnings caused by economic events (e.g., increased sales)[17]. If the pooling-of-interests is primarily associated with an increased valuation of a firm, the market is inefficient with respect to accounting convention.

The authors chose 1954 –1964 as the time frame for the sample. In this period, prior to the issuance of APB Opinion No. 16 of October 1970, business combinations accomplished by an exchange of securities could have been accounted for by purchase or pooling-of-interests. Such combinations were almost always nontaxable exchanges so that there would be no difference in the cash flows associated with using one method or the other. Hence, differences in reported earnings between the two methods, caused by amortizing goodwill under the purchase method but not under pooling, would not affect the valuation of the consolidated entity. In addition, post–1964 mergers were not considered, because the low incidence of purchase accounting in the late sixties would have led to a highly unbalanced sample.

To be admitted to the sample, the merger must take place by an exchange of shares. This means that the merger would have been a candidate for either purchase or pooling under ARB No. 48. This criterion rules out cash acquisitions and virtually taxable mergers. Details of accounting methods, book values, and market values of the acquired and acquiring companies were usually contained in proxy statements issued in connection with mergers. A total of 205 mergers satisfied all the criteria for selection.

Of the sixty-two purchases, thirty-seven amortized goodwill and reported lower earnings than would have been the case if pooling were used. The authors compared the stock returns of these firms with those of firms having positive acquisition goodwill but who opted to use pooling. There was little relation between the relative size of the firm and the amount of goodwill.

The familiar Sharpe-Fama model was then used to evaluate the performance of stocks around the merger dates. The results ran counter to the conventional wisdom and suggested that no abnormal gains were made by firms that used pooling, despite the large amounts of goodwill not being written-off by most firms. To the contrary, the market seems to have favored those firms electing purchase accounting (recall that the period studied preceded the issuance of APB Opinion No. 16, and the combinations studied qualified as either purchase or pooling, at management's option). Two possible explanations for the apparent advantage to purchase accounting are:

1. The market may interpret the choice of the more conservative (higher asset base, lower reported earnings) accounting method as information about management's forecast of future cash-generating ability, so that the market model residuals reflect a revision of the total information set impounded in securities prices. In sum, the market does not react naïvely to accounting numbers, but management's choice among accounting methods may itself be important information.

2. The purchase and pooling samples may differ systematically for reasons unrelated to the choice of accounting methodology. For example, firms electing purchase accounting may also be seen as more likely to restructure capital; in such cases the market model residuals would capture the effects both of merger and of capital restructure.

Given the assumptions of the Sharpe-Fama Model, *the Hong et al. study further suggests the absence of any measurable gain from business combination.* The results of other studies, also based on the market model, lead to the opposite conclusion. Ellert, for example, reported substantial gains to both the buyer and seller, as a result of merger[10]. However, there is an important difference in the sample population. In contrasting Hong's conclusions to those of other researchers, the Hong's sample is restricted to stock-for-stock exchanges, while the Ellert study does not impose this condition. Therefore, it is reasonable to assume that the "gains to merger" reported by Ellert and others are actually "gains to capital restructure." The situation merits further investigation.

It is important to remember, too, that the Hong *et al.* study does not lead to any conclusions on the presence or absence of gains to the shareholders of the selling corporation; that is, whether the wealth position of the selling shareholders has been enhanced or diminished.

CONCLUSION

The controversies outlined in this chapter persist. The Financial Accounting Standards Board has issued a discussion memorandum addressing the accounting issues in business combinations[11]. The FASB intends that the professional and industrial response, coupled with further research, will eventuate in a revised statement of the appropriate accounting principles to be applied in business combinations. In the meantime, since accounting options do exist and affect the valuation of assets and the bottom line on earnings, the accounting decision will necessarily figure in management's acquisition strategy. Whether security markets respond to accounting numbers or not, common sense would induce managers to opt for a higher earnings per share rather than a lower figure.

1. Accounting Principles Board, Opinion No. 10, *Omnibus Opinion, 1966.* American Institute of Certified Public Accountants (AICPA), 1967.

    —— Opinion No. 16, *Business Combinations, 1970.* AICPA, 1970.

    —— Opinion No. 17, *Intangible Assets, 1970.* AICPA, 1970.

    —— Opinion No. 18, *The Equity Method of Accounting for Investments in Common Stock, 1971.* AICPA, 1971.

    —— Opinion No. 23, *Accounting for Income Taxes-Special Areas, 1972.* AICPA, 1972.

    —— Opinion No. 24, *Accounting for Income Taxes-Investments in Common Stock Accounted for by the Equity Method, 1972.* AICPA, 1972.

    —— Opinion No. 28, *Interim Financial Reporting, 1973.* AICPA, 1973.

    —— Opinion No. 29, *Accounting for Non-monetary Transactions, 1973.* AICPA, 1973.

    —— Opinion No. 30, *Reporting the Results of Operation, 1973.* AICPA, 1973.

2. AICPA, *Accounting Research Bulletin No. 48-Business Combinations.* January 1957.

3. Anderson, John C., and Joseph G. Louderback III. "Income Manipulation and Purchase-Pooling: Some Additional Results." *Journal of Accounting Research.* Autumn 1973. pp. 338–343.

4. Backman, Jules. "An Economist Looks at Accounting for Business Combinations." *Financial Analysts Journal.* July–August 1970. pp. 39–48.

5. Briloff, Abraham J. "Dirty Pooling—How to Succeed in Business Without Really Trying." *Barrons.* July 15, 1968.

    —— "Grim Shelter." *Barrons.* October 25, 1971.

    —— "Much Abused Goodwill." *Barrons.* April 28, 1969.

    —— *Unaccountable Accounting.* New York: Harper & Row, 1972.

    —— "You Deserve a Break. . . ." *Barrons.* July 8, 1974.

6. Bullard, Ruth Harper. "The Effect of Accounting for Combinations on Investor Decisions." The University of Texas at Austin, August 1972.

7. Burton, John C. *Accounting for Business Combinations.* New York: Financial Executives Research Foundation, 1970.

8. Copeland, Ronald M., and Joseph F. Wojdak. "Income Manipulation and the Purchase-Pooling Choice." *Journal of Accounting Research.* Autumn 1969. pp. 188–195.

9. Currie, Edward W. "Acquisition Costing and the Bargaining Area." *Management Accounting.* September 1974. pp. 29–37.

10. Ellert, James C. "Mergers, Antitrust Law Enforcement and Stockholder Returns." *The Journal of Finance.* May 1976. pp. 715–732.

11. Financial Accounting Standards Board, *Accounting for Business Combinations and Purchased Intangibles.* August 19, 1976.

12. Foster, William C. "Does Pooling Present Fairly?" *The CPA Journal.* December 1974. pp. 36–41.

    —— "The Illogic of Pooling." *Financial Executive.* December 1974. pp. 16–21.

    —— "Setting Standards for Treasury Shares." *Financial Executive.* February 1974. pp. 48–52.

13. Gagnon, Jean-Marie. "Purchase vs. Pooling of Interests: The Search for a Predictor." *Empirical Research in Accounting: Selected Studies,* supplement to *Journal of Accounting Research.* 1967. pp. 187–204.

14. "Gimmick For All Seasons." *Forbes.* October 1, 1975. pp. 60–62.

15. Gunther, Samuel P. "Lingering Pooling Problems." *The CPA Journal.* June 1973. pp. 459–463.

16. Hawkins, David E. *Corporate Financial Reporting*. Homewood, Ill.: Richard D. Irwin, 1971.

17. Hong, Hai, Robert S. Kaplan, and Gerson Mandelker. "Pooling vs. Purchase: The Effects of Accounting for Mergers on Stock Prices," forthcoming in *The Accounting Review*.

18. Linter, J. "Expectations, Mergers and Equilibrium in Purely Competitive Securities Markets." *American Economic Review*. 1971. pp. 101–111.

19. Meyer, Philip E. "Accounting for Business Combinations—A Framework for Implementation." *The National Public Accountant*. February 1976. pp. 15–19.

20. Miller, Malcolm C. "Goodwill—An Aggregation Issue." *The Accounting Review*. April 1973. pp. 286–291.

21. Mosich, A. N. "Impact of Merger Accounting on Post-Merger Financial Reports." *Management Accounting*. December 1965.

22. Perlmutter, Louis. "Comparison of Tax, Accounting, and Securities Aspects of Business Combinations." *Journal of Corporate Taxation*. Autumn 1975. pp. 305–348.

23. Petz, David J. "Business Combinations, Pooling or Purchase." *Management Accounting*. February 1973. pp. 45–46, 50.

24. Pivar, Samuel. "Implementation of APB Opinions Nos. 16 and 17." *The CPA Journal*. October 1973. pp. 58–65.

25. Samuels, John Malcolm. *Readings on Mergers and Takeovers*. New York: St. Martins Press, 1972.

26. Sapienza, Samuel R. "Pooling Theory and Practice in Business Combinations." *The Accounting Review*. April 1962. pp. 263–278.

27. Seidman, J. S. "Pooling Must Go." *Barrons*. July 1, 1968.

28. Tearney, Michael G. "Accounting for Goodwill: A Realistic Approach." *The Journal of Accountancy*. July 1973. pp. 41–45.

29. Wakefield, B. Richard. "The Accounting Principles Board on the Wrong Track." *Financial Analyst Journal*. July–August 1970. pp. 33–36.

30. Wright, Robert Help. "Corporate Business Combinations. A New Look at the Basic Tax and Accounting Considerations." *The CPA Journal*. May 1973. pp. 361–368.

31. Wyatt, Arthur R. *A Critical Study of Accounting for Business Combinations*. New York: AICPA. 1963.

———— "Inequities in Accounting for Business Combinations." *Financial Executive*. December 1972. pp. 28–35.

———— "Discussion of Purchase vs. Pooling of Interests: The Search for a Predictor." *Empirical Research in Accounting: Selected Studies* supplement to *Journal of Accounting Research*. 1967. pp. 187–204.

ACQUISITION STRATEGY
Tax Options

Few decisions in financial management are devoid of tax consequences, and business combinations make no exception to the rule. Tax factors influence the attitudes of the management and stockholders of the acquiring and acquired corporations. Guardino notes:

> Probably the most important factor in casting the terms of the deal is attributable to the tax consequences, *but this should not be the controlling factor.* Rather business considerations should control, but in actual practice this is not usually the case . . . few of these considerations [business, legal, and financial] are as significant as the tax cost of the transaction . . . tax considerations play the key factor in acquiring corporations which should not be the case, since many acquisitions turn sour [Italics added][4].

This chapter highlights those features of the tax law that shape the acquisition strategy of the acquiring firm and the response of the acquired firm to what, on other grounds, may appear an attractive proposition. The chapter does not intend to offer a comprehensive review of the IRS code relating to mergers and acquisitions. For that level of sophistication, management must turn to *experienced* tax lawyers and accountants.

A strategy to minimize the tax liability of the combination may conflict with the choice of accounting options that offer the highest earnings per share. A cash transaction, for example, requires that the transaction be recorded as a purchase. The use of purchase accounting alters accounting profits and cash flow due to the recognition of certain gains, losses, and the assignment of new tax bases to assets and liabilities. Increased asset values, for example, create depreciation shields that improve cash flow.

ACCOUNTING STRATEGY AND TAX STRATEGY

161

On the other hand, the additional depreciation charge and the amortization of goodwill lower the accounting bottom line. The dichotomy between accounting and tax strategies arises from the differing criteria in the accounting standards and the IRS code. Specifically, the criteria for purchase and pooling differ from the criteria for taxable and tax-free exchanges.

TAXABLE AND TAX-FREE TRANSACTIONS

A business combination may be completely tax-free, partly tax-free, or completely taxable to the seller. In a sale of stock or assets, the seller has a recognized gain or loss, either capital or ordinary, depending upon the character of the assets transferred. *A taxable transaction usually involves an exchange of stock or assets by the acquiring company for stock or assets of the acquired company with little or no continuity of ownership by the shareholders of the acquired company.* The tax liability usually arises in the year in which the transaction takes place.

The tax-free transaction is really a misnomer. Tax deferral more accurately describes the transaction. At the time of purchase, the seller incurs no immediate tax liability. Tax liability arises when and if the shareholder subsequently sells the stock received in the exchange. When the seller disposes of the stock, the full gain is taxable in the year of sale, and the tax basis for determining gain or loss is that of the original stock.

> *Illustration:* Mr. Jones purchased stock in the Alpha Corporation in June 1976 at $100 market value. Four years later Alpha is taken over by Delta and Jones receives in exchange $200 in Delta stock. Jones incurs no tax liability at this point. However, Jones' tax basis in the new Delta stock is $100, not $200. In 1983, Jones sells his Delta stock for $500. Jones now has a taxable gain of $400 ($500 − $100).

TAX DEFERRED REORGANIZATION

The term "reorganization" also has a different connotation in tax law than in corporation finance. In the tax code, reorganization refers to a transaction in which a corporation acquires the stock or assets of another corporation, readjusts its capital structure by substituting equity for debt, or changes its name or place of incorporation. The term does not cover the mere purchase by one corporation of properties owned by another corporation, nor imply that the reorganization is the consequence of financial distress. There are particular features that characterize all tax deferred reorganizations. These are:

1. *Continuity of Interest:* The rule requires that selling shareholders retain a sufficient interest in the combined corporation, either preferred or common stock. Consideration is valued at fair market on the date of the exchange. The continuity rule stipulates that the consideration received by the selling stockholders be at least 50 percent of the value of all formerly outstanding stock of the acquired company. However, not all of the shareholders of the acquired corporation need receive stock in exchange.

LeTulle v. Scofield, 308 U.S. 415, 23AFTR789 (1940): The Court held that the
transfer of all the assets of the acquired corporation in exchange for $50,000 in cash and $750,000 in bonds of the acquiring corporation did not constitute a reorganization.

John A. Nelson Co. v. Helvering, 296 U.S. 374, 16AFTR1262 (1935): The transfer of the assets of a corporation for consideration composed of 38 percent preferred stock (nonvoting) and 62 percent cash constituted a reorganization even though the preferred was redeemable at stated intervals[1].

The reader will observe that under current accounting standards, both transactions would have to be recorded as a purchase.

2. *Business Purpose:* The transaction must be motivated by a business purpose other than the avoidance of tax. A warning: it is the corporation that must have a business purpose, not the shareholders.

3. *Step Transaction Doctrine:* The IRS will look at the separate steps of a transaction as forming a single transaction in order to determine whether the transaction as a whole meets the definition of a reorganization. The rule prevents the fragmentation of an exchange into a series of transactions that have both taxable and nontaxable features[4].

A corporation may simply purchase the stock or assets of another corporation without seeking any special tax status. The primary distinction between a reorganization and a simple purchase turns on the consideration paid the selling corporation. In a reorganization, the stock of the acquiring corporation is the sole or major portion of the consideration paid. By contrast, a purchase of stock or assets can be paid for by cash, debt instruments, stock or other assets, or any combination thereof. Moreover, a reorganization presupposes acquisition of all or substantially all of the acquired firm's assets. Finally, a reorganization frequently involves the extinction of the acquired firm; a purchase leaves the selling corporation free to pursue its business purposes with the proceeds of the sale. The purchase represents a taxable transaction. If management seeks a tax-free or partly-tax-free transaction it must structure the deal as a reorganization[1]. The IRS recognizes basically four types of tax deferred reorganizations: Types A, B, C, and D. Our interest, however, centers on Types A, B, and C.

Type A Reorganization: Statutory Merger or Consolidation:

A nontaxable merger or consolidation is one that has been effected in accordance with state or Federal merger or consolidation statutes. Generally, under statutory law negotiations take place between the respective managements, and the terms of the transaction are then submitted to the stockholders for their approval. The surviving corporation inherits all the assets and liabilities of the acquired firm(s). Subject to the continuity of interest rule, consideration may take the form of cash, debt, preferred and common stock, or some combination thereof. No taxable income accrues to the acquiring or acquired corporation. However, for the stockholders of the acquired corporation(s), the issuance of cash or debt instruments as part of the consideration package may result in a partial tax liability. A taxable gain to the stockholder will be recognized to the extent that the cash and value of other property received plus the value of an excess principal value of securities (other than stock or short-term debt) received exceeds the value of the securities surrendered. The excess is termed "boot."

Illustration: Suppose the Alpha Corporation takes over Delta. Mr. Jones owns $10,000 in Delta stock for which he receives $15,000 in Alpha common; $1,000 in Alpha preferred; a $1,000 debenture bond; and $1,000 in cash. What is Jones' tax liability?

Alpha Common	$15,000
Alpha Preferred	1,000
Alpha Debenture	1,000 } Boot
Cash	1,000
Consideration Received	$18,000
Original Cost of Delta Stock	10,000
Economic Gain	$ 8,000

Of the $8,000 gain, only the $2,000 boot (cash and the debenture) are taxable. In the absence of boot, the transaction would have been tax-free— tax deferred. Note the presence of cash, debt, and preferred stock in the consideration package would classify the transaction as a purchase for accounting purposes.

Case: Anaconda, ADC, Atlantic Richfield and Newco entered into a Plan and Agreement of Reorganization dated July 26, 1976. The "Plan," in accordance to which Anaconda became a wholly-owned subsidiary of Atlantic Richfield, and shares of Anaconda Common Stock were converted into Atlantic Richfield Common Stock and a right to receive cash, is described below.

The Mergers

By effecting the First Merger into ADC pursuant to the terms of the Agreement and Plan of Merger between Anaconda and ADC (the "First Merger Agreement"), Anaconda changed the place of its incorporation from Montana to Delaware. ADC became the surviving corporation with the same shareholders (other than those who exercised dissenters' rights), business, assets, and liabilities as Anaconda. The purpose of the First Merger was to reincorporate Anaconda in a state which, unlike Montana, permitted it to merge into a wholly-owned subsidiary of another corporation in exchange for capital stock of the parent corporation.

The Second Merger became operative as soon as practicable thereafter pursuant to the terms of the Agreement of Merger between ADC and Newco (the "Second Merger Agreement") . . . Upon completion of the Second Merger, the separate existence of ADC ceased. The assets and liabilities of Anaconda immediately prior to the Mergers were assumed by Newco, the name of which was changed to "The Anaconda Company."

Approval of the Merger

The Boards of Directors of Anaconda and Atlantic Richfield unanimously approved the Plan and the transactions contemplated thereby. The Board of Directors of Anaconda recommended approval of the proposal that resulted in Anaconda becoming a wholly-owned subsidiary of Atlantic Richfield on the terms stated in the Proxy Statement and that Anaconda be merged into its wholly-owned Delaware subsidiary.

Under Montana law, the affirmative vote of the holders of 66⅔ percent of the outstanding shares of Anaconda Common Stock was required for approval of the First Merger Agreement. Atlantic Richfield owned approximately twenty-seven percent of the outstanding shares of Anaconda Common Stock and agreed, under the Plan, to vote all such shares in favor of the adoption of the First Merger Agreement. Accordingly, the affirmative vote of holders of an additional approximately forty percent (representing more than a majority of the seventy-three percent of Anaconda's shares held by shareholders other than Atlantic Richfield) was required for approval and adoption of the First Merger Agreement. The First Merger Agreement was approved by Anaconda as the sole shareholder of ADC.

The Second Merger Agreement was approved by Anaconda and Atlantic Richfield as the respective sole shareholders of the constituent companies, ADC and Newco, and became effective as soon as practicable thereafter. Holders of Anaconda's Common Stock were not entitled to vote, or to demand appraisal rights for their shares in connection with the Second Merger. However, since the Second Merger was contingent upon the effectiveness of the First Merger, failure of the Anaconda shareholders to adopt the First Merger Agreement would prevent completion of the Second Merger.

No vote of the shareholders of Atlantic Richfield was required to approve either of the Mergers.

Exchange Ratio

By virtue of the Mergers, each share of Anaconda Common Stock outstanding immediately prior to the effective date of the First Merger, other than shares held by certain dissenting shareholders and by Atlantic Richfield or Newco, would be converted into one-half of a share of Atlantic Richfield Common Stock (after giving effect to the 100 percent Atlantic Richfield stock dividend distributed September 13, 1976) and a right to receive $6 in cash. The Mergers did not change the shares of Newco Common Stock, which would remain outstanding and would be owned only by Atlantic Richfield.

Based on the number of shares of Anaconda Common Stock outstanding on June 30, 1976, and without regard to the exercise of dissenters' rights and payments for fractional shares, Atlantic Richfield was required to issue approximately 8,069,000 shares of Atlantic Richfield Common Stock and approximately $96,826,000 in cash upon consummation of the Mergers.

Federal Income Tax Consequences

On July 22, 1976, Atlantic Richfield and Anaconda made application to the IRS for certain rulings regarding the Federal income tax consequences of the Mergers. The receipt of rulings on or prior to the Closing, satisfactory to Atlantic Richfield and Anaconda in form and substance, was an express condition to the completion of the Mergers:

1. The proposed transactions contemplated by the Plan will constitute a reorganization (or reorganizations) within the meaning of Section 368(a) of the Internal Revenue Code of 1954, as amended, and no gain or loss will be recognized to any of the corporate parties to the Plan as a result of the transactions.

2. The basis of the assets of Anaconda in the hands of Newco will be the same as their basis in the hands of Anaconda immediately prior to the

transactions and the holding period for the assets of Anaconda acquired in the transactions will include the holding period in the hands of Anaconda on the date of the transaction.

3. The gain, if any, realized by the Anaconda shareholders as a result of the transactions contemplated by the Plan will be recognized but in an amount not in excess of the cash received pursuant to the Mergers.

In addition, certain other rulings were requested from the IRS, the receipt of which was not a condition to the completion of the Mergers, including rulings, among others, to the effect that:

1. The portion of the recognized gain, if any, which is not in excess of an Anaconda shareholder's ratable share of the undistributed earnings and profits of Anaconda, will be treated as a dividend only to the extent it has the effect of the distribution of a dividend. Recognized gain, which does not have the effect of the distribution of a dividend, will be treated as gain from the sale or exchange of property and will be subject to the capital gain provisions and limitations of the Internal Revenue Code, provided the stock constitutes a capital asset in the hands of the shareholder.

2. The basis of the shares of Atlantic Richfield Common Stock (including any fractional share interests) received by the Anaconda shareholders in the exchange will be the same as the basis of the shares of Anaconda Common Stock surrendered, decreased by the amount of cash received and increased by the amount of gain recognized. The holding period of the Atlantic Richfield Common Stock (including any fractional share interests) received will include the holding period of the Anaconda Common Stock, provided the Anaconda Common Stock was held as a capital asset at the time of the exchange.

3. Each shareholder of Anaconda who receives cash in lieu of a fractional share interest in Atlantic Richfield Common Stock will recognize gain or loss measured by the difference between the basis of the fractional share interest and the amount of cash received. Provided the fractional share interest constitutes a capital asset in the hands of such shareholder, such gain or loss will constitute capital gain or loss in accordance with the capital gain provisions and limitations of the Internal Revenue Code.

4. The net operating loss carryovers of Anaconda will not be diminished in the hands of Newco by reason of Section 382(b) of the Internal Revenue Code.

Accounting Treatment

The transactions were accounted for under the "purchase" method of accounting. Atlantic Richfield's equity in the book value of net assets of Anaconda exceeded its investment by $528 million based upon the market value of Atlantic Richfield Common Stock on July 1, 1976. Following the Mergers Atlantic Richfield undertook a study to determine how such excess should be allocated to specific Anaconda assets acquired or liabilities assumed by Newco. Pending the completion of this study, the excess of book value over cost was included as a separate line item on the pro forma balance sheet. The market value of the Atlantic Richfield Common Stock issued in exchange for the outstanding Anaconda Common Stock was credited to shareholders' equity and the cash paid reduced working capital. The excess of the book value of Anaconda's net assets over Atlantic Richfield's investment will ultimately be amortized over the lives of the assets or liabilities to which the excess was assigned and was estimated to have a positive effect on earnings, but this would not result in additional cash flow to Atlantic Richfield[6].

The advantages of a Type A reorganization include:

1. The only requirement is that the merger conform to state law.
2. It is the most flexible of the tax-free reorganizations because the use of nonvoting stock is permitted along with combinations of cash, warrants, debentures, and other assets.
3. The tax attributes of the disappearing corporation(s)—net operating losses, capital losses, earnings and profits, depreciation, accounting and inventory methods—carry over to the surviving corporation.

The disadvantages of Type A include:

1. State law may confer special privileges on the minority (for example, the right to have their stock appraised and paid off in cash) that can impede the reorganization.
2. Approval of the stockholders of both corporations may be required and a two-thirds vote of the outstanding shares is a common stricture for stockholder assent.
3. All assets and liabilities (existing or unknown) are passed to the surviving corporation, including unwanted assets[4].

As in all Type A, B, and C reorganizations, the acquisition may be accomplished through a subsidiary using its parent's stock.

Type B Reorganization: Stock-for-Stock Acquisition: A Type B reorganization represents the "acquisition of stock of one corporation in exchange solely for part or all of the voting stock of either the acquiring corporation or its parent"[1]. The acquiring corporation must have control immediately after the acquisition. Control is defined as possessing at least 80 percent of the outstanding voting stock plus at least 80 percent of the total number of shares of all other classes of stock. The sole consideration that can be used is the voting stock of the acquiring company or its parent. Even a small amount of boot can disqualify the exchange as a Type B reorganization. However, under the *de minimis* rule small amounts of cash can be used to round off fractional shares.

The Type B reorganization constitutes an agreement between the acquiring corporation and the stockholders of the acquired corporation. A properly constructed tender offer could, therefore, qualify as a Type B reorganization. Figure 9–1 illustrates the Type B reorganization.

A Type B reorganization need not be completed in a single step. Guardino states the rule:

> . . . If X Corp. owns fifty percent of the stock of Y Corp. acquired with cash or any other type of consideration, the acquisition of an additional thirty percent in an exchange for stock will qualify as a B-type reorganization. If the fifty percent was acquired with cash and was found to be part of a plan of acquisition which included the additional thirty percent acquired a short time later, the two transactions could be combined under the step transaction doctrine, and the entire transaction could become taxable because it is no longer solely for voting stock acquisition. However, if the original fifty percent were acquired years before, the doctrine will be inapplicable[4].

Figure 9–1. Type B Reorganization

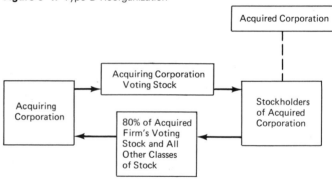

Minority stockholders, dissenting from the plan and holding 20 percent or less of the outstanding stock, *may* have their stock redeemed for cash or other property. But the acquiring corporation cannot make such a payment part of the original plan without invalidating the Type B arrangement[1].

The advantages of a Type B reorganization include:

1. Stockholders of the acquired corporation have no tax liability until they sell the stock received from the acquiring corporation.
2. Stockholder approval is not required pursuant to state law.
3. Minority stockholders do not have the *right* to require their stock be appraised and paid off in cash, a privilege reserved to them by state law in Type A reorganization.
4. The acquired corporation may continue to exist after the acquisition. This can facilitate later divestiture if the investment does not meet expectation.

The disadvantages of a Type B reorganization include:

1. Tender offers must comply with SEC regulations.
2. The 80 percent control stipulation could prove difficult to achieve.
3. Consideration is limited to voting stock of the acquiring firm or its subsidiary.

Case: General Signal Corporation designs, manufactures and sells specialty control equipment and systems incorporating one or more of the four basic control technologies—electrical, electronic, hydraulic, and pneumatic—in three product groups: (1) environmental and industrial process controls; (2) transportation controls; and (3) energy distribution and control. General Signal's products include specialty control equipment and systems for water and wastewater treatment and other industrial processes, railroads and rail mass transit, aircraft and ships and off-the-road mobile equipment, automobiles and trucks. General Signal also produces specialty control equipment and systems employed in the distribution, control and use of energy in electric form for the electrical and communications utilities, for electrical construction, and for industrial processing applications, as well as for the protection of persons and properties. Through a fourth product group, home appliances, General Signal manufactures floor care appliances and electric motors for small appliances.

Leed & Northrup is engaged in the development, manufacture, and marketing of a comprehensive line of electronic instrumentation and process control systems that measure, indicate, record, monitor, and control conditions critical to the efficient operation of diverse processes in a wide range of industries. The company pioneered and continues to maintain a strong position in the development of electronic instruments for industrial and laboratory applications. The Company is also recognized as a leading designer and developer of control systems and manufactures its own digital computer as a major component of systems delivered to customers around the world.

General Signal's corporate growth rested on an expanding control technology base with particular emphasis on markets of high social priority in the areas of water and air pollution control, railroads and rail mass transit, electric energy distribution and control, and life safety and property protection:

The objectives and criteria of the General Signal acquisition program were:

Objectives

1. To achieve a consistent trend of sales and earnings improvement, and provide a strong base for continued growth.
2. To provide additional management and resources, a broadened base of earning power, and consolidated financial strength.
3. To develop their present products and systems continuously and to expand into new markets of high social priority.

Acquisition Criteria

1. A leader in another market of high social priority (energy, productivity, or environmental).
2. A strong marketing force with broad product lines in a high growth industry.
3. Present management is willing to join General Signal and continue to run and develop their business.
4. A strategic position and addition to General Signal's potential for growth.
5. A company that will aid General Signal in expanding their technological base.

Financial

1. Maintains a good earnings record over a five-year period or more.
2. Sales of $100–$300 million in a business field that is already familiar to General Signal.

General Signal began their acquisition program by acquiring the plants and properties of the Taylor Signal Company of Buffalo and the Pneumatic Signal Company of Rochester, New York in June of 1904. Since that time, General Signal has acquired over thirty-five companies in the fields of energy distribution and controls, environmental and fluid process controls, transportation controls, and consumer products.

In June of 1978, General Signal purchased all of the Leeds & Northrup shares (1,301,940) held by the Cutler-Hammer Company for $40 per share. In announcing its purchase of Leeds & Northrup stock, General Signal stated its intention was to acquire the remaining L&N shares by way of a tax-free stock-for-stock exchange. A competing proposal was received by L&N from Reliance Electric Company and on July 6, 1978 Signal raised its proposed exchange ratio to 1.375 shares of Signal for each L&N share.

The L&N Board analyzed the proposals of Signal and Reliance and also the respective lines of business, past records, management, financial condition, and future prospects of each company. Representatives of Smith Barney were present or available to the L&N Board for consultation during much of the Board's deliberations. Such representatives provided the Board with information of a financial nature with respect to Signal and Reliance, and answered questions of the Board with respect to the structures and financial terms of the proposals of Signal and Reliance. In addition to the above, a major consideration in leading the L&N Board ultimately to recommend Signal's proposal was that it offered a tax-free exchange which, in the Board's judgment, would be in the best interests of most L&N shareholders. The L&N Board determined that a tax-free exchange could not be affected by Reliance because under the terms of the agreement between L&N and Signal entered into at the time Signal acquired the original L&N shares, any announcement by L&N of a proposal to merge with other company would permit Signal to go into the market to acquire additional shares of L&N common stock. The acquisition by Signal of additional L&N common stock sufficient to give it a majority of the total shares outstanding would both prevent a tax-free exchange and severely limit the opportunities for receiving other proposals.

At the effective date of the merger, Leeds & Northrup would cease to exist as a Pennsylvania corporation. A new Leednorth Company, being a wholly-owned subsidiary of Signal organized in Delaware, would succeed to the assets and liabilities of Leeds & Northrup Company, and the new Leednorth's name changed to Leeds & Northrup Company. Upon the merger of Leeds & Northrup, each outstanding share of Leeds & Northrup common stock would be converted into 1.375 shares of Signal common. General Signal would record the transaction as a purchase. After a review of the merger transactions, the Internal Revenue Service rendered an opinion that:

1. No gain or loss will be recognized by Leeds & Northrup or its shareholders upon the exchange of their shares of Leeds & Northrup common stock for Signal common stock.
2. No gain or loss will be recognized by Signal or the new Leednorth Company upon the exchange of Leeds & Northrup common stock for Signal common stock.
3. The basis to Leeds & Northrup shareholders of the shares of Signal common stock received by them, including fractional share interests to which they may be entitled, will be the same as the basis of the Leeds & Northrup common stock exchanged therefore.
4. The holding period for shares of Signal common stock received by each Leeds & Northrup shareholder will include the holding period for the shares of Leeds & Northrup common stock exchanged, therefore, provided that the shares so exchanged constitute capital assets in the hands of such holder.
5. The receipt of cash by a Leeds & Northrup shareholder in lieu of his fractional share interest in Signal common stock will be treated as a redemption of such fractional share interest subject to the provisions and limitations of Section 302 of the Internal Revenue Code of 1954, as amended to date.
6. The assumption by Signal of the qualified stock options of Leeds & Northrup outstanding under its stock option plans and the substitution therefor of Signal options will not constitute a modification, extension, or renewal of such options.
7. Signal common stock is presently exempt from existing Pennsylvania personal property taxes[3].

Type C Reorganization: Acquisition of Property for Voting Stock: A
Type C reorganization constitutes an acquisition by one corporation of
substantially all the properties of another corporation in exchange solely
for voting stock of the acquiring corporation, its parent, or in exchange
for voting stock and a limited amount of cash or other property.

The reasoning underlying a Type C reorganization is important to
an understanding of the tax implications. Type C reorganizations were
made tax-free to accommodate transactions that had the effect of mergers
but could not qualify, for some business reason, as a statutory merger or
consolidation. Hence, Type C transactions should exhibit a merger equiv-
alence. According to IRS guidelines for advanced rulings on proposed
transactions, therefore, "substantially all of the assets" means 90 percent
of the fair market value of net assets and 70 percent of the fair market
value of the gross assets[2].

> *Illustration:* Assume, for example, the Delta Corporation has $50,000 in assets
> at fair market value and $10,000 in liabilities.
>
> **1.** Alpha acquires all the assets of Delta ($50,000) and assumes the $10,000
> of liabilities. Alpha gives up voting stock with a market value of $40,000.
> Alpha acquires, accordingly, 90 percent of the fair market value of net
> assets [.90 × ($50,000 − $10,000)] and 70 percent of the gross assets
> [.70 × ($50,000)]. The deal qualifies as a tax-free Type C reorganization.
>
> **2.** Alpha acquires 90 percent of Delta's assets for voting stock and pays
> cash for the balance, $5,000. Alpha does not assume Delta's liabilities.
> The voting stock exchanged by Alpha is valued at $40,000 which exceeds
> 90 percent of Delta's net asset ($36,000) and 70 percent of Delta's gross
> assets ($35,000). The transaction qualifies as a tax-free Type C exchange.
>
> **3.** Alpha acquires 90 percent of Delta's assets for voting stock valued at
> $40,000, assumes Delta's liabilities ($10,000) and pays $5,000 in cash.
> The liabilities (considered the equivalent of cash) and the cash now
> exceed 10 percent of the fair market value of Delta's net assets ($4,000)
> and equal 30 percent of Delta's gross assets. Under IRS guidelines, the
> transaction would not qualify as a tax-free Type C exchange.

Mechanical calculations provide a guide to the "substantially all"
test. But the facts and circumstances of each case are ultimately controlling: the nature of the properties retained, the purpose of the retention,
and the amount thereof. For example, if the assets retained by the seller
are used to continue the business, doubt will exist as to whether the
"substantially all" test has been met; conversely, transfer of all the operating assets except cash creates a *prima facie* case that the test has been
satisfied. The retained assets, however, should not exceed 10 percent of
the seller's assets necessary to redeem the stock of the minority shareholders as provided by state law.

In a Type C reorganization, depicted in Figure 9–2, negotiations
take place between the managements of the respective corporations. The
advantages of a C Type reorganization include:

1. Buying corporation may assume some or none of the liabilities of the selling
corporation.

Figure 9–2. Type C Reorganization

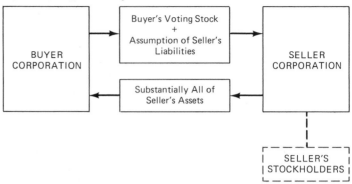

2. A limited amount of boot is allowed.

3. Type C may be a useful device for setting up a wholly-owned subsidiary or a personal holding company since the selling corporation's only remaining asset may be the stock of the acquired corporation.

The disadvantages of the C Type option include:

1. Under state law, if the sale of corporate assets is such as to significantly alter the nature of the business, the consent of the stockholders will be required.

2. As a corollary, the transaction may give rise to minority rights of appraisal and payment in cash.

3. Unlike the B Type reorganization, the assets acquired in a Type C must constitute a single transaction.

TAX CONSEQUENCES OF NONTAXABLE REORGANIZATION

The basic principle behind the nontaxable exchange is that paper profits are nontaxable and the tax bases of the transferred assets are unchanged unless boot is issued. In that event, the tax bases are increased to the extent of the gain recognized by the stockholders of the acquired corporation. In a tax-free exchange, net operating loss carryovers transfer to the acquiring corporation; in a taxable exchange, such losses remain with the seller and can be applied against any gain on the sale of the assets.

In a Type A reorganization, no gain or loss accrues to the shareholders of the acquired corporation, so long as the consideration received by them consists of stock or other securities of the acquiring corporation. The tax basis of the securities received is the same as the tax basis of the old securities and the holding period of the old securities is transferred to the new securities. However, the exchange becomes partially taxable to the extent of any boot received.

In a Type B reorganization no gain or loss accrues to the acquiring corporation or to the acquired corporation and its shareholders. The acquiring corporation receives the stock of the acquired corporation at a tax cost equal to the tax cost of the stock to the shareholders of the acquired corporation. The holding period of old stock transfers to the stock issued in exchange. Similarly, the shareholders of the acquired corporation have no taxable gain or loss in giving up their stock for the stock of the acquiring corporation. Boot provisions have no application to Type B reorganizations, for only voting stock is exchanged.

Similar to the Type A reorganization, no gain or loss accrues in Type C to the shareholders of the acquired corporation, as long as the consideration received consists of stock or other securities of the acquiring corporation not in excess of the principal amount of securities of the acquired corporation given up. If cash or property in addition is received as boot, the gain (if any) is taxable as ordinary income. The tax consequences to the corporation may be somewhat more involved.

> No gain or loss is recognized to a corporation that is a party to a reorganization when it exchanges property solely for stock or securities in another party to the same reorganization. Thus, the acquired corporation would not recognize any gain or loss on the transfer of its assets in exchange for voting stock of the acquiring corporation if it should liquidate. If the corporation is not liquidated, then the basis to the acquiring corporation for the assets received is the basis to the acquired corporation increased by the gain recognized to the acquired corporation. The gain recognized to the acquired corporation is recognized to the extent that the consideration received and retained by it consists of cash or property other than stock or securities of the acquiring corporation or its parent. On the other hand, if such boot is distributed by the transferor corporation to its shareholders, no gain will be recognized to them[4].

TAX STRATEGIES

The tax objectives of the selling corporation depend on the purchase price of the assets to the seller and their tax bases. If the purchase price of the assets is less than their tax bases, the seller will likely seek a taxable transaction. Conversely, if the purchase price exceeds the tax bases, the seller has an advantage in seeking a tax-free transaction.

> *Illustration:* Assume Delta were a closely held corporation with an original investment of $10 million. Delta can now be sold for $50 million. In a taxable transaction, Delta has a taxable gain of $40 million in ordinary income or a possible capital gain approximating $8 million depending upon the circumstances.

Apropos of the buying corporation, if the purchase price of the acquired assets exceeds their tax bases, a taxable transaction is advantageous to the buyer. In the opposite case, the buyer would wisely seek to structure a tax-free reorganization.

> *Illustration:* Assume Delta Corporation has $5 million in assets. If Alpha Corporation agrees to purchase these assets for $8 million and the price is entirely allocated to depreciable assets, Alpha acquires new tax bases, the result of a taxable transaction. However, if the transaction were a tax-free exchange, Alpha's tax bases on the assets acquired would be $5 million as per the books of Delta.

Allocation of the purchase price among the assets acquired may lead to conflict of interest between the acquiring and the acquired corporations. The acquiring corporation will tend to resist allocating purchase price to goodwill and land, both nondepreciable assets for tax purposes. Buyers will prefer to allocate purchase price to equipment, plant, patents, leases, and inventories—all representing a charge against revenue and creating tax shields thereby.

Similarly, the seller in the case of land and buildings will attempt to allocate more of the purchase price to land where the sale of the building creates taxable income. The seller will also resist allocation to inventory when the allocation exceeds the tax basis and results in ordinary income. In general, the seller will prefer the capital gains tax to the tax on ordinary income.

TAX CONSEQUENCES OF TAXABLE REORGANI-ZATIONS

Circumstances may dictate that both parties agree to a taxable transaction. A taxable transaction occurs by the purchase of the acquired firm's stock from its stockholders for cash or nonvoting securities of the acquiring firm or by the purchase of the acquired firm's assets for cash or nonvoting stock of the acquiring firm. In the first case, the transaction could create a capital gain liability for the stockholders of the selling corporation. In the second case, the selling corporation may have a taxable gain and also a situation of double taxation. However, the selling corporation in the latter event can avoid double taxation by adopting a plan of complete liquidation and distributing its assets within twelve months from the date of adoption of the plan. In this event, no gain or loss will be recognized to the selling corporation.

From the standpoint of the acquired firm, therefore, it is generally a matter of indifference whether the merger is taxable or nontaxable, since the liability most often involves the stockholders of the selling corporation. In addition, a taxable deal may offer positive advantages to the acquiring firm: it may be easier to transact; it may not be necessary to transfer voting stock; if the fair value of the assets approximates the purchase price, the purchase price is above book value of the seller's assets, or for accounting purposes the transaction is recorded as a purchase, a taxable transaction may be acceptable to the buyer. The seller, too, may opt for a taxable transaction if the purchase price is less than the tax basis of the assets[2].

Where a tax liability results from the combination, the installment option may assist the parties in negotiating their differences. For example, the acquiring firm may not be able to pay the full cost of the acquired assets in cash. Assuming voting stock is ruled out, the buyer may offer cash and debt securities to cover the purchase price. As a consequence, the seller may not realize sufficient cash to cover the tax liability on the transaction. If the transaction qualifies for installment sales treatment, the income taxes due will be payable when the proceeds of the sale are actually realized.

To qualify for installment sales treatment, the deal must include the sale of real property or personal property (excluding inventory). The taxable portion of the payments received in any year is that portion of

those payments that the gross profit (the profit realized when all payments are completed) bears to the contract price of the acquired assets.

Illustration: Alpha acquires 100 percent of Delta's stock under the following terms:

Purchase Price	$1,000,000
Tax Cost of Delta's Shareholders Stock	900,000
Gross Profit to Delta Shareholders	$ 100,000

Alpha pays $300,000 in cash and nonnegotiable notes of $700,000 ($100,000 falling due in each of the next seven years).

$$\text{Gross Profit Percentage: } \frac{\$100,000}{1,000,000} = 10\%$$

Tax Liability of Selling Stockholders:

Year	Amount
1	$300,000 × .10 = $ 30,000
2	100,000 × .10 = 10,000
3	100,000 × .10 = 10,000
4	100,000 × .10 = 10,000
5	100,000 × .10 = 10,000
6	100,000 × .10 = 10,000
7	100,000 × .10 = 10,000
8	100,000 × .10 = 10,000
	Total Tax Liability $100,000

The selling stockholders report 10 percent of each year's installment payment as taxable income.

Case: Alco Standard Corporation (ASC) and The Drug House (TDH). Alco Standard Corporation was formed on November 22, 1965 when Alco Chemical Corporation merged with V and V Companies of Cleveland, Ohio. Alco Chemical was a manufacturer of synthetic latex for fabric backing and also synthetic thickeners for viscosity control. V & V Companies manufactured metal processors for stampings, weldments, and machined parts. These companies formed the backbone of a developing conglomerate enterprise. The newly formed Alco Standard Corporation eagerly entered the acquisition market, expanding its product market to include capital goods; food service equipment; rubber and plastic products; and paper products. The acquisition of paper products companies was Alco's first step away from its basic line of manufactured products. In the 1970's Alco continued to diversify with acquisitions in the metal products field; distilled spirits and wines; glassware and plastic and metal containers; automotive and marine parts and equipment; and the operation under long-term contract of mining properties. The acquisition of The Drug House was an effort by ASC to move into a new product market within its distribution sector. In the ten-year period from 1966 to 1976, revenues grew 95 percent (71 percent restated for addition of results of acquisitions), net income grew 94 percent (76 percent restated), and net working capital grew 94 percent.

The Drug House

The Drug House Incorporated had been in business as a wholesale pharmaceutical distributor since 1929. In 1968, TDH acquired by merger Philadelphia Wholesale Drug Company; and in 1972 purchased Hensel & Son. With these additions, TDH had four divisions serving the areas of Philadelphia, Harrisburg, and Johnstown, Pennsylvania and Wilmington,

Delaware. Unlike ASC, however, TDH had not been able to make these investments pay off, experiencing only modest growth in revenues (20 percent) and earnings (23 percent) for the five years prior to 1977. But the major shortcoming, at least from the shareholders' viewpoint, was that dividends had not increased for the same five-year period. ASC's dividends by contrast increased 66 percent for the comparable five-year period. The Purchase and Sale Agreement between Alco Standard and TDH was completed on September 30, 1977. For $6,710,000 in cash, TDH sold to Alco Standard all of its assets except:

1. $152,000 cash that would be used by TDH to pay the expenses of Kidder, Peabody & Co., its investment banking firm.
2. $300,000 of Federal and State Prepaid Income Taxes.
3. All carry-back tax claims and all carry-forward tax claims arising by reason of the sale.

In turn, ASC agreed to assume substantially all of the liabilities of TDH, including, but not limited to, certain items not included on the TDH balance sheet:

1. All unfunded pension plan liability.
2. All contingent liability on certain customers' notes receivable discounted at a bank.

ASC did not assume any Federal State, or Local corporation income, capital stock or franchise taxes payable by TDH.

To complete the purchase, ASC established a wholly-owned subsidiary, Alco Wholesale Drug Distribution Company, which would purchase the assets of TDH under the Purchase and Sale Agreement negotiated between the two companies. The agreement, besides establishing the identity of assets to be purchased and liabilities to be assumed, also included a clause whereby TDH would make a tender offer, after the sale, to its shareholders to purchase all outstanding shares of its common stock, except those belonging to four of their board members. At the time of the agreement, TDH had outstanding 838,563 shares of no par value, $1 stated value, common stock. Of the 838,563 shares outstanding, the amount belonging to the four board members whose shares would not be tendered totaled 705,811 shares. The remaining 132,752 shares would be purchased at the tender price of $10.25 per share, computed as follows:

	Total	*Per Share
Cash received from Alco	$6,710,000	$7.92
Prepaid Federal and State taxes	300,000	.35
Recoverable Federal Income Tax	1,450,000	1.71
	$8,460,000	$9.98
Maximum Possible Additional Retained Profits, Years 1978–84, by reason of $1,550,000 carry-forward loss computed @ 48% ($.88 per share)	744,000	
Since the realization of this $.88 is not assured, TDH is offering approx. 30% thereof, or		.27
Total Offer Per Share,		$10.25

*Per Share numbers calculated on total expected outstanding shares on September 30, 1977 of 847,563.

Because TDH was incorporated in the state of Pennsylvania, a majority of shareholders approval was needed to approve the Purchase and Sale Agreement. This majority was obtained with the approval by the four board members. All dissenting shareholders were entitled to have their shares purchased at fair market cash value. In light of the fact that previous to the agreement, the reported bid price of TDH Common Stock was $4 per share and had been trading within a quarter of that price in the Over-the-Counter Market for the previous two years, the price of $10.25 per share was fair. This opinion was also expressed by Kidder, Peabody & Co., the investment banking firm retained by the board of directors of THD.

For accounting purposes, ASC recorded the acquisition as a purchase. In applying the purchase method, the assets acquired are recorded at cost less the liabilities assumed. But, as explained in APB No. 16:

"the sum of the market or appraisal values of identifiable assets acquired less liabilities assumed may sometimes exceed the cost of the acquired company. If so, the values otherwise assignable to noncurrent assets acquired (except long-term investments in marketable securities) should be reduced by a proportionate part of the excess to determine the assigned values. A deferred credit for an excess of assigned value of identifiable assets over cost of an acquired company (sometimes called 'negative goodwill') should not be recorded unless those assets are reduced to zero value." (p. 318, paragraph 87)

EXHIBIT 9–1
Excess of Equity Over Cost of
Acquired Company

Total Assets	$19,548,183	
Less: cash and prepaid taxes not assumed	452,000	
	$19,096,183	
Less: deferred income taxes not assumable per APB 16	70,000	
	$19,026,183	
Less: prerecorded goodwill not assumable per APB 16	145,089	
Net Adjusted Assets		$18,881,094
Total Liabilities	$19,548,183	
Less: Shareholders Equity	12,056,934	
	$ 7,491,249	
Less: Federal and State income taxes not assumed	87,320	
	$ 7,403,929	
Plus cash payment	6,710,000	
Net Adjusted Liabilities		14,113,929
Excess of assets over liabilities and cash		$ 4,767,165
Subsequent writedown of noncurrent assets as required by APB 16		1,637,483
Excess of Equity over cost of acquired company		$ 3,129,682

*Given the fluctuation of asset values between the negotiation date and the 1976 Annual Report, the calculated amount is approximately $3,000,000.

This was the case with the acquisition of TDH. ASC qualified for a "bargain purchase," acquiring the assets of TDH at substantially below replacement cost. Recording the transaction in conformity with APB No. 16 necessitated the creation of an account entitled, "excess of equity over cost of acquired company," for the amount of approximately $3,000,000 that would be amortized as revenue over a ten-year period. This amount is approximately calculated in Exhibit 9–1 using December 31, 1976 figures for TDH. The amortization of the excess equity over cost resulted in ASC reporting higher earnings. Since the amortization of excess equity over cost was not taxable, the added accounting earnings were tax-free.

The acquisition was a taxable exchange. For TDH, the acquisition created a loss in the amount of $5,580,000, the amount that ASC charged against inventory. This loss was then carried back against the income of 1974, 1975, and 1976, in the amount of $3.3 million, thereby setting a tax refund of approximately $1,450,000. The remainder of the loss was to be carried forward against any income of TDH for the years 1978 through 1984.

The sale of stock by the shareholders of TDH under the tender offer also represented a taxable transaction. If all shareholders tendered their shares, the transaction will be treated as a capital gain. If only a portion of the shares are tendered, the transaction could be considered as a dividend and consequently taxable as ordinary income.

SUMMARY

This chapter presented a few basic concepts in tax law that affect acquisition strategies by creating "profit opportunities" from tax avoidance that might not otherwise exist in a noncorporate environment. Tax options to corporations and shareholders heavily influence the structure of merger deals. Indeed, such options may actually encourage certain business combinations or shape the form of the combination. For example, the separate tax treatment of debt, dividend income, and capital gains conceivably creates incentives for conglomerate mergers. Ideally, tax considerations should have a neutral effect on business judgment. The reality is something else.

Each situation must be considered on its merits in order to determine whether a taxable or nontaxable transaction is the best course. But the complexities of the IRS code warrant the employment of *experienced* legal and accounting advise in taking the best advantage of what Congress has bequeathed to the business community. Prior clearing with IRS will provide further assurance on the tax status of the combination.

NOTES

1. Bittker, Boris I., and James S. Eustice. *Federal Income Taxation of Corporations and Shareholders.* Boston, Massachusetts: Warren, Gorham & Lamont, 1971. pp. 14–26 and 32–41.

2. Bradley, James W., and Donald H. Korn. *Acquisition and Corporate Development.* Lexington, Massachusetts: Lexington Books, 1981. p. 31–32; 176–177.

3. Finnie, Denise M. *The General Signal Corporation and Leeds & Northrup Company Merger.* Unpublished MBA seminar paper, Drexel University, 1983.

4. Guardino, Joseph R. *Accounting, Legal and Tax Aspects of Corporate Acquisitions.* Englewood Cliffs, N.J.: Prentice-Hall, 1973. pp. 20, 70, 75, 122, 35–36.

5. Helfrich, Steven. *The ALCO and The Drug House, Inc. Merger.* Unpublished MBA seminar paper, Drexel University, 1983.

6. The Anaconda Company. *Proxy Statement.* October 20, 1976. pp. 7–11.

Liability to Antitrust Action

10

Chapter 2 described the ebb and flow of merger activity. On three occasions, the Federal Government sought to deter the growth of corporate size to preserve the competitive market. The spirit behind Federal policy was "a desire to preserve to the nation the benefits of industrial competition in the belief that the economies of production on a large scale would be accomplished through the self-interest of the manufacturer"[3]. In 1890, Congress passed the Sherman Antitrust Act; in 1914, the Clayton Act; and in 1950, the Cellar-Kefauver Amendment to Section 7 of the Clayton Act. Today, Congress is again faced with demands for new legislation to assure the benefits of competition. However, what Congress should do and whether the economy has grown more or less competitive since 1890 has inspired much debate but no consensus on a new policy.

The purpose of this chapter is to survey the principle legislation to curb restraints on trade and the guidelines set down by the Department of Justice (DOJ) in deciding whether or not to challenge a particular business combination. The discussion focuses on the implications of the antitrust law for the development of company acquisition strategy. It is not a definitive analysis of antitrust law and practice (a specialty unto itself) and will not impart the wisdom to allow the reader to judge his own situation. Hopefully, it will encourage those with corporate authority to consult with *experienced* lawyers in the field *before* implementing the firm's acquisition strategy.

SHERMAN ANTITRUST ACT (1890) The Act applies to interstate and foreign trade. Section 1 declares unlawful "every contract, combination in the form of trust or otherwise, or conspiracy in restraint of trade or commerce among the several states or with foreign nations." Section 2 declares that every person shall be guilty of a misdemeanor, subject to fine and/or imprisonment, if he shall monopolize, attempt to monopolize, combine, conspire with others to monopolize any part of our interstate or foreign trade. Enforcement may take the form either of a criminal prosecution or a civil suit for an injunction by the Department of Justice. Also, any person injured in his business or property by reason of a violation of the Sherman Act may sue for three times the amount of damage actually proved[8].

Strong words, full of sound and fury. The Supreme Court thought otherwise. In the first test of the law, the Court held that the Sherman Act did not apply to manufacturing and mining but only to commerce [U.S. v. E.C. Knight Company, 156 U.S. 1 (1895)]. In 1911, the Court held that only unreasonable restraints of trade were illegal under Section 1 [Standard Oil Company v. United States, 221 U.S. 1 (1911)]. Restraints that were merely ancillary to normal- and efficiency-producing business practices were exempt. Dewing observed: "There is little doubt that, had the issue been so raised, a merger to achieve an economy would have been deemed reasonable"[3]. In 1920, the Court held that U.S. Steel had not violated Section 1, for the company had not achieved its purpose of a monopoly [United States v. United States Steel Corp., 251 U.S. 417 (1920)]. As interpreted, the Act could not prevent mergers of less than monopolistic dimensions.

CLAYTON ACT (1914)

In the words of the Court, the Clayton Act "aims to strike down a monopoly at its inception, when the first step is taken," as distinguished from the Sherman Act, which aims to strike it down "after it has become more virile." [United States v. Besser Mfg. Co., 96 F. Supp. 304, 308 (1951)]. The practices outlawed by the Clayton Act include:

1. *Price Discrimination:* Section 2 of the Clayton Act prohibits price discrimination between different purchasers "where the effect . . . may be to substantially lessen competition or to tend to create a monopoly in any line of commerce." (In 1936, this section was amended by the Robinson Patman Act that allowed price differences in the absence of restraint or monopolistic effect; or where justified by differences in grade and quality; or where justified by quantity purchases; or in the case of changing conditions; or by the necessity to meet competition; and by cooperative associations[8].)

2. *Tying Contracts:* Section 3 makes it unlawful for a person to lease or sell goods on the condition that the lessee or purchaser refrain from doing business with a competitor(s) of the lessor seller, where the effect may be to "substantially lessen competition or tend to create a monopoly"[8].

3. *Stock Acquisition of Competitors:* Section 7 of the Clayton Act prohibits a corporation from acquiring all or part of the stock of another corporation where the effect substantially lessens competition between the acquiring and acquired corporation or restrains commerce or tends to create a monopoly[3].

4. *Interlocking Directorates:* Section 8 prohibits any director from serving

on the boards of two or more competing corporations where the elimination of competition would violate the antitrust laws. Section 8 applies only where one of the corporations has capital, surplus, and undivided profits of more than $1,000,000.

5. *Enforcement:* Enforcement of the Clayton Act is vested in the Federal Trade Commission established in 1914. In addition, private individuals may now sue and have injunctive relief against threatened loss or damage because of a violation. Unlike the Sherman Act, private individuals need not wait until they have sustained damage before suing.

> For example, under this provision, the Chrysler Corp. submitted a memorandum to the FTC charging that the General Motors-Toyota Motors Corp. joint venture to produce a small car violates antitrust laws and could constitute an illegal price-fixing arrangement. The memo stated that the joint venture:
>
> —Violated Justice Department standards for industry concentration.
>
> —Could reduce incentives at GM and Toyota for research and development.
>
> —Could lead to an alliance between GM and Toyota that would last beyond the twelve year life of the agreement.
>
> Chrysler's hope was that the FTC would rule the joint venture anticompetitive[14].

The primary defect in the Clayton Act lay in Section 7 that covers *stock* acquisitions but neglected *asset* acquisitions. Steiner cites a further deficiency in the opinion of antitrust experts that the language focusing on competition between the acquiring and acquired companies limits the Act to horizontal acquisitions[13].

Cellar-Kefauver Act of 1950: Cellar-Kefauver amended Section 7 to include the acquisition of all or part of the *assets* of another corporation where the effect substantially lessens competition between the acquiring and acquired corporations or *elsewhere* or restrains commerce or tends to create a monopoly [italics added][13].

In a series of decisions the Court used the Cellar-Kefauver amendment to severely restrict horizontal and vertical combinations as well as to endanger the validity of many product-extension and market-extension conglomerates.

• U.S. v. The Philadelphia National Bank, 374 U.S. 312 (1963): the Court blocked a bank merger that would have resulted in control of 30 percent of the commercial banking business in the four-county Philadelphia metropolitan area.

• Brown Shoe Co. v. U.S. 370 U.S. 294 (1962): the Court blocked the acquisition of Kinney which would have given Brown control of 7.2 percent of the nation's total retail shoe outlets.

• U.S. v. E. I. duPont deNemours & Company, 353 U.S. 586 (1957): the Court held that DuPont's acquisition of 23 percent of General Motors stock foreclosed one-third of the total market for automotive finishes and one-fourth of the total market for automotive fabrics.

• United States v. Pabst, 384 U.S. 546 (1966): Despite the contrary testimony of economists, the Court held that Wisconsin, by itself, is "a distinguishable and economically significant market for the sale of beer."

• United States v. El Paso Natural Gas Co., 376 U.S. 651 (1964): El Paso's acquisition of Pacific Northwest Pipeline Company was held to have violated Section 7.

• United States v. Aluminum Co. of America, 377 U.S. 271 (1964): ALCOA's acquisition of Rome Cable (primarily a manufacturer of copper cable) was held to have violated Section 7.

• United States v. Continental Can Co., 378 U.S. 441 (1964): the Court held Continental's acquisition of Hazel-Atlas Glass, a manufacturer of glass bottles, ran contrary to Section 7.

• U.S. v. Proctor & Gamble Co. 386 U.S. 568 (1967): P & G's acquisition of Clorox Chemical Company violated Section 7 since bleach was sufficiently related to the P & G product line that P & G could have expanded internally to become a major competitor in the bleach market had it not acquired Clorox.

A common thread of philosophy runs through these cases. In each case, the Court not only looked at the extant level of competition within a defined market area but also the *potential* competition that might develop if the acquisition were aborted. Potential competition could mean either the elimination of the acquiring firm as a new entrant into the industry or the establishment of a position by the acquiring firm in the industry such as to discourage entry by other firms. Thus, as the decade of the 1960s drew to a close any company formulating an acquisition strategy would have to approach with caution even loosely horizontal or vertical combinations[13]. Only the pure conglomerate type seemed *relatively* immune to the probing eye of DOJ.

MERGER GUIDELINES

Legislative enactments and case law while historically interesting do not tell management whether the combination under discussion is likely to attract the attention of DOJ. This gap is partially filled by the issuance of DOJ Guidelines which spell out DOJ's understanding of the law. Thus on May 30, 1968, DOJ issued *Merger Guidelines*:

> to acquaint the business community, the legal profession, and other interested groups . . . with the standards currently being applied by the Department of Justice in determining whether to challenge corporate acquisitions and mergers under Section 7 of the Clayton Act.

Exhibit 10–1 summarizes the principal provisions of the 1968 Guidelines.

In referring to the Guidelines, however, it is well for management to bear in mind their limited significance. Antitrust cases are decided by judges not prosecutors. The Guidelines do not cover suits by private individuals. DOJ lacks the facts in a particular case prior to litigation. The Guidelines apply to the prelitigation phase and are, accordingly,

EXHIBIT 10–1
Department of Justice Merger Guidelines, 1968

Horizontal Mergers

1. Where the share of business held by the leading four firms is 75 percent or more, a merger will ordinarily be challenged if the firms involved possess the following market shares:

Acquiring firm	Acquired firm
4 percent or more	4 percent or more
10 percent or more	2 percent or more
15 percent or more	1 percent or more

2. Where the concentration ratio is less than 75, a merger will ordinarily be challenged if the firms involved possess the following market shares:

Acquiring firm	Acquired firm
5 percent or more	5 percent or more
10 percent or more	4 percent or more
15 percent or more	3 percent or more
20 percent or more	2 percent or more
25 percent or more	1 percent or more

3. Other mergers may be challenged where the acquired firm has 2 percent or more of the market, if the acquiring firm is among the eight largest in that market and the market share of any grouping of the two to eight largest firms has increased 7 percent or more in the preceding ten years.

Vertical Mergers

1. Mergers will ordinarily be challenged where the firm supplying inputs accounts for 10 percent or more of sales in its market and the purchasing firm accounts for six percent or more of the purchases in the same market.
2. Other mergers may be challenged outside the limits above if there is a significant trend toward vertical integration by merger.

Conglomerate Mergers

1. Merger by a potential entrant into a market will ordinarily be challenged where: (a) the acquired firm has 25 percent or more of the market; (b) the acquired firm is one of the two largest in the market and the top two have 50 percent or more of the market; (c) the acquired firm is one of the four largest in a market in which the top eight have 75 percent of the market and the acquired firm at least 10 percent; (d) the acquired firm is one of the largest eight in a market where the largest eight have 75 percent or more of the market.
2. Mergers that create a significant danger of reciprocal buying will ordinarily be challenged.
3. Acquisition of a leading firm may be challenged where the acquisition may increase that firm's market power, raise barriers to entry, or produce a very large disparity in size.
4. Other conglomerate mergers that on specific analysis appear anticompetitive may be challenged.

Source: Department of Justice, "Merger Guidelines."

EXHIBIT 10–2
Department of Justice Merger Guidelines
1982

I—*Purpose and Underlying Theme*:

   A. The merger should not be permitted to create or enhance 'market power' or to facilitate its exercise.

   B. Mergers play an important role in a free enterprise economy by penalizing inefficient management and encouraging more efficient redeployment of productive assets; the guidelines are not inherently hostile to merger activity.

   C. Guidelines explicitly adopt an economic approach to merger analysis.

   D. The guidelines are consistent with the modified structural analysis reflected in recent court decisions.

II—*Horizontal Mergers:*

   A. Horizontal mergers are the most likely category of mergers to attract enforcement attention.

   B. The following standards are set for the analysis of horizontal mergers:

     1. *Concentration and Market Share:* As an aid in assessing the degree of market concentration, DOJ will use Herfindahl-Hirschman Index (HHI) described in Exhibit 10–3.

     2. DOJ will consider both the postmerger market concentration and the increase in concentration resulting from the merger.

     3. Markets with a postmerger *HHI score of 1000 or less* will be considered unconcentrated—having at least the equivalent of ten equally sized firms.

     4. Markets with a postmerger *HHI between 1000 and 1800* will be considered concentrated, the degree of concentration increasing as the HHI score rises to 1800. DOJ, however, is not likely to attack mergers producing an increase in the HHI of less than one hundred points. DOJ is more likely to attack mergers in this region which increase HHI by more than one hundred points.

     5. Markets with a postmerger HHI *above 1800* are deemed highly concentrated. The DOJ is likely to challenge mergers in this category which increase the HHI by one hundred points or more; depending upon the particular circumstances, DOJ may challenge mergers producing an increase in the HHI of fifty to one hundred points; below a fifty-point increase in the HHI, the Department is unlikely to proceed against the merger.

     6. Under the *leading firm concept*, DOJ is likely to challenge the merger of any firm with a market share of at least 1 percent with the leading firm in the market, provided the latter has a market share of at least 35 percent and is approximately twice as large as that of the second largest firm in the market.

     7. If entry into a market is sufficiently easy such that existing competitors could not succeed in raising price for any significant period of time, DOJ is unlikely to challenge mergers in that market.

     8. When the relevant product in the market is completely homogeneous or undifferentiated, the probability of a DOJ challenge to the merger increases; the probability of a challenge decreases as the product line becomes more differentiated.

     9. Where the products in the market area are close substitutes and/or the location of the next most distant seller is relatively close

EXHIBIT 10–2

continued

to the last seller included in the market area, the probability of challenge also increases.

10. If the plants and facilities of the merging firms are particularly good substitutes, the Department is more likely to challenge the merger.

11. If market conditions are conducive to the enforcement of collusive agreements, the probability of a DOJ action against the merger increases.

12. The prior conduct of the merging firms relative to anticompetitive practices will figure in the judgment to proceed against the merger.

III—*Nonhorizontal Mergers:*

Nonhorizontal mergers involve firms that do not operate in the same market. The following are the principal *theories* under which DOJ is likely to challenge this category of mergers:

A. *Potential Competition:* By eliminating a significant present competitive threat that constrains the behavior of the firms already in the market or by eliminating the possibility of entry by the acquiring firm, the merger might result in an immediate deterioration of market performance or result in a lost opportunity for improvement in market performance by the addition of a significant competitor.

B. *Competitive Problems from Vertical Mergers:* As with the Potential Competition Standard, this standard is concerned with the possibly adverse consequences to entry. Three conditions can create objectionable barriers to entry: (1) the degree of vertical integration between the two markets must be so extensive that entrants to one market (the primary market) also would have to enter the other market (secondary market); (2) the requirement for entry at the secondary level must make entry at the primary level significantly more difficult and less likely to occur; (3) the characteristics of the primary market must be so conducive to noncompetitive performance that increased difficulty of entry is likely to affect its performance. The following criteria determine whether these conditions are satisfied:

1. *Need for Two-Level Entry:* If the postmerger sales by unintegrated firms in the secondary market would be sufficient to service two minimum-efficient-scale plants in the primary market, DOJ is unlikely to oppose the merger. As the unintegrated capacity declines, the probability of DOJ opposition increases.

2. *Increased Difficulty of Simultaneous Entry to Both Markets:* If entry at the secondary level is easy, the requirement of simultaneous entry is less likely to adversely affect entry into the primary market and DOJ is less likely to attack the combination. The converse is also true. Barriers to entry in the secondary market can arise from excessive increases in the cost of capital and the amount of capital required to develop a minimally-efficient-scale plant.

3. *Structure and Performance of the Primary Market:* Is the structure of the primary market conducive to monopolization or collusion? If the HHI of the primary market exceeds 1800, DOJ is likely to oppose the merger. Primary considerations include the power of primary producers to monitor retail prices or the elimination of a disruptive buyer or the use of vertical integration to evade rate regulation by public utility commissions.

EXHIBIT 10–2
continued

IV—*Defenses*

    A. *Efficiency:* DOJ will not accept efficiency as a specific defense in the case of a merger that would otherwise be challenged. The reasons for the general rule are:

       1. Most mergers resulting in significant efficiencies are permitted under the guidelines.

       2. Plausible efficiencies are far easier to allege than to prove.

       3. Even if measureable, it is impossible to know *in advance* whether savings will outweigh potential loss from an increase in concentration.

    B. *Failing Firm:* The Department will closely scrutinize an anticompetitive merger when justified by the argument that one of the combining firms will otherwise fail. The allegedly failing firm must demonstrate that:

       1. It probably would be unable to meet its financial obligations in the near future.

       2. Probably would not be able to reorganize successfully under Chapter 11 of the Bankruptcy Act.

       3. Has made unsuccessful good faith efforts to elicit reasonable alternative offers of acquisition that would both keep it in the market and pose a less severe danger to competition than does the proposed merger.

Source: Department of Justice

---

intended to assist lawyers representing clients subject to prosecution by spelling out DOJ criteria for initiating an action. Using the Guidelines, the firm's attorneys can obtain DOJ's *opinion* as to whether the combination is in violation of existing law. The opinion will not, on the other hand, stay suit by a private party claiming injury by reason of the combination's actual or potential adverse effect on the state of competition.

The Guidelines, according to Steiner, identified for attack:

> any acquisition of a significant-sized firm by an already large diversified firm under one or more of the bases—potential competition, reciprocity, or entrenchment—that were regarded as predicting probable competitive harm. At the same time the guidelines rejected efficiency defenses[13].

But events moved quickly to obsolete the 1968 Guidelines. The Court rejected the use of mechanical formulas for determining the illegality of horizontal mergers; a growing body of academic and legal research cast new light on the causes and effects of industrial concentration; and a change of guard in the Antitrust Division of DOJ favored review of the Department's criteria for prosecution[2]. On June 14, 1982, DOJ issued a new set of Guidelines.

Exhibits 10–2 and 10–3 summarize the new guidelines. The *Wall Street Journal* (June 15, 1982) heralded the new guidelines as "U.S. Eases Mergers Guidelines, Allowing Somewhat More Concentrated Markets." **187**

EXHIBIT 10–3
Herfindahl-Hirschman Index (HHI)

Calculation: HHI is calculated by summing the squares of the individual market shares of all the firms included in the market. For example, suppose there were seven firms in an industry with the following market shares:

Firm	Market Shares (S)	S^2
A	.30	.0900
B	.20	.0400
C	.15	.0225
D	.15	.0225
E	.10	.0100
F	.05	.0025
G	.05	.0025
Total	1.00	.1900

To shift the decimal, multiply S^2 by 10,000:

$$\text{HHI} = S^2 \times 10,000$$
$$= .1900 \times 10,000$$
$$= 1900$$

Suppose F and G merge:

Firm	Market Share	S^2
A	.30	.0900
B	.20	.0400
C	.15	.0225
D	.15	.0225
E	.10	.0100
F–G	.10	.0100
Total	1.00	.1950 ($\times$ 10,000)
Premerger HHI		1900
Postmerger HHI		1950
Increase in HHI		50 Points

"HHI reflects both the distribution of the market shares of the top four firms and the composition of the market outside the top four firms. It also gives greater weight to the market shares of the larger firms, which probably accords with their relative importance in any collusive interaction" (Department of Justice *Guidelines*). The Index should be contrasted with the traditional four firm concentration ratio spelled out in the 1968 Guidelines.

DOJ divides the spectrum of market concentration measured by the HHI into three regions:

	HHI
Highly Concentrated	Over 1800
Moderately Concentrated	Between 1000 and 1800
Unconcentrated	Below 1000

DOJ calculations using actual market shares in actual industries indicate that a four-firm concentration ratio (CR_4) of 50 percent corresponds roughly to a Herfindahl index (HHI) of about 1040, a CR_4 of 60 percent corresponds to a HHI of about 1410, and a CR_4 of 70 percent corresponds to a HHI of about 1820. Conversely, a HHI of 1000 corresponds to a CR_4 of about 49 percent, a HHI of 1200 corresponds to a CR_4 of about 54 percent, and a HHI of 1600 corresponds to a CR_4 of about 64 percent.

Management might react less enthusiastically after perusing the complexities of Exhibits 10–2 and 10–3. In all events, DOJ did not linger in applying its new criteria. On June 14, 1982, the Department challenged the acquisition of Pabst Brewing Co. by G. Heileman Brewing Co. on the grounds that merger would have added 112 points to the Herfindahl-Hirschman Index (HHI) and raised the index to 1834[14]. Exhibit 10–3 explains the calculation of the Index.

Some points of contrast between the 1968 and 1982 Guidelines are worth noting:

• The new Guidelines in describing areas within which DOJ is not likely to challenge a merger go a long way toward creating "safe harbors" that reduce the risks and costs of certain combinations.

• The 1968 Guidelines measured market concentration by adding the percentage of sales held by the four largest companies. A market was considered highly concentrated if four companies accounted for 75 percent of the sales. Under the new Guidelines, an HHI of 1800 corresponds to a market where four concerns hold about 70 percent of the sales.

• For dominant firms (firms accounting for 36 percent of the market and twice the size of the largest competitor) the new Guidelines are more restrictive. Even small acquisitions (1 percent of the market) by dominant firms are likely to be challenged.

• Conglomerate mergers are not specifically targeted unless they violate the general criteria set forth in the new Guidelines. These would encompass cross subsidization, tie-in sales, reciprocity agreements, and other collusive practices that diminish the competitiveness of a market.

Federal antitrust law is not the sole legal barrier to business combinations. The Securities and Exchange Commission is charged with assuring full and fair disclosure in the issuance of new securities and prohibiting fraud therein. The Williams Act of 1968 strengthened the hand of SEC in dealing with tender offers. Under the Williams Act, if a tender offer would achieve control of 5 percent or more of the target's stock, detailed information prior to the offer must be filed with SEC concerning:

OTHER REGULATORY INHIBITIONS TO MERGER

• Identities and backgrounds of the purchaser.
• The number of shares presently owned by the bidder.
• The offeror's plans for the acquired firm if the tender is successful.
• The source and amount of funds to be used to finance the acquisition.
• Details of any agreements with other persons concerning the affairs of the target company.

Similar information must be provided by any group that achieves a 5 percent stock holding and by the management of the target company if it recommends to the shareholders how to respond to the tender offer. Tender offers are to remain open for a minimum of seven days and a maximum of sixty days[13]. In addition, the Hart-Scott-Rodino Act requires the filing of a premerger notification with FTC and DOJ for all combinations where one of the companies has sales or assets in excess of $100 million and the other company has sales or assets in excess of $10 million. Under the Act, completion of an acquisition cannot occur until thirty days after the notification. H-S-R also applies to acquisition of 15 percent of the outstanding stock of a company or $15 million in stock or assets involving a large company.

In special cases, other Federal agencies may become involved. Bank mergers may involve Federal Reserve review; similarly the Civil Aeronautics Board has jurisdiction over the nation's airlines; and the Interstate Commerce Commission, over rail and motor transportation. Conceivably, the Environmental Protection Agency's mandate may be grounds for asserting its authority in a merger situation[1].

The reader should also bear in mind that most states have similar antitrust and regulatory statutes on the books. Although Federal activity enjoys the spotlight, state law cannot be ignored with impunity. Indeed, state laws, if applicable, may be more restrictive than Federal legislation. Some states, for example, have moved to curtail hostile tender offers by requiring supermajorities (80 percent of more) for the completion of the deal[14].

To recapitulate, good acquisition strategy requires that management and an *experienced* attorney ascertain the status of the planned merger under the:

> Sherman Antitrust Act
> Clayton Act
> Cellar-Kefauver Act
> Williams Act
> Hart-Scott-Rodino Act
> Securities Act
> DOJ Guidelines
> Relevant state law

and consult before the fact with appropriate enforcement agencies:

> Federal Trade Commission
> Department of Justice
> Interstate Commerce Commission
> Civil Aeronautics Board
> Federal Reserve.

Premerger review will not guarantee immunity from subsequent civil prosecution but it will reduce the risks and costs of the combination and the likelihood of criminal prosecution.

IS THE ECONOMY MORE OR LESS COMPETITIVE?

Few nations have put as much effort as the U.S. into the maintenance of a competitive market. How effective have been these legal ayes and nays? After nearly a century of antitrust legislation, is the economy more or less concentrated? Some pertinent statistics are:

1. Of the fifty largest industrial corporations in the world, twenty-one are American companies and twelve of these are oil companies[5]. The
remaining eight include: General Motors, Ford Motor, IBM, General Electric, DuPont, ITT, Tenneco, U.S. Steel, and United Technologies. Of the eight, only ITT was classified by Lynch as an aggressive conglomerate, although Tenneco and United Technologies were active participants in the Post–World War II merger waves[10]. DuPont raised its ranking from 38th to 16th by the acquisition of Conoco. Since the oils account for twenty-two of the select fifty, a representation of eight companies out of a net twenty-eight is not disproportionate to the size of the U.S. economy vis-à-vis the world market. Moreover, nonU.S. firms in the top fifty have more than doubled their number since 1967. In 1967, twelve foreign firms ranked in the top fifty; by 1981, twenty-seven were nonU.S. firms with sales and/or assets equal or exceeding their U.S. competitors[2].

2. Domestically, in 1929 the 200 largest nonfinancial corporations accounted for 49.4 percent of corporate assets; the figure rose to 57 percent in 1933 and declined to 39.5 percent in 1975. The share of nonfinancial assets held by the fifty largest firms declined from 24.4 percent in 1958 to 23.4 percent in 1972. Both groups showed larger percentage declines in their share of corporate after-tax profits over the corresponding periods.

With reference to manufacturing production, the fifty largest manufacturing corporations made up 28 percent of the output in 1937; this declined to 25 percent by 1977. But the 200 largest showed a rise from 41 percent of manufacturing production to 45 percent in 1977[2].

However, several caveats attach to the use of concentration ratios. Concentration ratios do not *per se* correspond to antitrust criteria of competitiveness and resource utilization; the data base includes the foreign investments of U.S. firms; and the fifty, one hundred or 200 largest firms are not a fixed membership. For example, membership in the fifty largest manufacturing firms turned over nearly 50 percent between 1947 to 1977[2].

3. Studies by Markham, Lorie and Halpern, and White agree that total concentration in the U.S. economy has not increased[11,9,15]. White concluded his study with the comment:

> Has aggregate concentration in the U.S. economy increased in the 1960s and 1970s? The answer, very clearly, is no. . . . The available date, when properly compiled, will simply not support any assertions that aggregate concentration is increasing; if anything, the trends appear to be in the opposite direction[15].

Markham found that the merger wave of the 1960s had no appreciable effect on total concentration[11].

Dennis C. Mueller, on the other hand, takes a longer perspective on the impact of merger activity. He contends that the first two merger waves increased both overall and industry concentration levels but since the Cellar-Kefauver Act horizontal merger activity has been inconsequential and industry concentration "levels have exhibited no pattern of change that seems to be merger related." But, Mueller sees overall concentration creeping slowly upward. The percentage of manufacturing assets held by the 200 largest manufacturing firms increased from 55.4 percent in 1959 to 60 percent in 1982[12].

4. As Exhibit 10–4 illustrates, despite the arguments over the level of concentration in the American economy, the population of the business community continues to increase.

The evidence, therefore, on whether the U.S. economy is becoming more or less concentrated is ambivalent at best. One can argue for or against the hypothesis depending upon the concentration ratio used: non-financial assets, manufacturing assets, corporate profits, number of firms, number of employees, market shares, value added, etc. Manufacturing data should in all cases be used with caution. The U.S. economy is undergoing dramatic change. The service industries gain in importance as the manufacturing sector declines. U.S. imports of manufactured goods have increased substantially since 1960. Consequently, it is quite possible that U.S. sales of manufactured goods by the 200 largest manufacturing firms could have declined while their share of U.S. production and manufacturing assets could have increased.

Also the data overlaps domestic and foreign markets. Should concentration ratios be based upon the domestic market or include foreign

---

EXHIBIT 10–4
Number of Returns, Receipts, and Net Income,
by Type of Business: 1960 to 1980

[Figures are estimates based on samples; see Appendix III. See also *Historical Statistics, Colonial Times to 1970*, series V 1–12. For further information regarding corporations, see tables 907–909]

Item	Unit	1960	1965	1970	1975	1976	1977	1978	1979	1980
Number	1,000	11,172	11,416	12,001	13,979	14,536	14,741	15,629	16,187	16,793
Receipts[1]	Bil. dol...	1,095	1,469	2,082	3,685	4,170	4,699	5,377	6,345	7,159
Net income (less deficit)[2]....	Bil. dol...	73	111	109	196	245	283	320	361	302
Proprietorships, number[3]......	1,000	9,090	9,078	9,400	10,882	11,358	11,346	12,018	12,330	12,702
Business receipts[1]	Bil. dol...	171	199	238	339	375	394	443	488	506
Net income (less deficit)[2]....	Bil. dol...	21	28	33	45	50	51	59	61	55
Partnerships, number........	1,000	941	914	936	1,073	1,096	1,153	1,234	1,300	1,380
Total receipts[4].............	Bil. dol...	74	75	93	147	160	177	219	258	292
Net income (less deficit)[2]....	Bil. dol...	8	10	10	8	10	13	14	15	8
Corporations, number	1,000	1,141	1,424	1,665	2,024	2,082	2,242	2,377	2,557	2,711
Total receipts[4].............	Bil. dol...	849	1,195	1,751	3,199	3,635	4,128	4,715	5,559	6,361
Net income (less deficit)[2][5] ..	Bil. dol...	44	74	66	143	185	219	247	285	239

[1]See footnote 1, table 890.
[2]See footnote 2, table 890.
[3]Individually owned businesses and farms.
[4]Total taxable receipts before deduction of cost of goods sold, cost of operations, and net loss from sales of property other than capital assets.
[5]Beginning 1965, includes constructive taxable income from related foreign corporations.

Source: Bureau of the Census, *Statistical Abstract of the United States: 1984*, p. 532.

sales and foreign investments? That the latter can reinforce the domestic position of a U.S. producer is illustrated by the current position of Ford Motor.

To argue that mergers contribute to business concentration is a defensible position; to assert that business combinations are the primary cause of the present level of concentration is not a provable hypothesis. Recall from Chapter 1, internal growth historically outweighs growth by merger. The factors contributing to the emergence of "bigness" lie in technology, the size of the market area, capital formation, and so forth. Antitrust legislation did not and could not have prevented the development of big business. At best, antitrust legislation may have prevented short term excesses in the degree of market control and affected the form of business growth. FTC described the influence of antitrust policy on the brewing industry:

> The fact that mergers have accounted for such a small share of the increase in concentration is directly a result of very strict antitrust enforcement by the Justice Department. But this policy may have . . . promoted higher national concentration in two ways: (1) by foreclosing the merger route to national brewers, it forced them to expand internally . . . their large, new breweries are more efficient than the older ones . . . (2) The Department has blocked merger of smaller brewers. This may have had the effect of weakening the competitive position of the latter group . . .[4].

The forced investment in new breweries created a 40 percent excess capacity in the industry which, for the most part, was written off.

Given a dubious link between merger activity and industry concentration, the argument comes down to political philosophy. Some Americans hold to the Jeffersonian ideal of small businessmen and farmers. Others see this vision as contradictory to the requirements of modern technology that presupposes large amounts of capital. All the same, the clock will not be turned back. More technology, not less, is needed to support a growing world population at even minimal standards of living.

SUMMARY

Antitrust laws are stronger in saying what cannot be done than in providing a clear guide as to what can be done. The negative connotation to the laws, the nuances of the adjudication process, the political feature of enforcement policy—all contribute to the business risk of mergers. Management deals with uncertainty by devising a strategic plan to cope with the possible outcomes. Thus, in the antitrust arena, management should seek to ascertain the prevailing attitude of Federal and state enforcement officials regarding the combination and any potential future liability down the road. A business combination, which at the time of formation may be judged not to diminish competition, may have within it the seeds of future liability. To avoid the pitfalls of the future, management has to keep informed on emerging trends in the philosophy underlying enforcement and the sentiments in the legislature regarding the quality of market competition. As with tax strategies, this is an on-going assignment. Antitrust enforcement has a tendency to select the more profitable combinations for prosecution.

NOTES

1. Arthur D. Little. *Acquisition and Merger Trends and Their Implications for Corporate Development*. 1978.

2. Brozen, Yale. *Mergers in Perspective*. Washington, D.C.: American Enterprise Institute for Public Policy Research, 1982. pp. 2–3, 60–61, 88.

3. Dewing, Arthur Stone. *The Financial Policy of Corporation*. Vol. 2, New York: The Ronald Press, 1953. p. 882.

4. Federal Trade Commission, Bureau of Economics. *The Brewing Industry*. 1979. pp. 64–65.

5. *Fortune*. May 3, 1982.

6. Hammond, Michael J. *Industrial Concentration and Recent Changes in Government Merger Guidelines*. Unpublished MBA seminar paper, Drexel University, 1983.

7. Kelly, William A., Jr. "A Generalized Interpretation of the Herfindahl Index." *Southern Economic Journal*. July 1981. pp. 50–57.

8. Lavine, A. Lincoln. *Modern Business Law*. Englewood Cliffs, N.J.: Prentice-Hall, 1963. p. 764–765.

9. Lorie, James H. and Paul Halpern. "Conglomerate: The Rhetoric and the Evidence." *Journal of Law and Economics*. April 1970. p. 157.

10. Lynch, Harry H. *Financial Performance of Conglomerates*. Boston: Division of Research, Graduate School of Business, Harvard University, 1971. p. 73.

11. Markham, Jesse. *Conglomerate Enterprise and Public Policy*. Boston: Graduate School of Business Administration, Harvard University, 1983. p. 119.

12. Mueller, Dennis C. "Do We Want a New, Tough Anti-Merger Law?", in Michael Keenan and Lawrence J. White. *Mergers and Acquisitions*. Lexington, Massachusetts: Lexington Books, 1982. pp. 170–173.

13. Steiner, Peter O. *Mergers*. Ann Arbor: University of Michigan Press, 1977. pp. 152–155, 159, 163–171.

14. The *Wall Street Journal*. April 28, 1983; May 26, 1983; June 15, 1982.

15. White, Lawrence J. "Mergers and Aggregate Concentration." in Michael Keenan and Lawrence J. White. *Mergers and Acquisitions*. Lexington, Massachusetts: Lexington Books, 1982. pp. 107–110.

Takeovers

11

Some current wisdom asserts that in the years before 1973 "mergers" was a game reserved for gentlemen. The rules called for personal contacts between the two managements followed by negotiations to devise a mutually beneficial deal. If the negotiations proved fruitful (a process that might take six months or more), ownership rights would then be transferred. The "respectable" corporation would not violate tradition by appealing directly to the stockholders of the acquired firm without reference or prior notice to its management. Tender offers were few in number[4].

Like most Colonel Blimp tales this represents a rather fanciful view of American corporate history. One need only recall some of the rough and tumble tactics accompanying nineteenth century railroad combinations. (To cite an extreme case, Morgan's attempt in 1869 to retain control of the Albany and Susquehanna Railroad actually resorted to physical violence.) Nonetheless, whatever our view of business history, tactics did change after 1973. The 1974–75 bear market and inflation led to very low stock prices which, according to some observers, had companies selling below their intrinsic earning power as well as book values. On the other side, corporate managers were striving to rebuild profit margins and maintain a reputation for growth. The conventions of the game appeared incompatible with these immediate objectives. Under pressure and with the assistance of the investment banking community, a number of corporate managements decided to deal directly with the stockholders of target companies. To induce a positive response, they offered substantial premiums over the low values of the shares sought. The approach became respectable in polite society:

It is no longer the LTV's, Leascos, and other upstart conglomerates that are going after companies for the sake of a quick boost to earnings. It is **195** the likes of Mobil (with its takeover of Marcor), International Paper (General Circle Oil Co.), North American Phillips (Magnavox), and International Nickel (ESB) that are acquiring, usually for long-term reasons[14].

NONNEGO- TIATED TAKEOVERS

In an unfriendly or hostile takeover, the acquisitor bypasses the target company's management in either of two ways: by proxy or by a nonnegotiated tender offer. The former tactic begins by acquiring shares in the target firm on the open market and appealing to the mass of stockholders for their proxies in order to oust the incumbent management. However, statistics show that the "ins" hold the "trump cards" because of their control of company policy and financial resources. Nevertheless, the history of corporate finance contains some dramatic, if costly, proxy contests: Nineteen fifty-four was marked by a struggle for the control of the New York Central Railroad. Robert R. Young and a group of influential friends took on the management headed by William White, the company president. Young's group had personal holdings of 1,118,880 shares or 17.4 percent of the outstanding shares. White's group held 106,000 shares or 1.6 percent of the total outstanding. It was estimated that Young's group spent $500,000 in soliciting proxies. When the results were tallied, Young's group received the vote of 3,407,512 shares (52.9 percent of the total outstanding); White's group received 2,340,237 votes (36.3 percent of the shares outstanding); and 699,659 shares (10.8 percent of the total) were not voted. About 40 percent of Central stock was held under "street" names and over 60 percent of these voted for the Young's group[7].

An interesting study in proxy tactics is provided by the contest for control of Curtiss-Wright. Formed in 1929 through a merger of concerns founded by aviation pioneer, Glen Curtiss, and by Orville and Wilbur Wright, Curtiss Wright became a leading aviation manufacturer. During World War II, the company produced 26,000 airplanes and 143,000 aircraft engines. The company was perhaps the dominant American aircraft-engine producer. However, the company failed to get government funding to develop a jet engine and hard times set in. In 1948, T. Roland Bernier waged a proxy battle blaming management for the corporation's troubles and further charging management with a niggardly dividend policy. Bernier proposed, if elected, to pay a high dividend or have the company buy back half of its shares at a premium price. Either alternative would help defray Bernier's expenses in waging the proxy contest and still leave him in control of Curtiss-Wright. Mr. Bernier lost the proxy battle but won the war. Because of the sizable number of votes cast for his position, he was given a seat on the board and in 1960 became both chairman and president of Curtiss-Wright[16].

The Annual Report of the Securities and Exchange Commission for 1966 recorded thirty-seven proxy contests: twenty-four for control of the boards of directors and thirteen for representation on boards. Of the control contests, the "ins" won ten; the "outs" won six; two were settled by negotiation; and six were in the pending file. Of the thirteen representation cases, six were victorious for the incumbent management; the opposition won in six cases; and one was settled by negotiation. All the same, the opening years of the 1980s witnessed renewed interest in the proxy route to corporate control.

As an alternative to the proxy contest, the acquiring firm might simply buy up enough shares on the open market to secure control or make a tender offer to stockholders to purchase a specified percentage of the outstanding common shares, at a specific price, within a stipulated time period. The tender may consist of a stock consideration, cash or a combination of the two. If the tender is previously negotiated with the target company's management (in some cases a tender may be actually solicited by the target), it represents a friendly takeover. If placed on the table with minimal or no prior notice to the target company's management, it represents a hostile takeover attempt. Exhibit 11–1 lists the number of tender offers for the period 1956–1983.

EXHIBIT 11–1
Number of Inter-Firm Tender Offers
1956–1983

Year	Number
1956	2
1957	0
1958	3
1959	4
1960	7
1961	8
1962	10
1963	21
1964	12
1965	35
1966	45
1967	86
1968	62
1969	49
1970	15
1971	6
1972	29
1973	80
1974	68
1975	71
1976	132
1977	181
1978	166
1979	116
1980	83
1981	123
1982	94
1983	77

Source: Douglas V. Austin and Michael Jackson, "1983 Tender Offers," Paper presented to Eastern Finance Association Annual Meeting (Spring 1984).

Indicative of the switch in merger tactics is the resurgent influence of investment banking houses in promoting corporate combinations. Although suffering a relative decline in power and prestige following World War I and in the Great Depression, the investment banker, throughout his long history, contributed to the growth of large scale enterprise. In the latter half of the nineteenth century,

> a new system often called 'finance capitalism' gradually emerged and became rather typical of the American business scene . . . The moving force behind finance capitalism was the banker, especially the investment banker, and it was his attitude and philosophy that now began to permeate the American business scene . . . his spirit was one of 'live and let live!' Unlike the industrial capitalists, his interests were spread over many businesses rather than specialized in one. He placed dividend payments above plowing back earnings . . . His talents lay more in the direction of reorganizing and consolidating existing business rather than creating and building new ones[8].

Fees and commissions from the sponsorship of business combinations and the sale of securities filled the coffers of the House of Morgan, Drexel and Co., Kidder, Peabody and Co., and their allies in the banking system. Morgan led the group with such combinations as U.S. Steel, General Electric, International Mercantile Marine, Equitable Life Assurance Company, International Harvester, and American Telephone and Telegraph. But more than money motivated investment banking. Sponsoring combinations also meant directorships and in a few instances control.

Investment banking, of course, was never the staid institution pictured in the public mind, and the at times blatant misbehavior of the nineteenth century has given way to more sophisticated conduct. In the computer age, the battle lines are held by analysts (graduates of the nation's leading business schools) led by such luminaries as Felix Rohatyn of Lazard Freres, Robert F. Greenhill of Morgan Stanley, Joseph R. Perella and Bruce Wassertein of First Boston. The aggressive firm in the new mode does not eschew accepting hostile takeover situations or in shopping bids. The latter refers to the practice in which one bidder is told the current high price on the table in an effort to get him to try to top that price—in essence creating an auction market for the client. And the returns are lucrative. The *Wall Street Journal* (December 3, 1982) reported that Merrill Lynch & Co. would collect $250 million in merger fees for 1982; Goldman Sachs about $83 million; and First Boston about $100 million for 1981–82. Exhibit 11–2 reproduces an advertisement of First Boston in *Foreign Affairs* listing their more prominent clients and claiming to be "Number 1 in 1981."

Some play the game more conservatively. For example, with the objective of building a reputation for even handed dealing, Goldman Sachs follows a policy of not shopping bids or taking on the management of any tender offer that is apt to be opposed by the target company management. The firm restricts itself to non-hostile transactions. The honest broker policy also pays off. In 1982, Goldman Sachs acted as a merger adviser in the $4 billion combination of Connecticut General Corporation and INA Corporation and in the $548.2 million merger of Morton-Norwich

EXHIBIT 11–2
Leadership in Mergers and Acquisitions: Number 1 in 1981

Acquiring Companies	Acquired or Divesting Companies	Assignment or Form of Transaction	Approximate Size of Transaction
E. I. du Pont de Nemours and Company	Conoco Inc.	Offer for Cash and Common Stock	$7,570,000,000
United States Steel Corporation	Marathon Oil Company	Cash Tender Offer followed by Merger for Notes	6,264,000,000
Fluor Corporation	St. Joe Minerals Corporation	Cash Tender Offer followed by Merger for Common Stock	2,733,000,000
Freeport-McMoRan Inc.	Freeport Minerals Company; and McMoRan Oil & Gas Co.	Merger for Common Stock	2,540,000,000
Kuwait Petroleum Corporation	Santa Fe International Corporation	Merger for Cash	2,537,000,000
Union Pacific Corporation	Missouri Pacific Corporation	Merger for Common and Preferred Stock	1,000,000,000
Ensource Inc.	Certain Oil and Gas Interests	Common Stock Exchange Offer	625,000,000
CSR Limited	Delhi International Oil Corporation	Cash Tender Offer	610,000,000
Allegheny International, Inc.	Sunbeam Corporation	Cash Tender Offer followed by Merger for Preferred Stock	548,000,000
Sulpetro Limited	St. Joe Minerals Corporation	Divestiture of CanDel Oil Ltd.	460,000,000
The Prudential Insurance Company of America	Bache Group Inc.	Cash Tender Offer	386,000,000
E. I. du Pont de Nemours and Company	New England Nuclear Corporation	Merger for Common Stock	348,000,000
The Prudential Insurance Company of America	Connecticut General Mortgage and Realty Investments	Cash Tender Offer	340,000,000
Allied Corporation	Fisher Scientific Company	Cash Tender Offer followed by Merger for Preferred Stock	320,000,000
Amcon Group, Inc., a Subsidiary of Consolidated Gold Fields Limited	Newmont Mining Corporation	Purchase of 22% Interest	309,000,000
Chemical New York Corporation	Florida National Banks of Florida, Inc.	Merger for Common Stock	291,000,000
Credit and Commerce American Holdings, N.V.	Financial General Bankshares, Inc.	Cash Tender Offer	241,000,000
Brascan U.S.A., Inc., a Subsidiary of Brascan Ltd.	Scott Paper Company	Purchase of 20.5% Interest	235,000,000
M.I.M. Holdings Limited	ASARCO Incorporated	Purchase of 16% Interest	198,000,000
Bucyrus-Erie Company	Western Gear Corporation	Cash Tender Offer	175,000,000
San Cristobal, an affiliate of Scott Paper Company	Grupo San Rafael	Merger for Cash	167,000,000
Liberty National Insurance Holding Company	Continental Investment Corporation	Merger for Cash	166,000,000
Gulf Oil Corporation	Republic Steel Corporation	Sale of 50% Interest in Certain Coal Properties	155,000,000
First Bank System, Inc.	Banks of Iowa, Inc.	Merger for Cash	150,000,000
Ennia N.V.	National Old Line Insurance Company	Merger for Cash	144,000,000
United Canso Oil & Gas Ltd.	Great Basins Petroleum Company	Divestiture of Canadian Oil and Gas Properties	128,000,000
Mercantile Texas Corporation	PanNational Group Inc.	Merger for Common Stock	124,000,000
The St. Paul Companies	City Investing Company	Divestiture of Seaboard Surety Company	85,000,000
Swissair	Loews Corporation	Purchase of Loews Drake Hotel	73,000,000
Argyll Foods Limited	RCA Corporation	Purchase of Oriel Foods Ltd.	70,000,000
Celanese Corporation	Virginia Chemicals, Inc.	Merger for Cash and Common Stock	67,000,000
City Investing Company	GDV, Inc.	Cash Tender Offer	62,000,000
Witco Chemical Corporation	The Richardson Company	Cash Tender Offer	61,000,000
Agfa-Gevaert N.V., a Subsidiary of Bayer AG	Compugraphic Corporation	Cash Tender Offer	60,000,000
Communications Satellite Corporation	Amplica, Inc.	Merger for Cash	57,000,000
The New York Times Company	Cable Systems Incorporated; and Audobon Electronics, Inc.	Mergers for Cash and Notes	55,000,000

EXHIBIT 11–2 continued

Terson Co., 50% owned by C. I. Mortgage Group	Ward Foods, Inc.	Leveraged Buyout	54,000,000
Bank America Corporation	Charles Schwab Corporation	Merger for Common Stock	53,000,000
Hudson Bay Mining and Smelting Co., Limited	Terra Chemicals International, Inc.	Merger for Cash	52,000,000
NuCorp Energy, Inc.; Total Petroleum, Inc.; and Transco Exploration Company	DEPCO, Inc., a Subsidiary of DEKALB AgResearch, Inc.	Sale of Certain Joint Venture Interests in Oil and Gas Leases	45,000,000
Citizens and Southern Georgia Corporation	Citizens and Southern Group banks	Mergers for Cash, Common Stock and Notes	44,000,000
Peoples Energy Corporation	Austin Companies	Purchase of the assets of Austin Drilling Companies	41,000,000
WACI, a corporation organized by management and First Boston	The Wine Group of The Coca-Cola Bottling Company of New York, Inc.	Leveraged Buyout	32,000,000
Carolin Mines Ltd.	Great Basins Petroleum Company	Divestiture of Columbian Northland Exploration Ltd.	30,000,000
Virginia National Bankshares, Inc.	New Virginia Bancorporation	Merger for Cash	30,000,000
Union Pacific Corporation	The Western Pacific Company	Cash Tender Offer followed by Merger for Cash	28,000,000
Kobe Steel, Ltd.	Harnischfeger Corporation	Sale of 10% Interest	26,000,000
The Mitsubishi Bank of California	First National Bank of San Diego County	Merger for Cash	26,000,000
Cipher Data Products, Inc.	Perkin Elmer Corporation	Divestiture of Memory Products Division	20,000,000
Clyde Petroleum plc	City Investing Company	Divestiture of City Petroleum Company and City Exploration Company	Undisclosed
Dobson Park Industries Limited	Marathon Industries, Inc.	Merger for Cash	Undisclosed
Dover Corporation	City Investing Company	Divestiture of Tipper Tie Division	Undisclosed
Jardine, Matheson & Co., Limited	The Prudential Insurance Company of America	Divestiture of Bache Insurance Services, Inc.	Undisclosed
Levingston Industries, Inc.	Sun Company, Inc.	Divestiture of Sun Ship, Inc.	Undisclosed
SIG Swiss Industrial Company	NJM, Inc.	Merger for Cash	Undisclosed
Sun Life Assurance Company of Canada	Massachusetts Financial Services Company	Merger for Cash	Undisclosed

Source: The First Boston Corporation

Products and the Thiokol Corporation. Goldman Sachs represented all four parties.

However, while Goldman Sachs collected $5 million for representing four parties, in the Bendix-Martin Marietta imbroglio, First Boston collected $7 million in fees from Bendix, and Lehman Brothers Kuhn Loeb received $5 million for representing a single client.

The Morton-Norwich Products and the Thiokol Corporation is a good illustration of the Goldman Sachs approach and the pattern of today's investment banking operation.

Goldman Sachs had been assisting Morton-Norwich and Thiokol for over a decade in developing a long-term business strategy. Norwich informed Goldman Sachs of their wish to divest their Norwich Eaton division. Goldman solicited several offers in 1981 from which Morton-Norwich chose Proctor & Gamble Co.'s $371 million bid. Morton then had the problem of how to use the $371 million. Management evidenced an interest in acquiring the Thiokol Corporation's specialty-chemicals business. The combination would make Morton-Norwich an important competitor in a lucrative segment of the chemicals business. Both firms in turn requested Goldman Sachs to represent them in structuring a 'merger of equals' . . . For the purpose, Goldman organized a project team that included Robert H. Conway who had worked closely over the years with Morton-Norwich and Robert J. Hurst who serviced the Thiokol account. Both were Goldman Sachs partners. The final terms involved the formation of Morton Thiokol. Morton-Norwich paid $50 cash for half of Thiokol's stock and exchanged 13,507 shares of Morton-Norwich for each of the remaining Thiokol shares. After the merger, the shares of Morton-Thiokol rose from $32.65 prior to the merger to $53, equivalent to approximately $72 for each Thiokol share exchanged for Morton-Norwich stock[16].

If the first order of business in implementing an acquisition strategy is to set up a merger team, then the second order is to assure the participation of a well-connected investment banking house to identify target companies, devise a bidding strategy, and structure the deal. Some investment banking houses have become so adept at tender offers that success or failure of the offer depends on who retains them first, the acquiring company or the target firm[4,14].

THE CASH TENDER OFFER

As business moved through the 1970s, the cash tender offer gained popularity. Corporations had become more liquid and there was a greater availability of bank loans to finance tender offers. Moreover, as *Business Week* noted:

> With most stocks selling at bargain prices at or below book value, with the dollar continuing to fall against most foreign currencies, and with the climate for corporate investment in physical assets unlikely to improve markedly . . .[3]

the acquisition movement picked up steam. It was cheaper to buy a company for its fixed assets than to build those assets from scratch. For example, Tesoro Petroleum, through a cash tender offer, purchased Commonwealth Oil Refining for $82 million. Commonwealth's properties had a book value of $300 million and an estimated replacement cost exceeding $800 million[3]. Exhibit 11–3 presents the dollar amounts of cash tender offers from 1978 to 1983.

A major appeal of cash tender offers is the speed. Stock swaps may require several months to complete due in part to SEC registration requirements. Negotiated mergers may require up to a year for completion. By contrast, cash tender offers may be consummated in less than three weeks[4].

On the other hand, cash tender offers are not without risk. The buyer receives no contractual protection in the tender purchase of a company. If the bidding company's research and evaluation of the target company is incorrect, the firm may end up shackled to an overpriced white elephant. Also, tender offer bids necessarily include a premium over and

EXHIBIT 11–3

Tender Offer-Cash Offers–Calendar Year

Year	Quarter	Total $ Amount of Tender Offers ($000)
1978	1	1,440,176
	2	2,332,680
	3	2,994,449
	4	3,439,872
1978 Totals		10,157,177
1979	1	1,299,026
	2	1,635,482
	3	2,606,060
	4	3,423,166
1979 Totals		8,963,734
1980	1	1,198,747
	2	1,928,448
	3	3,521,220
	4	1,823,033
1980 Totals		8,471,448
1981	1	4,757,772
	2	17,769,714
	3	52,395,048
	4	14,849,458
1981 Totals		89,771,992
1982	1	2,324,000
	2	9,825,981
	3	9,177,632
	4	4,309,388
1982 Totals		25,637,001
1983	1	1,192,457
	2	4,057,139
	3	1,492,108
	4	2,317,421
1983 Totals		9,059,125

Source: Douglas V. Austin and Michael Jackson. "1983 Tender Offers," Paper presented to Eastern Finance Association Annual Meeting (Spring 1984).

above the market price of the company. This premium may end up higher than the amount that would have been paid in a negotiated transaction[14]. To hedge against some of the inherent risks of a cash tender offer, before making tender bids, corporations frequently purchase stock on the open market to lock up their position. If their tender price is bid up by some other competitor, and the company loses the tender offer, they can still get out ahead of the game by tendering their holdings at the higher bid price. Crane Company did just that in its bidding contest with Arco for control of Anaconda stock. Crane lost the bid but sold its Anaconda stock to Arco and netted $42 million for its efforts[3]. Exhibit 11–4 presents the outcomes of cash tender offers from 1956 to 1983 and Exhibit 11–5 for all tender offers in the same period.

EXHIBIT 11–4
Tender Offer Outcomes—
Cash Tender Offers
1956–1983

Year	Successful No.	Successful %	Partially Successful No.	Partially Successful %	Unsuccessful No.	Unsuccessful %	Combined Successful & Partially Successful No.	Combined Successful & Partially Successful %	Total No.
1956	1	100.0	–	–	–	–	1	100.0	2
1957	–	–	–	–	–	–	–	–	–
1958	1	33.3	1	33.3	1	33.3	2	66.7	3
1959	3	75.0	1	25.0	–	–	4	100.0	4
1960	4	80.0	–	–	1	20.0	4	80.0	5
1961	3	50.0	1	16.7	2	33.3	4	66.7	6
1962	5	62.5	2	25.0	1	12.5	7	87.5	8
1963	16	84.2	1	5.3	2	10.5	17	89.5	19
1964	4	44.4	1	11.1	4	44.4	5	55.5	9
1965	26	83.9	–	–	5	16.1	26	83.9	31
1966	17	58.6	6	20.7	6	20.7	23	79.3	29
1967	45	59.2	11	14.5	20	26.3	56	73.7	76
1968	15	45.4	2	6.1	16	48.5	17	51.5	33
1969	10	52.6	2	10.5	7	36.9	12	63.2	19
1970	6	85.7	–	–	1	14.3	6	85.7	7
1971	1	100.0	–	–	–	–	1	100.0	1
1972	5	45.5	4	36.4	2	18.2	9	81.8	11
1973	32	56.1	16	28.1	9	15.8	48	84.2	57
1974	24	45.3	18	34.0	11	20.7	42	79.3	53
1975	15	60.0	6	24.0	4	16.0	21	84.0	25
1976	58	63.7	17	18.7	16	17.6	75	82.4	91
1977	32	52.5	17	27.9	12	19.8	49	80.4	61
1978	94	68.6	23	16.8	20	14.6	117	85.4	137
1979	76	76.7	7	7.1	16	16.2	83	83.8	99
1980	42	62.7	12	17.9	13	19.4	54	80.6	67
1981	52	53.1	21	21.4	25	25.5	73	74.5	98
1982	44	59.4	13	17.6	17	23.0	57	77.0	74
1983	38	56.7	10	14.9	19	28.4	48	71.6	67*
1956–1983 Totals:	627	58.4	192	17.9	254	23.7	819	76.3	1073
1980–1983 Totals:	176	53.3	56	17.0	98	29.7	232	70.3	330

*Three tender offers are pending or have no information available on their outcome.

Source: Douglas V. Austin and Michael Jackson. "1983 Tender Offers," Paper presented to Eastern Finance Association Annual Meeting (Spring 1984).

EXHIBIT 11–5
Tender Offer Outcomes
1956–1983

Year	Successful No.	Successful %	Partially Successful No.	Partially Successful %	Unsuccessful No.	Unsuccessful %	Combined Successful & Partially Successful No.	Combined Successful & Partially Successful %	Total No.
1956	2	100.0	–	–	–	–	2	100.0	2
1957	–	–	–	–	–	–	–	–	–
1958	1	33.3	1	33.3	1	33.3	2	66.7	3
1959	3	75.0	1	25.0	–	–	4	100.0	4
1960	5	71.4	–	–	2	28.6	5	71.4	7
1961	4	50.0	2	25.0	2	25.0	6	75.0	8
1962	6	60.0	2	20.0	2	20.0	8	80.0	10
1963	18	85.7	1	4.8	2	9.6	19	90.5	21
1964	6	50.0	1	8.3	5	41.7	7	58.3	12
1965	30	85.7	–	–	5	14.3	30	85.7	35
1966	29	64.4	9	20.0	7	15.6	38	84.4	45
1967	53	61.6	11	12.8	22	25.6	64	74.4	86
1968	37	59.7	2	3.2	23	37.1	39	62.9	62
1969	33	67.3	2	4.1	14	28.6	35	71.4	49
1970	13	86.7	–	–	2	1.3	13	86.7	15
1971	6	100.0	–	–	–	–	6	100.0	6
1972	13	65.0	4	20.0	3	15.0	17	85.0	20
1973	31	55.4	16	28.6	9	16.0	47	83.9	56
1974	27	49.1	18	32.7	10	18.2	45	81.8	55
1975	15	60.0	6	24.0	4	16.0	21	84.0	25
1976	63	63.6	18	18.2	18	18.2	81	81.8	99
1977	34	50.7	19	28.3	14	20.9	53	79.1	67
1978	103	68.7	23	15.3	24	16.0	126	84.6	150
1979	81	77.1	7	6.7	17	16.2	88	83.8	105
1980	49	65.3	12	16.0	14	18.7	61	81.3	75
1981	61	52.6	25	21.6	30	25.8	86	74.1	116
1982	49	59.0	13	15.7	21	25.3	62	74.7	83
1983	43	58.1	12	16.2	19	25.7	55	74.3	74*

1956–1983 Totals

	Successful No.	Successful %	Partially Successful No.	Partially Successful %	Unsuccessful No.	Unsuccessful %	Combined No.	Combined %	Total No.
	815	63.2	205	15.9	270	20.9	1020	79.1	1290

1980–1983 Totals:

	Successful No.	Successful %	Partially Successful No.	Partially Successful %	Unsuccessful No.	Unsuccessful %	Combined No.	Combined %	Total No.
	202	58.1	62	17.8	84	24.1	264	75.9	348

*Three tender offers are pending or have no information available on their outcome.

Source: Douglas V. Austin and Michael Jackson. "1983 Tender Offers," Paper presented to Eastern Finance Association Annual Meeting (Spring 1984).

Here the attacker has the upper hand. Since the acquiring firm knows the objective, it generally has time on its side in preparing the assault. The attacking firm can, furthermore, camouflage its intentions, at times up to the point of the actual tender offer. On the other hand, the victim, though it may realize its vulnerability to a takeover, may not be able to discern the direction of the "blitz" and make ready a timely defense. However, once the opening move is made, the aggressor must accomplish the objective expeditiously. The defending management then moves to buy time to arrange a successful counter strategy[11].

Once a buyer settles on a possible takeover target, he usually seeks confirmation of his decision from the investment banker. The latter will undertake an industry and financial statement analysis; review filings with SEC; and, using his contacts, attempt to determine the common stock distribution of the target company. Interest, in this respect, centers on the extent of public ownership, institutional holdings, the existence of concentrations of holdings, and whether or not shareholders are experiencing gains or losses. Such data are essential to an estimate of the price at which shareholders will likely offer their stock.

PICKING THE TARGET

The tender price comprises two elements: the present market value of the stock plus a premium to attract the requisite number of shares to assure control. The decision on tender price not only determines the success or failure of the takeover effort but also has a definite bearing on the profitability or unprofitability of the enterprise after the combination. Raymond S. Troubh suggests that:

SETTING THE TENDER PRICE

> . . . a fair bench mark starting premium over the norm price is 20 percent to 40 percent. The lower the market price the higher the premium required. Moreover, if a battle for control is anticipated, the premium must be set high enough to attract shares. On the other hand, if the target company is attractive enough to merit competitive bids, the offeror should have a reserve so that he can top other bids. Also, a reserve will allow him to raise the initial offer in order to meet the target company's usual defense that the offer is inadequate. Several of the major tender offer battles of 1975— involving Otis Elevator Co, Gorlock, American Chain & Cable Co., and Commonwealth Oil Refining Company—were won by an increase in the original offer of $2 to $3 per share[14].

The limit to the size of the premium is determined by the parameters of the bargaining area described in Chapter 5. A premium that takes the tender price above the maximum exchange ratio of the acquiring company reduces the wealth position of its shareholders.

Before making the tender offer public, the aggressor company may judge that the target company's management is not all that hostile but simply holding out for a higher price and will bend under pressure. The aggressor may therefore seek to feel out the target as to how receptive it would be to a tender offer. This type of approach has been called a "teddy bear

SHOULD FOREWARNING BE GIVEN?

EXHIBIT 11–6
Glossary of Takeover Terminology

Arbitrageurs—Dealers who purchase large quantities of the target firm's stock at prices below the tender offer. They can sell the stock to the raider at the tender offer plus a fee for their services, or to a rival bidder if one should appear.

Bear Hug—A public or private takeover proposal to induce the board of the target company to act quickly. Frequently, the acquiring firm secures a large position in the target firm's stock before applying the bear hug. This forms a hedge against other bids. If higher bids are made by other aggressors, the initial acquirer may simply sell his stock at a profit.

Fair Price Clauses—Amendments to the corporate charter that require a raider to pay an equivalent price for all shares. A defense against two-tier offers.

Golden Parachutes—Agreements between potential target firms and their managements which protect the latter in the event of a change in control. Usually provide generous compensation if a manager is displaced by the acquiring firm or decides to opt out of the new situation. Increases the cost of a takeover and may threaten the acquiring firm with the loss of top management personnel in the target corporation.

Gray Knight—An unsolicited second bidder seeking to take advantage of troubles between the target firm and the first bidder.

Leveraged Buyout—A defense against a hostile takeover. A friendly group, frequently including the management of the target firm, puts up a small amount of money and uses the company's assets as collateral for loans to finance the purchase of the target firm's stock. If the hostile takeover is defeated, the target firm's cash flow will then be used to pay off the debt.

Pac-Man Defense—Target firm retaliates against a hostile tender offer by making a counter bid for the stock of the raider.

Poison Pill—To defeat a hostile tender offer, the target firm may declare a stock dividend in convertible preferred stock to the existing shareholders. In the event the hostile tender offer succeeds, the preferred automatically becomes the preferred of the surviving company and convertible into that company's voting stock. Conversion then dilutes the control position of the shark. The threat may defeat the tender offer.

Saturday Night Special—A direct tender offer, placed on the table without warning, and expiring within a week. Usually made on a Friday with the intention of inducing shareholders to unload their stock on the next business day. Subject to provisions of the Hart-Scott-Rodino Act and State laws.

Shark Repellants—Charter amendments to make more difficult the task of raiders. These include: staggered directorships, supermajorities for approval of a merger, changing state of incorporation.

Show Stopper—A defensive maneuver by the target company that completely stops a takeover attempt.

Smoking Gun—An offense mistake by the raider that gives the target firm's management time to shore up its defenses.

Two-Tier or Front-End Loaded Tender Offer—Raider offers a generous cash bid for a controlling share of the target's stock and a lower amount—usually in stock or debentures—for the remaining shares. The objective is to induce the shareholders to tender their shares post haste.

White Knight—A friendly firm brought in by the target to help fend off another bidder.

Sources: Business Week, May 16, 1977; The *Wall Street Journal*, sundry issues.

pat." The target company is informed by letter that the aggressor is prepared to make an offer. No price is mentioned in the letter, thereby avoiding any requirement by the SEC that a public announcement of the tender offer be made. This action lets the target know that the aggressor is serious, yet leaves open the possibility of negotiating a friendly deal. When it is clear that a friendly acquisition is impossible, the raider resorts to a "bear hug." Unlike the pat, the bear hug includes a specific price. The hope, more often forlorn, is that the target's board will endorse the order. Ordinarily, however, the target sues[5].

Harry Gray, the Chairman of United Technologies, used the bear pat and bear hug techniques in his effort to acquire Babcock and Wilcox:

> . . . That episode began with his (Gray) decision to buy a maker of steam generators. The first choice was Combustion Engineering. In 1975 and 1976 Gray tried to persuade Arthur Santry of Combustion to merge with United, but Santry wasn't interested. Gray concluded that a hostile offer for Combustion (its code name at United was "Alpha") was beyond his means, and he began looking elsewhere.

> In December, 1976, Paul Hallingby, the chairman of White Weld, suggested that United go after Babcock (code name "Gamma"). By February of last year, Gray had decided to make an offer. He met twice with Babcock's chairman, George Zipf, but Zipf wasn't any more accommodating than Santry had been. Babcock, however, appeared affordable. On the afternoon of March 28, Gray called Zipf in New York to tell him that a helicopter was on its way from Hartford and that on it was a letter offering to buy the company.

> Babcock responded to this "bear hug" by suing United in federal court and complaining to the Ohio securities commissioner. While United was clearing those hurdles, J. Ray McDermott bought up 9.9 percent of Babcock's stock on the open market and said it was entering the bidding. In the ensuing contest, United went all the way from its initial price of $42 a share to $59.75, but lost to McDermott's offer of $65. (The stock had been in the mid-thirties before United's first offer.)

> There was a lot of speculation afterward that Gray had let himself get caught up in the auctionroom atmosphere of the contest and bid higher than he had intended. Not so, says Gray. A Kidder, Peabody analysis of the steam-generator industry—that hinged on President Carter's ambitious plans for coal—persuaded Gray that Babcock was worth $60 a share. Given the likely dismal fate of Carter's energy bill, Gray is a happy loser[5].

The Gray episode illustrates how a bidding war pushes up the premium on a tender offer. It also suggests if the buying firm suspects that its advances may not be welcomed by the target company it should not disclose its plans until a public announcement is ready[4]. Exhibit 11–6 presents a glossary of takeover terminology.

MAKING THE PUBLIC TENDER ANNOUNCEMENT

The day of reckoning comes when the aggressor company makes the public announcement of its tender offer. If all preparations have been conducted properly and fortune smiles, news of the tender offer can come as a surprise to the target company's board of directors. Normally a tender offer is only open ten to fourteen days and as such gives the unsuspecting and unprepared management little time to mount a counter offensive. The Williams Act and New York Stock Exchange rules require tender offers be open at least ten days[14].

The number of shares that are normally solicited in a tender will vary. Obviously 51 percent gives a controlling interest; but in companies where no shareholder has a significant stock position, the required number may be reduced to approximately 40 percent, thereby lowering the overall cost of the tender[14].

The success of the tender offer also pivots on how quickly the offer is transmitted to the shareholders. The task is simplified if the aggressor has a copy of the shareholder list. Where this is not the case, the offer is transmitted via a news release. Here the public relations expert can make a significant contribution. His presentation has a carrot and stick aspect. The presentation to the shareholders stresses the fairness of the tender offer; but, should the tender be successful, those left holding the stock may find the stock delisted and/or dividends reduced or eliminated.

If the company is fortunate to obtain a shareholder list, it usually turns over the list to regional brokerage houses to solicit the equity owners on behalf of the acquiring company. For this service, the soliciting broker receives a fee of approximately 2 percent of the purchase price in addition to the normal commission[14].

Arbitrage dealers can affect the prospects of a tender offer. These dealers traditionally attempt to profit by a price spread in a security between two markets or between related securities. In a merger situation, arbitrageurs may scent a profit opportunity by interjecting themselves as intermediaries between the offeror and the target's shareowners; that is, by entering bids at levels somewhere between the pretender market price and the tender price.

The exact bid by the arbitrageurs depends upon their assessment of the offer's prospects for success; normally, the greater the certainty the higher the bid. When the arbitrage bid lies close to the tender price, it will attract shares from investors unwilling to risk snags (such as, legal intervention or proration) that lie in the path of the tender offer. Arbitrageurs take the shares thus accumulated and tender them to the buying firm at the tender price (plus any soliciting fees they may attach).

For example, assume an aggressor firm has announced a $20 tender offer for a stock with a market value of $14. An arbitrage house could pay as much as $20 and still profit, provided two things happen: (a) It receives a solicitation fee of $.50 or thereabouts per share; (b) The offer goes forward without interruption. Under these circumstances, the house would realize a minimum gross profit on investment of approximately 65 percent on an annualized rate ($[.50 \div 20] \times 26$). If the shares could be obtained for $18 or $19 and tendered for $20, or if the offer should be contested and a bidding war set off, arbitrage profits would rise accordingly. However, if the offer should fail, the price of the target shares can tumble and the arbitrageur may incur substantial losses. On this note, when the Gulf Oil Corp. abruptly ended a $4.8 billion bid for Cities Service Co., arbitrage dealers faced the possibility of sustaining an all-time high loss on a single stock. The dealers had tendered about fifteen million shares of Cities Service stock, acquired at an average cost of $53, for the $63 tender price. Gulf's offer ran into antitrust problems and the company withdrew the bid. Cities Services stock fell to $37.25 with a predicted drop to $28. The latter left risk arbitrageurs with a potential $400 million loss[14,16].

Risk arbitrageurs also lost in the Burlington-Northern takeover of El Paso. Burlington originally placed a hostile tender of $24 per share of El Paso on the table. The tender sought 25.1 million shares of El Paso (a 51 percent stake) by December 30, 1982, the proration deadline. The tender largely achieved its objective. However, Burlinton then did an about face and entered into negotiations with the El Paso management. As a result, Burlington signed a peace agreement with El Paso ten days later, terminated the original tender, and substituted a new tender that sought only twenty-one million shares at $24. The new offer was anticipated to draw 80 percent of El Paso's fifty million shares, since it now enjoyed the support of the El Paso management. The arbitrageurs, therefore, faced the prospect of having almost half of their accumulated shares returned[16].

DEFENSIVE STRATEGIES

In a business environment in which the hostile takeover has become an acceptable mode of behavior, it is as important to have a defensive strategy as it is to have an acquisition strategy. Similarly, a defensive strategy cannot be formulated on an *ad hoc* basis when the need arises. A defensive strategy requires an objective examination of your relationships. How do you stand with your shareholders? With large institutional holders? With security analysts who will recommend the stock for sale or retention? With the people who will influence the decisions of others?

How much support is in reserve for you in the communities where you live and work? Will they view your action as a threat, or as a welcomed development? How about the media, which are potentially your primary means not only of extending your message, but of influencing others through their editorial stands? Will they support you, or will the tone of their coverage be negative? This can be very, very important.

Then there are third parties that one does not normally think about: how will they react? For example, how will the union—or unions—view your proposed action? Will they fight for, or against, a takeover? Or will they sit and do nothing, which might be worse[13]?

Steps in the preparation of a defensive strategy include:

1. *Determining the Vulnerability of the Company to a Hostile Takeover:* The company should analyze its position to see if it exhibits those characteristics most looked for by aggressor companies. The most important of these include: undervalued assets, highly liquid financial condition, unused borrowing capacity, limited insider control, limited total market value, book value per share greater than the market value per share, and low price earnings ratio. Peter F. Drucker in The *Wall Street Journal* (January 5,

1983) indicates the strong, prosperous, medium-sized company, with sales of $75 million to $400 million, and excellent long-range growth prospects stands the greatest liability of a takeover attempt.

A survey of seventy takeover targets by *Barron's* in 1978 drew a corporate profile likely to attract an aggressor firm:

- Total assets of the target averaged $250 million.
- Annual sales averaged $260 million.
- Seven out of ten firms had a current ratio of 2-to-1 or better.
- Forty percent of the targets had cash and cash equivalents equal to 10 percent of total assets.
- In thirty-seven of the seventy cases, profits had risen by 25 percent in their latest fiscal year.
- Growth rates for forty-eight of the seventy companies exceeded the 12.3 percent five year average rate of growth for the Standard and Poor's 400 Stock Index.
- The return on equity for the target group also exceeded the S & P Index, 16.2 percent to 14 percent.
- A "good-fit" or the opportunity to diversify also lured the aggressor.
- For most target companies, market values per share exceeded book values per share (contrary to the conventional wisdom).
- P/E multiples of the targets were only slightly higher than the average for the market.
- Ninety percent of the targets had fewer than ten million shares outstanding; in other cases, a considerable amount of the stock was held by family interests, management, and directors.
- Once holders of a substantial number of shares accepted the offer, the remainder tended to follow[9].

The attractiveness of a particular corporate profile varies, of course, with time and circumstance. The business cycle, antitrust attitudes, tax legislation, technological trends, fiscal and monetary policy, and so on— all operate to shape the opinion of the acquiring firm regarding an appropriate acquisition.

2. *Setting Up a Defense Team:* If a hostile takeover attempt appears in prospect somewhere down the road, the firm should move now to set up a defensive team. This unit normally includes key officers of the firm, the firm's accountants and lawyers, the investment banker, and the firm's public relations counsel. The latter, frequently ignored in the formulation of acquisition and defensive strategies, has in reality a vital role in achieving the corporate objective.

A defensive strategy necessarily covers a broad front. The economic and legal issues inherent in the situation must be interpreted in a light favorable to the firm under attack. There is a selling job to be done to: hold the local community in line, cultivate worker and stockholder support, win the favor of local politicos and their colleagues in Washington, and handle the media. Such tasks fall in the purview of public relations. Moreover, the firm's relations with these constituencies are matters of long-term interest. A firm, which has ignored the wider ramifications of the enterprise, may find it has few supporters in time of need. The defensive team needs to inventory all assets that will affect public opinion and, as an ongoing project, move positively to condition public opinion[13].

To maintain an alert defensive posture, many firms construct a "black book" which contains a checklist of items comprising the defensive strategy, directories and reference material, and the firm's contacts with key personages and groups[4].

3. *Know Thy Stockholders:* Since the fate of the company, in the event of a tender offer, lies in the hands of the stockholders, it is essential for the target company's management to know the characteristics of its stockholding family. Stockholder lists and transfer sheets provide significant information. Reviewing these data on a regular basis keeps management informed as to: who owns the stock, the price of which the stock was purchased, and what kinds of activity and changes of ownership are occurring. In this respect, a distribution of stock purchase prices gives management some insight as to the probability of the shareholders accepting a tender offer. Exhibit 11–7 presents pertinent information on the IBM stockholder profile.

Also, if a growing proportion of the stock is registered under street names management has cause for concern on two counts: one, there may be an unknown buyer building up holdings in anticipation of a tender offer; two, the company management will be less able to communicate its side of the story in the event of a tender[12].

EXHIBIT 11–7

Who Owns IBM:

Type of stockholder	Number of accounts	Number of shares	Percent of total shares
Men	149,845	47,831,008	8.2
Women	172,090	52,896,711	9.1
Joint tenants	107,308	11,723,587	2.0
Fiduciaries	112,122	19,998,398	3.4
Brokers	800	52,044,493	8.9
Bank nominees	3,289	339,029,485	58.1
Partnerships and corporations	4,447	13,804,421	2.4
Insurance companies	563	7,926,239	1.3
Investment organizations	729	512,816	.1
Banks and trust companies	227	6,646,003	1.1
Other organizations and associations	9,865	9,807,011	1.7
Employees and directors	145,446	21,354,609	3.7
Scrip	—	4,551	—
Totals	706,731	583,579,332	100.0

Capital stock as of the record date for the Annual Meeting, March 10, 1980.

Source: *Report to IBM Stockholders.* Annual Meeting, April 28, 1980.

Large institutional holdings of the firm's stock represents another problem for management. Institutional investors tend to hold the stock for short-term profit and appeals by management may fall on deaf ears when these investors are confronted with a premium tender offer.

A company can shore up the stockholder defenses by keeping its lines of communication to shareholders open—telling the shareholder what is happening and why. The management can, in addition, encourage investment by friends; that is, by employees, directors, and officers. Along these lines, the executive stock option plan may prove a valuable asset in fending off an aggressor:

> . . . Hi-Shear Corp. is a Los Angeles maker of fasteners that has been fighting off a tender offer by one Frank A. Klaus for many months. The battle, raging both in the marketplace and in the courts, was nip and tuck until January, when the company quietly announced that two officers and eleven employees had exercised options representing 39,000 common shares. In most tender offers, 39,000 shares would not be nearly enough to tip the scales. But for Hi-Shear and others, the ploy apparently paid off. In the showdown at the annual meeting, management tallied 51 percent of the vote, the Klaus slate a frustrating 49 percent[11].

Similarly, company pension plans, profit sharing, thrift plans, and employee stock ownership programs are possible allies in the battle. A useful device in this category is the employee stock ownership trust (ESOT). The trust holds stock of the firm for the employees but the shares are voted on by the company. Initially conceived as tax shelter and financing strategems, ESOT plans have become defensive weapons in takeover battles. If the management can tell an aggressor that 40 percent or more of the stock is tied up in an ESOT, a takeover battle may be aborted.

4. *Legal Defense:* Both the Federal securities law and antitrust legislation provide defenses in the event of a hostile takeover attempt. These were discussed in greater detail in Chapter 10. The present discussion relates to the requirements bearing on tender offers.

It was not until 1968 that Congress moved to regulate tender offers. As amended in 1970, the Williams Act requires that anyone who intends to make a tender offer that would produce personal ownership of more than 5 percent of the outstanding stock of a target company to provide the SEC with a statement (Schedule 130) disclosing: the purchaser's identity, the source and amount of funds for the purchase (including details about borrowings), the purpose for which the purchase is being made, the number of shares the purchaser owns, and details on any arrangements the would-be purchaser has made with others with respect to the acquired stock. Further, the statute requires persons making recommendations to security holders of target firms with regard to the acceptance of tender offers to file an information statement with the SEC (Schedule 14D).

The Anti-Trust Premerger Notification Act of 1977 (Hart-Scott-Rodino Act) provides the Justice Department and the FTC, which share enforcement responsibility for the Clayton Act, with the authority to challenge proposed mergers that "may substantially lessen competition," before they are completed. The Act requires that certain major acquisitions by

tender offer be delayed for a fifteen-day waiting period to permit the
government to examine the antitrust implications of the proposed merger.
The waiting period may be extended by the departments for an additional
ten days. The law affects companies of $100 million or more in sales or
assets that expect to merge with companies of $10 million or more in sales
or assets.

> Gulf Oil Corporation entered a $4.8 billion bid for Cities Service Co. The
> acquisition would have been the third largest takeover in U.S. business
> history. The FTC objected to the merger on the grounds it would adversely
> affect competition. Rather than make the adjustments stipulated by the
> FTC, Gulf withdrew the $63 per share tender offer[16].

> The Justice Department challenged on antitrust grounds the proposed
> acquisition of Pabst Brewing Co. by a company controlled by Irwin L.
> Jacobs, a Minneapolis investor. The Jacobs group made an unwelcome
> tender for all of Pabst's shares; the offer paid $22 per share if Pabst completed
> the acquisition of Olympia Brewing Co. and $24 a share if Pabst called off
> the transaction. The Justice Department felt that Pabst might not remain
> a viable competitor in the Western states after the merger. A federal district
> court issued a temporary restraining order[16].

In addition to Federal legislation, over half of the states (twenty-nine as
of July 1, 1977) have enacted takeover laws to improve the protection
afforded local stockholders by the Williams Act. These individual statutes
differ from one another and from the federal approach in various respects.
Some make provisions for lengthy "cooling-off" periods; others, for hearings by state examiners—procedures without parallels under the Williams
Act. Under the New York statute, for instance, an offeror must file disclosure information with the state's attorney general. This information is
filed twenty days before an offer for 5 percent or more of the stock of a
company either incorporated or having its principal place of business or
substantial assets in the state can be made. The attorney general may
schedule hearings and, under certain circumstances, may even require the
bidder to discontinue the offer[4].

The likelihood of FTC or Justice Department (DOJ) intervention
in a proposed merger correlates in some degree to the prevailing mood in
Congress. Hence, the defending firm must not only be aware of the nuances
in dealing with FTC or DOJ but also properly read the temper of Congress.
The following proposals regarding mergers reflect a growing annoyance
with hostile tenders in the Ninety-Seventh Congress:

- H.R.4145—*Foreign Takeovers:* would eliminate the advantage to foreign purchases of securities by extending the margin requirements to foreign securities purchases.
- H.R.5517—Would deny a tax deduction for interest on indebtedness incurred
  to finance corporate acquisitions.
- H.R.6604—*Tax Motivated Takeovers:* would (a) prevent filing consolidated
  tax returns by affiliates for the first three years of affiliation; (b) require
  gains in liquidation of large corporations acquired by other large corporations to be taxed as sales; (c) extend from twelve to fourteen months the
  required holding period for nonrecognition of gains or losses on stock redeemed
  by distribution of appreciated property.

- S.2547—*Gains Resulting from Corporate Mergers:* would (a) require an acquiring corporation to assume liability for recapture of excess depreciation and tax credits of a target corporation; (b) require recognition of gains or losses in mergers by stock redeemed by distribution of appreciated property.
- H.R.5719—*Merger Tax Act:* imposes an excise tax of 15 percent of the consideration paid in corporate acquisitions involving a corporation whose gross receipts exceed $2 billion in the taxable year preceding the acquisition.
- H.R.6605—Imposes a tax surcharge equal to one percent of annual gross income of the acquiring firm and the target(s) in the year following acquisition.
- S.1925—Imposes a ten-year moratorium on acquisitions or control of oil industry companies or their assets by a major producer.
- H.R.4409—*General Moratorium on Corporate Mergers:* prohibits both mergers of two corporations with $350 million in annual assets and sales and mergers involving one corporation with $350 million in assets or sales and another company that has 20 percent or more of sales in any significant market.
- H.R.3310—*National Foreign Investment Control Commission:* establish a comprehensive scheme of Federal regulation of national foreign investment by the establishment of a National Foreign Investment Control Commission to review and approve foreign investment in a broad range of U.S. industries.

Most of these bills will not make it through the legislative process but they measure the political repercussions of widely publicized merger battles, such as Mobil's attempt to takeover Marathon Oil and the Bendix-Martin Marietta fiasco.

In short, the target company has legal defenses to fend off an aggressor but the use of these weapons requires personnel experienced in the ways of the FTC and the DOJ plus a large dose of Congressional savvy. Washington will not likely come out in favor of virtue without the reward of political advantage.

5. *Implementing Precautionary Measures:* The target company has the option of implementing various precautionary measures. Some of these tactics may not necessarily prevent a tender offer from taking place but may delay the tender-completion date, thereby giving the target needed time to get its story out to the stockholders, mount a counter-offense, or find a higher and friendlier bidder for the company.

Reincorporating in states that have enacted takeover statutes may be a useful delaying tactic. Whereas the Williams Act requires that a tender remain open ten days, some states' statutes may require as much as sixty days. Many of these statutes have been designed to protect local corporations from outside tender offers and as such they protect incumbent management by forestalling takeovers. Their constitutionality, however, is being tested in the courts because it is argued that they are preempted by the Williams Act. The intent of the Williams Act was that tender offers be settled in the marketplace. In any event, while the lawyers argue the target firm gains time[2].

Another precautionary measure would change the bylaws of the corporation to require a supermajority (for instance 70 percent) of stockholders to approve a merger. This tactic lowers the risk of a takeover but may restrict the present management from implementing an acquisition strategy[4].

Other impediments which can be effective involve: (a) instituting complex succession requirements for the board of directors whereby it may take a raider two or three years to get his people on the board; (b) use of restrictive covenants written in loan agreements making the note due and payable in the event of a merger. Again these tactics may discourage an aggressor but tie the hands of the company in other situations. Finally, the target company may keep a list of friendly companies to acquire in the event of a hostile tender offer. Acquiring a small company in an industry comparable to the aggressor's industry could provide a basis for enjoining the takeover as detrimental to competition[4].

6. *Responding to a Tender Offer:* Following announcement of an unfriendly tender, the target firm should focus on three principal considerations: price, the bidder's intentions regarding the future of the business, and the treatment of shareholders who refuse the tender. We may assume that in pondering these matters management will not ignore the issue of self-preservation. Assuming, however, that management acts primarily to foster interests of the shareholders, the target has three options:

- Accept the offer.
- Remain neutral and allow the shareholders to decide the issue.
- Fight the tender and urge the shareholders to retain their shares.

The target may choose to fight the takeover in principle or simply because the management believes the offering price is too low. Apropos of the latter, the fact of a tender offer *per se* may induce the management of the target firm to reassess the values of the company. The tender offer tells the world that the firm is currently undervalued or at least that its value can be substantially enhanced by association with another organization. In this event, the target firm may attempt to negotiate a higher price with the aggressor or shop around for another bidder (the White Knight). While shopping around for a White Knight, the target firm also moves to gain time using the tactics discussed in the preceding paragraphs. The Bendix Corp.'s unfriendly offer for Martin-Marietta Corp. illustrates how a tender offer, met with a determined defense, can set in motion consequences unintended by the participants.

In August 1982, Bendix Corp. announced a $43 per share bid for Martin-Marietta shares. Mr. Agee, president of Bendix, attempted to call Mr. Pownall, president of Martin-Marietta, prior to the announcement of the tender but Pownall sensed the purpose of the call and refused to accept it. Actually, Mr. Agee had picked a target headed by a man determined to keep Martin-Marietta independent and especially out of the hands of Mr. Agee.

Backed by a strong cash position and a line of credit, Mr. Agee upped his bid to $48 per share fearing that the initial tender would not attract a sufficient number of Martin-Marietta shares. Mr. Agee had now put himself in the position of bidding against his original tender.

In due course Bendix acquired 70 percent of Marietta's shares. Believing turnabout to be fair play, Martin-Marietta offered to purchase Bendix stock at $75 per share before Agee could move to oust the Marietta board. Marietta eventually acquired nearly half the Bendix stock.* The antagonists now faced a stalemate and a time consuming series of court battles.

Representatives of both companies then attempted to fashion a negotiated settlement. The session failed on the intransigent position of Marietta and another Agee blunder. At an October meeting, Mr. Agee brought one Mary Cunningham (a former Bendix officer and current executive at Seagram Co.) along as an adviser. The breach of protocol rather upset the Marietta team.

Kidder, Peabody & Co. represented Martin-Marietta in the struggle which now pulled into its vortex outside parties. Mr. Pownall induced United Technologies to initiate a rival takeover bid aimed at Bendix—a variation of the White Knight strategy. Mr. Gray, president of United Technologies, saw in Bendix the opportunity to make United a $20 billion conglomerate and gain $100 million cash with little risk. United Technologies offered $75 a share for 50.3 percent of Bendix (11.9 million shares), buying to commence on September 28. Mr. Agee now had two determined opponents, Mr. Gray and Mr. Pownall.

Before the Marietta tender for Bendix became effective, however, the Allied Corp. agreed to purchase Bendix for $1.9 billion in cash and stock. Allied would pay $85 per share for 51 percent (13.1 million shares) of Bendix and swap 1.3 Allied shares for each remaining Bendix share plus $27.50 in Allied convertible securities. Agee would become president of Allied and retain his position with Bendix. The Allied-Bendix agreement included a separate pact covering the possible sale by Bendix to Allied of Bendix's aerospace electronics group for $800 million in cash plus liabilities. This would further discourage Marietta's pursuit of Bendix.

If Mr. Agee had agreed to the Allied proposition a day earlier, the Marietta purchase of Bendix stock would have been held up under Federal law for ten days—giving Bendix some breathing time. Agee missed the deadline and in his haste to force quick approval of the Allied proposition by the Bendix board, four directors resigned: William P. Tavoulareas, president of Mobil Corp.; Wilbur J. Cohen; Donald H. Rumsfeld; Hugo E. R. Uyterhoeven.

On the other hand, Marietta was dealt an earlier blow when Citibank, acting as trustree for the Bendix Salaried Employee Stock Ownership and Savings Plan, withdrew the 4,479,000 Bendix shares previously tendered to Marietta. This left Marietta with 13,288,912 shares of Bendix in its pool. Marietta announced it would purchase all remaining shares in its pool despite the Allied offer[16].

At this point, the reader might justifiably ask who stayed at home to run business. Ego trips and "dirty tricks" seemed to abound although all sides claimed some justifying corporate purpose for joining the struggle.

---

*The purchase of the aggressor's stock by the acquiring company or the issuance of securities convertible into the stock of the target firm is referred to as the poison pill strategy. Its execution either leaves the target with little cash and large debt or dilutes the target's common stock.

Mr. Agee apparently sought to build Bendix into a high technology enterprise through acquisitions. United saw an opportunity for quick growth in size and increased cash holdings. Marietta put a high premium on independence. Allied, after several acquisition attempts, sought to redeem its reputation as a worthy suitor. Some of the side events included:

- A Bendix move against its own employees. Twenty-three percent of the outstanding Bendix shares (4.5 million shares) were held by the Bendix Salaried Employee Stock Ownership and Savings Plan under the trusteeship of Citibank. Citibank, acting in its fiduciary capacity, tendered the stock to Marietta at the latter's $75 offering price. Bendix ordered Citibank to withdraw the stock unless it had specific authorization from the employee to place his stock in the Marietta pool. Mr. Agee then sent a letter to each employee warning that tendering the stock to Marietta would cause mandatory cessation of contributions to the ownership and savings plan for six months.
- Marietta charged coercion of the employees and sued Bendix.
- Marietta informed the Department of Defense that a takeover by Bendix would not be in the national interest. It also informed key members of Congress along the same lines. DOJ responded with a letter to Bendix and Marietta that it neither supported nor opposed the takeover. This actually improved the Bendix position.
- Bendix's law firm of Hughes Hubbard and Reed hired investigators to monitor the activities of United Technologies and Mr. Gray. Nothing seamy was apparently found.
- Bendix moved to change its by-laws to repel a takeover by either United or Marietta.
- Bendix sent its story to shareholders on September 9 but wouldn't show a list of Bendix shareholders to Georgeson & Co. (United's proxy solicitor) until September 10. On that date, Bendix only allowed Georgeson to photograph the list made up of 10,000 pages with three names per page.
- Edward L. Hennessy, Jr., chairman of Allied Corp., was given a tailor made situation to "gain a measure of revenge" on his old boss, Mr. Gray of United Technologies[16].

It is not possible at this writing to total the financial losses to the antagonists and the political losses to the business community. Some kind of Congressional action appears almost certain to result from this less than edifying display of takeover tactics. Yet, while bloody battles make the headlines, the Bendix-Allied v. Marietta-United encounter is not typical of merger activity. W. T. Grimm & Co. counted 2,395 acquisitions and divestitures in 1981 and 2,346 in 1982. Of these, there were seventy-five tender offers for publicly traded companies in 1982 and sixty-eight in 1981. Of the tender offers, twenty-nine were contested in 1982 and twenty-eight in 1981[16].

Tender offers fail, but even in failure there may be gains to the target company. In a sample of ninety-seven unsuccessful tender offers, target stockholders realized an average capital gain of 45 percent. The average post-offer return exceeded the average premium of these rejected offers by 29 percent[1]. These data would indicate that target managers may be acting in the interests of their stockholders by opposing a tender when they believe a higher bid could be obtained or higher valuation placed on the firm by the disclosure of information.

Conversely, Bradley reports negative returns to the unsuccessful bidder. Out-of-pocket expenditures can be substantial; for example, ninety-seven unsuccessful bids represented an average cash liability of about $90 million. In addition, the unsuccessful bidder may suffer loss of prestige, gain a reputation as an undesirable suitor, and experience a decline in the market value of its shares.

7. *Protecting Management:* Under the best of circumstances, a takeover, whether friendly or hostile, creates a period of uncertainty for the incumbent management. The acquiring company may choose to place its team at the helm or eliminate redundant positions altogether. Executives of acquired companies who do not lose their jobs may nevertheless find themselves in a new corporate environment with diminished responsibilities and few prospects of advancement. Companies that appear to be good prospects for a takeover, therefore, may find themselves losing quality managers and/or unable to recruit qualified personnel before an actual takeover is even attempted.

To allay the fears of management—usually top management—many firms have resorted to "golden parachute" contracts. These become operative when there is a change in control of the company. If, as a result of the change of control, the executive is fired without cause or suffers diminished responsibilities, the contract guarantees him a specified number of years of salary and other benefits. "Golden parachute" settlements are payable by the acquired company. About 15 percent of the 1000 largest U.S. corporations have instituted "golden parachute" contracts[15,16].

The agreement may take two forms: a "sweetheart contract" with very liberal walk away provisions far exceeding what the executive earned in the past; or a contract setting the amount of compensation and benefits at a level the executive could reasonably expect to receive in the absence of a change of control.

Not unnaturally the appearance of "golden parachute" agreements has stirred some controversy and at least one law suit. The advocates of the approach argue the following advantages:

- •Desirable takeover targets are able to hire and retain capable managers.
- Takeover offers that do materialize can be weighed dispassionately by management and not automatically opposed without regard to the interests of the stockholders.
- The acquiring company also has a mutual interest with the target firm in assuring continuity of management during the transaction period. The acquiring firm certainly does not wish to inherit a corporate shell devoid of key management personnel.

Critics, on the other hand, contend that "golden parachute" agreements:

- Do not always assume dispassionate examination of tender offers and negotiations in the stockholders interest. For example, all participants in the Bendix-Martin-Marietta match were protected by "golden parachutes." Mr. Agee of Bendix for one was guaranteed $4,020,000 if worse came to worst. The Bendix parachute, packed in the midst of battle, covered sixteen executives with a potential total liability of $15.7 million[10].

EXHIBIT 11–8
Employment Agreements:
Principal Policy Decisions to be Made

1. Term of agreements

   a. Should term run from date of execution or date of change in control?
   b. Length of term: 5 years? 10 years? Less? More?
   c. Age cutoff: 55, 60, 65?
   d. Should the term be extended annually by an evergreen provision that would automatically extend the term each year unless notice not to extend is given?

2. Effective date of agreement

   a. Should agreement take effect immediately or on change in control?
   b. The term "change in control" must be defined—how many shares of stock would be required to change hands or how many new directors would be required to replace present directors over what period of time?

3. Employment commitment

   a. Should the company be obligated to continue to employ the executive in no lesser a position than his present position with present title(s) and responsibilities, or only to employ him in a "senior-executive capacity" (that could leave open the possibility of demotion)?
   b. Should the agreements provide that the executive is to continue on the Board of Directors, with failure to reelect the executive to the Board constituting a breach of the agreement by the company?

4. Base salary

   a. Present rate guaranteed as minimum?
   b. Present practice for salary increases to be continued?
   c. Should some reference be made to adjustments for inflation?

5. Annual bonus: Total of salary and bonus should be no less than for a given year such as 1981?

6. Long-term Performance Bonus: Bonus should be pro-rated on an appropriate basis for incompleted cycles. On what basis? Should a minimum amount be guaranteed if the plan is not continued? How do you assure the same bonus opportunity if the operations of the company are materially changed?

7. Continuation of employee benefit plans

   a. What specific plans are to be continued?
   b. Plans can be amended or terminated but at least the same benefits and levels of benefits must be continued.

8. Termination other than for cause (which will be defined)

   a. Should executives be allowed to choose between an agreement that requires mitigation of damages and provides pay and benefits for balance of term in the event of termination, and one that does not require mitigation of damages but provides pay and benefits for a fixed period such as one or two years? How long should such fixed period be? If so, should such choice between mitigation and nonmitigation be made now or at the time of a termination of employment?
   b. Possible severance allowance: an additional 6 to 12 months' pay?
   c. Should payments be made in a lump sum or in installments? If in installments, should all installments be accelerated if the company defaults on any payments, or upon a default should the company be required to fund the unpaid installments to assure against future defaults?

EXHIBIT 11–8

continued

> If funding is desirable, what funding vehicle should be used?

> **d.** Should payment of deferred compensation be accelerated in the event of a change in control?

> **e.** Should options, including unexercisable options, be bought out by the company upon a termination? Should exercisability be accelerated or should the executive be given service credit for option exercise purposes instead? If a service credit approach is used, should the option plan(s) be amended or should the agreement set forth a phantom arrangement instead?

> **f.** Should termination payments be conditioned on noncompetition even though the company had breached the agreement?

9. Who is to receive employment agreements?

10. Supplemental Pension

> **a.** Should the agreements provide for a supplemental pension, or should such a pension be provided by a separate stand-alone supplemental pension plan?

> **b.** Should the supplemental pension commence at age 55 (assuming expiration of the agreement) if the executive has 15 years of company service or should another age and number of years of service be used? How much should the pension be: 40% of final average compensation? 50%? Should the supplemental pension be offset by 50% of social security benefits even though the qualified plan benefit may be offset by a lesser percentage?

> **c.** Should the supplemental pension be forfeitable in the event of competition?

> **d.** What, if any, provision should be made in the event of default in payment of the supplemental pension by the company? Upon such a default should the company be required to pay the executive an actuarially discounted lump sum, purchase an annuity to be owned by the executive or fund the supplemental pension with a disinterested third party? If funding is desirable, what funding vehicle should be used?

11. Reimbursement of legal expenses

> **a.** Should the company pay legal expenses relating to the agreement? If so, should the executive be required to pay his legal expenses if he loses a controversy concerning the agreement or only if he pursued the matter in bad faith?

> **b.** Should a "deductible" be imposed or should the company pay 100% of the legal expenses? If a deductible is used, how much should it be: 10%, 15%, 20%?

> **c.** Should the company be required to fund its obligation? If so, should there be a ceiling amount and when should funding be required: upon a change in control or upon a dispute arising after a change in control? What funding mechanism should be used? When should the fund revert to the company? How much should the company be required to fund: a year's salary, half a year's salary? Should the company be required to replenish the fund as it is expended?

Source: Copyright © 1983 by Practicing Law Institute and reprinted with permission of PLI, and the author, V. Henry Rothschild II. This article originally appeared in the PLI handbook *Executive Compensation 1983*, published in conjunction with a seminar of the same title. It is based on the forthcoming *Current Trends in Executive Compensation* by V. Henry Rothschild II and Arthur D. Sporn, which will be published by the Practicing Law Institute.

- Represent another form of executive nest feathering at the expense of the stockholders. The "sweetheart contract" is especially vulnerable on this score.
- Federal security laws do not require approval by stockholders of "golden parachute" agreements and their provisions need not be spelled out in proxy materials.
- The "sweetheart contract" may actually deter tender offers because of the cost involved or by inducing a flight of management in the event of a takeover. The acquiring firm may find itself without any management to run the business.
- The contracts may not stand up under legal scrutiny. If the agreement covers the chief executive officer and directors, the parties may lack the degree of independence and disinterest required in the exercise of their duties[15,16].

Perhaps the real cause of concern over "golden parachute" contracts is that many contracts are put through in haste during a takeover attempt when there is little time to consider the issues or carefully define the terms. It is, for example, important to define a change of control that triggers the parachute. Some companies define a change of control as a change in the majority of the directors within a specific time frame, or when some percentage of the outstanding securities is acquired by an individual or group acting in concert; still others, when the employing company ceases to be publicly held or to have a designated number of stockholders. But some contracts never get around to defining the term. In all events, a well drawn agreement should cover a very considerable range of questions and options. Exhibit 11–8 indicates the scope of a "golden parachute" agreement.

CORPORATE KIDNAPPING

Corporate jitters over hostile takeovers open the door to an apparently legal form of extortion. Assuming not all tender offers are made in good faith, the scenario would allow a person or group to buy up a significant block of stock (say 7 to 8 percent) at the market value to force the so-called target company (1) to buy back its shares at a premium under the threat of a proxy battle for control or (2) sale of the stock to a *bona fide* takeover group or (3) to organize a dissident group of stockholders to bedevil management. To avoid trouble, management will frequently pay up. Exhibit 11–9 lists some prominent 1980 buyback transactions.

Although such maneuvering may be legal, it does transfer wealth from the general group of stockholders to the dissident block and can represent a waste of corporate assets. In the limited sample shown in Exhibit 11–9, to avoid trouble managements paid an average premium of almost 25 percent—a lower premium than acceptable in the typical takeover situation. Perhaps the willingness to accept a relatively low premium may reveal a less than genuine takeover attempt[16].

EXHIBIT 11–9

Sample of 1980 Buy-Back Transactions

1	2	3	4	5	6
Company	*Average Price Paid Per Share*	*Target Company*	*Repurchase Price*	*Premium over Market*	*Percent of Premium over Column 2*
Gulf & Western	$21.72	Robertshaw Controls	$24.00	$4.25	19.6%
Gulf & Western	11.79	Oxford Industries	17.00	3.00	25.4
Walco National	18.64	McNeil Corp.	20.66	4.16	22.3
Walco National	10.17	Reece Corp.	12.00	3.00	29.5
Walco National	29.55	Standard-Coosa-Thatcher	33.75	1.38	4.7
Icahn Group	7.20	Saxon Industries	10.50	2.37	32.9
Care Corp.	7.90	Treadway Companies	9.00	2.50	31.6
Reliance Group	21.18	Penn Central	26.24	1.49	7.0
Clabir Corp. Group	16.75	General Host	25.00	7.12	42.5
General Host	12.12	Ponderosa System	16.95	3.83	31.6
		Premium over Average Purchase Price Per Share			24.71%

Source: Adapted from The *Wall Street Journal.* January 19, 1983.

SUMMARY

This chapter has discussed the tactics frequently employed in hostile takeovers. From the viewpoint of the potential target, the best defense lies in advance preparation rather than *ad hoc* arrangements after the call to battle has sounded.

The acquiring company has more to consider. Will the tender premium erode the wealth position of its stockholders? Does a better organization emerge from the consequences of a hostile takeover or from the less spectacular route of patient negotiation?

There are larger issues emerging. Peter Drucker (The *Wall Street Journal,* January 5, 1983) writes that fear of a hostile takeover places a premium on short-term planning rather than the implementation of long-term strategies. However, he does not advocate the type of legislation proposed above to curb hostile takeovers. Drucker proposes instead that the Comptroller of the Currency stop bank lending to finance unfriendly takeovers:

> Unfriendly takeovers need such huge amounts of cash that they cannot succeed without massive bank loans. Even DuPont, one of the most liquid and financially healthy of American businesses, had to borrow $3.9 billion to acquire Conoco, and then had to borrow an additional $1.4 billion to refinance Conoco's debts . . . To take over Conoco . . . DuPont raised its debt ratio from a conservative 20 percent to a risky 42 percent, increasing its total debt from $2 billion to $7.3 billion, which it had to borrow at a prohibitive 20 percent interest rate. In the end it suffered a sharp decline in its credit rating—which means a greatly impaired ability to borrow for other purposes.

NOTES

1. Bradley, Michael. "Interfirm Tender Offers and the Market for Corporate Control." in Michael Keenan and Lawrence J. White. *Mergers and Acquisitions.* Massachusetts: Lexington Books, 1982.

2. "State Takeover Statutes and the Williams Act." *Business Lawyer*, November
   1976.

3. "The Great Takeover Binge." *Business Week*. November 14, 1977.

4. Davey, Patrick J. *Defenses Against Unnegotiated Cash Tender Offers*. New York: The Conference Board, 1977.

5. Ehbar, A. F. "Corporate Takeovers are Here to Stay." *Fortune*. May 8, 1978.

6. Hayes, Samuel L. III, and Russell A. Taussig. "Tactics of Cash Takeover Bids." *Harvard Business Review*. March–April 1967.

7. Husband, William H., and James C. Dockeray. *Modern Corporation Finance*. Homewood, Illinois: Richard D. Irwin, 1966.

8. Krooss, Herman E. *American Economic Development*. Englewood Cliffs, New Jersey: Prentice-Hall, 1955. pp. 276–281.

9. Merjos, Anna. "Takeover Targets." *Barron's*. May 15, 1978.

10. Nossiter, Daniel D. "Oh, Those Golden Parachutes." *Barron's*. November 29, 1982.

11. Perham, John C. "The New Game of Takeovers." *Dun's Review*, August 1975.

12. Robinson, J. William. "To Counter Tender Offers TLC for Shareholders." *Harvard Business Review*. January–February 1976.

13. Russo, Michael B. Vice-President, The Superior Oil Company. Remarks to conference on Acquisitions and Mergers in the Energy Industry, December 7, 1982.

14. Troubh, Raymond S. "Purchased Affection: A Primer on Cash Tender Offers." *Harvard Business Review*, July–August 1976. Reprinted by permission of the *Harvard Business Review*. Copyright © 1976 by the Harvard President and Fellows of Harvard College; all rights reserved.

15. Salwen, Jack B. "Providing Management Continuity." Address to conference on Acquisitions and Mergers in the Energy Industry, December 7, 1982.

16. The *Wall Street Journal:* December 3, 1982; August 9, 1982; July 23, 1982; September 22, 1982; September 23, 1982; September 24, 1982; January 14, 1983; December 8, 1982; April 8, 1978; January 19, 1983.

Index